THE CONFEDERATE CIPHER
THE DUELIST
BOOK ONE

LARRY B. LAMBERT

Copyright © 2026 by Larry B Lambert
All rights reserved.

No part of this book may be reproduced in any form or by any electronic or mechanical means, including information storage and retrieval systems, without written permission from the author, except for the use of brief quotations in a book review.

This is a work of historical fiction. In this novel, historical figures from the 1800s interact with characters drawn from the author's imagination. No connection with any living person is made, implied, or should be inferred. Any reference that might be drawn to a living individual is merely coincidental.

Artificial intelligence was not used in the creation of this book or the series of books, of which this is the first.

❋ Formatted with Vellum

For respected colleagues with whom I served:

Supv. Deputy District Attorney Mark Sevigny
Lieutenant Donovan Dunnion, JD, US Navy
Superintendent Michael Watson, Australian Federal Police
Special Agent Herbert M. Brown, FBI
M. Cordell Hart, Central Intelligence Agency/Colonel, US Army
Donald J. Bennett, Central Intelligence Agency
Mathis B. Central Intelligence Agency
Sandra Buchan, Central Intelligence Agency
Detective Lieutenant Jack (Wo Fat) Willoughby, New Orleans PD
Special Agent Ken Sanz, Florida DOJ
Detective Sergeant Tom Perdue, San Francisco PD

People want to know why the South is so interested in the Civil War. I had maybe, it's a rough guess, about fifty fistfights in my life. Out of those fifty fistfights, the ones that I had the most vivid memory of were the ones I lost. I think that's one reason why the South remembers the war more than the North does. - Shelby Foote

NOTES

Language - I wrote this historical novel in twenty-first-century English, which differs from the nineteenth-century English spoken during the period. I have attempted to eliminate some expressions in everyday use today from the work to make it flow better and feel more comfortable to the reader. I hope that you can settle into the time period with a readable and enjoyable bit of fiction. If I had written it in the standard syntax of the day, it would not have flowed, and it would have been distracting. I included as much of the common terminology of the 1850-70 time period as I could while telling the story. And it's all about storytelling.

* * *

Research - Anything that anyone writes about the heavily researched American War of Northern Aggression/Civil War/War of Southern Secession/War Between the States comes under heavy scrutiny. I appreciate the *Henry Huntington Library*, San Marino, California, for their permission to consult their extensive book collection as a "reader",

NOTES

including the *War of the Rebellion* (Official Civil War History) series. I did not include a bibliography in this work because it is primarily a work of fiction based on historical fact.

The story includes the developing relationship between George Custer and Elizabeth Bacon and is not historical. The best information available has the couple meeting at Thanksgiving in Monroe, Michigan, in 1862. Their relationship is not key to the story, and I took considerable literary license while still trying to keep many key historical events as they occurred. I don't ask for your permission or approval, and hope you enjoy the *novel* as presented.

* * *

This is the first novel in a series. They were written to be read in order as part of a series. While these volumes can be taken individually, I expect that you'd enjoy them more by embracing the context that the serial provides.

It begins here with **The Confederate Cipher** (Volume 1) as Henry Hudson is pushed by his father into the US Military Academy at West Point in the hopes of avoiding a scandal and finding a place for himself in life. Henry, who is personable, talented, intelligent, and has family means, is courted by the British in their unconventional machinations of empire in the Americas. It ends in the early days of the Peninsula Campaign as the Federal Army attempts to break the Confederacy in its march to Richmond.

In **Hudson's Scouts** (Volume 2), there is more British meddling as the rebellion takes greater shape and develops momentum. His relationship with Victoria McKay becomes clearer, and we learn more about the characters as they navigate historical events through the Battles of Fredericksburg, Chancellorsville, Chickamauga/Chattanooga, and other events in the West, ultimately leading to the gold fields in Georgia at the conclusion of 1863.

In The Crow Creek Expedition (Volume 3) Hudson's Scouts are sent West on a mission of vengeance.

* * *

Principal Characters (in general order of their appearance)
Historical Characters marked **

Henry Laughton Hudson - (born 1841) The central figure and narrator in the story. We follow him on his journey through the tumultuous years of the Southern Rebellion in America, and beyond in subsequent volumes.

Judge Charles James Hudson - Henry's Father. The presiding judge sitting on the Federal Bench (Circuit Court) for the District of Michigan. His family interests include shipping, banking, railroads, and the press.

Margaret Louise Forsyth Hudson - Henry's mother, and a woman whose family connections run deep in the financial elite in America. Her family owns the Michigan Central Railroad and a commercial shipping company.

Robert Hudson - Henry's older brother, a lawyer who will inherit the family businesses.

Louise Hudson - Henry's older sister, who married into a steel manufacturing fortune.

Marie DuPont Cholmondeley - the young wife of Detroit Alderman Amos Cholmondeley, with whom Henry Hudson has had an illicit love affair.

Judge Daniel Stanton Bacon ** - A judge in the Michigan State Courts (Monroe) and father of Elizabeth Bacon.

Elizabeth Bacon Custer ** - Married George Armstrong Custer, a US Army (Cavalry) Officer who made a name for

NOTES

himself in the War of the Southern Sesession, and the expansion of the Old West.

Elijah Hudson - Henry's paternal grandfather, the founder of the Farmers' and Mechanics' Bank. Elijah Hudson invested the profits in railroad construction, which resulted in extensive ownership shares. Elijah's family owns three newspapers in Michigan and Indiana, which imparts political clout.

Leslie Forsythe - Henry's maternal grandfather, a former U.S. Ambassador to France, and a partner in the shipping business with Cornelius Vanderbilt. Owns the Michigan Central Railroad.

Samuel Hudson - Henry's uncle, a resident of Boston, a gambler, and majority stockholder in the Peninsular and Oriental Steam Navigation Company.

SS *Seraphim* Leslie Forsythe's steam-powered, armed screw packet is completing construction in Liverpool at John Laird Sons & Co's - Birkenhead Iron Works.

Colonel William Joseph Hardee ** - A career U.S. Army and Confederate States Army officer. For the U.S. Army, he served in the Second Seminole War and in the Mexican–American War, where he was captured and exchanged. He served as Superintendent of the United States Military Academy at West Point with the rank of lieutenant colonel. During the American Civil War, he sided with the Confederacy and rose to the rank of general. Hardee's writings about military tactics were widely used on both sides in the conflict. After the war, Hardee settled at his wife's Alabama plantation. After returning it to working condition, the family moved to Selma, Alabama, where Hardee worked in the warehousing and insurance businesses. He eventually became president of the Selma and Meridian Railroad.

Sergeant Major Arlund Bisbee (Artillery) - Born in Fort Smith, Arkansas, the youngest of nine children, he attended

Saint Mark's Normal School for Boys at Fort Smith. Enlisted in the US Army during the Mexican-American War. Commissioned first lieutenant (Artillery) in the Army of Northern Virginia, Confederate States of America. Seconded as an artillerist to the Confederate States Navy.

Cadet Nathaniel (Nate) Green Beaufort III, West Point Class of 1863 (left for CSA Service 1861), Captain, Company B of the 6th South Carolina Infantry Battalion, CSA, and after 1862, Santee Light Artillery

Cadet George Armstrong (Autie) Custer ** West Point Class of 1861, Brevet Major General of Volunteers during the War of the Rebellion, during which time he held the regular Army rank of Captain (Cavalry). Later promoted to Lieutenant Colonel in the regular army, taking command of the newly formed 7th U.S. Cavalry Regiment. The stated mission of Custer's 7th Cavalry during the Great Sioux War (1876) was to force renegade Northern Cheyenne and Sioux tribes back onto reservations after they failed to report to their agencies by a federal deadline.

Major Robert Anderson, US Army (Artillery) ** He was the Union commander in the first battle of the American Civil War at Fort Sumter in April 1861 when the Confederates bombarded the fort and forced its surrender, starting the war. Anderson was celebrated as a hero in the North and was promoted to brigadier general, given command of Union forces in Kentucky.

Owain Rowley-Conway, eleventh Baron Langford, Rear Admiral of the White.

Edmond Roche, newly raised Baron Fermoy, Lord Major, Royal Horse Guards Regiment

Colonel Nathaniel Green Beaufort II, 5th Regiment (Carolina Panthers), South Carolina Militia (Infantry), Port Royal, South Carolina

Victoria McKay, Niece of Major Sir Iain McKay, eventu-

NOTES

ally marries Henry Hudson and becomes a central character in her own right in this story.

Captain Ezra Pervis, Carolina Panthers, South Carolina Militia (Infantry) - Killed in a duel, Christmas Eve 1859, at Port Royal, South Carolina, by Cadet Henry Hudson, USMA.

Major Sir Iain McKay, Second Battalion, Coldstream Guards Regiment

Richard Bickerton Pemell Lyons ** 1st Earl Lyons, the British Queen's Ambassador in Washington City, District of Columbia.

Lieutenant Colonel Martin Smythe-Armbruster, of the Calcutta Light Horse

Brigadier General Fitz John Porter, USV ** Was a career United States Army officer who was called into question during his performance at the Second Battle of Bull Run. Although Porter served well in the early battles of the Civil War, his military career was ruined by a controversial trial called by his political rivals.

Lieutenant General Wade Hampton III CSA ** was an American politician from South Carolina. He was a prominent member of one of the wealthiest families in the antebellum South. He resigned from the South Carolina Senate to enlist as a private in the South Carolina Militia. The governor of South Carolina insisted that Hampton accept a colonel's commission. Although he had no military experience, his years of managing plantations and serving in state government were considered signs of leadership. Wealthy men were often commissioned based on social standing (in the North and South) and expected to finance military units. Hampton organized "Hampton's Legion", which consisted of six companies of infantry, four companies of cavalry, and one battery of artillery. He paid for all the weapons for the unit. Hampton proved a natural cavalryman—brave, audacious, and a superb horseman. Of officers without previous

NOTES

military experience, he was one of three to achieve the rank of lieutenant general.

Major General George Brinton McClellan USV ** was an American military officer, politician, and engineer who served as the 24th governor of New Jersey from 1878 to 1881 and as Commanding General of the United States Army from November 1861 to March 1862.

First Sergeant Horatio Fontaine (Rash) Nelson (Cavalry).

Major Fahrtzinger, USV (Engineers), (also known as Fart-slinger), forty years of age, with a round face and a long, waxed mustache. He had been an engineer officer in the Prussian Army and volunteered to fight for the Union.

Gideon Welles ** was an American government official who served as the United States Secretary of the Navy from 1861 to 1869, a cabinet post he held after supporting Abraham Lincoln in the 1860 election. Although opposed to the Union blockade of Southern ports, he duly carried out his part of the Anaconda Plan, essentially sealing off the Confederate coastline and preventing the exchange of cotton for war supplies. This is viewed as a significant cause of Union victory in the Civil War, and his achievement in expanding the Navy almost tenfold was widely praised. Lincoln nicknamed him his "Neptune".

★ ★ ★

Weapons

Düsack Sword - from Czech *tesák* "cleaver; hunting sword" - is a single-edged sword of the cutlass or saber pattern, used as a sidearm in Germany and often also as a German martial fencing weapon. Though somewhat more elaborate than the U.S. Model 1860 Light Cavalry Saber or the Model 1840 Cavalry Saber (frequently called the "wrist

NOTES

breaker," or the 1850 Army Staff & Field Officer's Sword. In this story, Henry Hudson prefers it because it's lighter and quicker, particularly in use as a dueling weapon.

Grape Shot Revolver, developed in New Orleans in 1856 by Jean Alexandre Le Mat, whose manufacturing effort was backed financially by an engineer, Colonel P. G. T. Beauregard. John Krider of Philadelphia made the revolver under license. It fired a 0.42-caliber ball; the shotgun option was a 16-gauge, and any shot size would do, depending on the desired outcome. 2,900 were produced in Liège, Belgium, and Paris, France, under license. The European-made pistols were shipped through Birmingham, England, where they were proof-tested and marked. About 900 revolvers were shipped to the Confederate States Army and 600 to the Confederate States Navy through Bermuda to avoid the Southern Naval Blockade.

Blue steel Belgian 7mm Pinfire Pocket Revolver with a folding dagger. The revolver featured a 3-inch folding dagger that was mounted on a spring-loaded mechanism with a push-button release. It also had a folding trigger, a deeply rifled bore, and Belgian proofs on the cylinder, which are common.

* * *

Notes on Savate

Savate is a French word for "old shoe or boot". Savate fighters wear specially designed boots. A male practitioner of savate is called a tireur.

Savate originated in France, where sailors practiced it in the southern port of Marseille in the 17th century. According to historians, sailors acquired their fighting style during their trips to the countries of the Indian Ocean and the China Sea. Subsequently, in every bar fight in French

NOTES

ports, it was common to see the savate kicks. Sailors called this type of combat "Chausson", in reference to the slippers usually worn on board.

Kicks

1 *fouetté* (literally "whip", roundhouse kick making contact with the toe—hard rubber-toed shoes are worn in practice and bouts), high (figure), medium (médian), or low (bas)

2 A *chassé frontal* (front kick)

3 *chassé* (side ("chassé lateral") or front ("chassé frontal") piston-action kick, high (figure), medium (médian), or low (bas)

4 *revers*, frontal or lateral ("reverse" or hooking kick), making contact with the sole of the shoe, high (figure), medium (médian), or low (bas)

5 *coup de pied bas* ("low kick", a front or sweep kick to the shin, making contact with the inner edge of the shoe, performed with a characteristic backwards lean)

Punches

1 *direct bras avant* (jab, lead hand)

2 *direct bras arrière* (cross, rear hand)

3 *crochet* (hook, bent arm with either hand)

4 *uppercut* (either hand)

Subjects Taught at West Point - late 1950s and early 1960s

1. Military Engineering and Science of War

2. Mineralogy and Geology

3. Law and Literature

4. Practical Military Engineering

5. Tactics of Artillery, Cavalry, and Infantry, and Equitation [ACIE]

NOTES

    6. Ordnance and Gunnery
    7. Ethics
    8. Chemistry
    9. Drawing - Landscape
    10. Tactics of ACIE, Strategy, Outpost Duty, and Military Organization and Administration
    11. Natural and Experimental Philosophy
    12. French Language
    13. Spanish
    14. Drawing - Human Figure, Topography
    15. Tactics of Artillery, Cavalry, and Infantry

CHAPTER 1

Detroit, Michigan
Spring 1858

The morning started well, but took an uncomfortable turn when I entered the sunroom for breakfast. Only my father sat at the table, dressed in his business suit, reading the newspaper, and sipping coffee from his oversized white china cup. My father, Judge Charles James Hudson, was tall and lean, in his forties, with slightly receding, graying, black hair and a strong chin. Unlike many of his contemporaries, he kept his hair carefully trimmed weekly and washed daily. He also remained clean-shaven. Intense, intelligent, blue eyes looked up at me over the top of half-moon eyeglasses.

I realize you might not find anything amiss in this, but Father had a rigid schedule that did not include breakfast alone at nine a.m. He waited for me. Patiently. Judge Charles James Hudson was not known for his patience.

"Please join me, Henry."

I looked around furtively for an escape, but there was none.

"You've returned from Georgetown, graduated from the Jesuit school, and your mother told me you did not become a kneeler."

"No, Father, I'm still a good Lutheran despite the seminary's efforts." I wasn't particularly avid about engaging in rituals or following the tenets of the faith. I think that he suspected as much because of where the conversation seemed to be headed.

He set the newspaper aside and picked up a portfolio with postage stamps affixed, adjusting his reading glasses as he did so. "Your grades are not *all* splendid, but they are commendable and good enough to get you into Dartmouth if you wish to read the law. They rate your horsemanship as the best in the school, and your athleticism is likewise excellent. You had your Spanish horses stabled there? The Andalusians you favor?"

"I've had Bayard and Glory in Georgetown for the last two years. They've come and gone with me on the train."

"Yes, of course, the trains. Your grandfather spoiled you with the purchases. Let me get to the matter. I'm concerned about sponsoring you for a career in the law that your brother Robert follows."

"Sir?"

"What of this situation you have created with Mrs. Cholmondeley since you have returned this past month?"

"Sometimes we ride together if we meet by chance."

"There are witnesses, son; thank God they are discreet witnesses. They confirm that a more ardent form of *riding* is done and done often."

I am sure that I blushed beet red.

"You are seventeen, she is at most twenty-five, and her

husband, Amos, is sixty and an alderman. As appealing as this arrangement may be to you, it has no future. I take it from your dress that you intended to ride this morning."

I don't recall nodding, but I'm sure that I did.

"Get it out of your system, go on, go. But muster the resolve to end your affair *this* day. Your mother has invited the prominent judiciary, industrialists, upstanding parents, and their suitable daughters to dine with us, beginning this Sunday and *continuing every Sunday* until a match is made. You will join us and behave. Do I make myself clear?"

"Yes, Father."

"Go."

I left the sunroom, walked right, and then right again into the scullery closet, which abuts the sunroom, and put my ear against the thin wall.

My mother and father were speaking.

"You heard what I told the boy?"

My mother answered, "Yes, I heard. It would be best to put an immediate end to the affair between Henry and Marie Cholmondeley. You were not nearly strong enough."

"What would you have me do, Margaret?"

"Lock him away."

"Seriously, it's not as if he was impregnating one of the colored help or scandalizing and ruining a young teenage girl he met at The Church of the Holy Trinity from a prominent family with a good upbringing and a reputation to uphold. This married woman may have as much to lose as he does if it comes to a publicly noticed scandal."

"Marie is a harridan, which is why her family married her off to Alderman Cholmondeley." Mother pronounced Marie's name as the French would do, rather than the British *Chumley*.

Father replied quietly. "If she becomes pregnant, Amos will strut like a cock of the walk."

"How can you speak that way?"

A rustling of papers and, "Look at his grades. Gold medal in competition saber, another gold medal in horsemanship, and I've seen him shoot with a pistol, rifle, and fowling piece. If Amos calls him out in a duel of honor, Henry will kill the man with a well-placed shot and then marry the widow. I know my son. He's too damned much like me for his good."

I couldn't help but smile as I listened. The thought of a duel, legally fought, occurred to me. Father understood. I'd kill the old man where he stood and take Marie. Amos Cholmondeley had a palsy in his chubby hands. He'd only hit the broad side of a barn with a pistol ball if God guided the bullet.

Mother said, "Dueling is now illegal."

Father laughed. "Honor is honor and must be satisfied despite the rules laid down by the legislature. If Amos called him out, Henry would answer and plant him in the ground, whether by blade or ball."

She changed focus, "His ethics, rhetoric, mathematics, and English composition grades are well above average."

"To my point, Margaret, he excels at what he loves, like all young men. Henry has never been bookish the way Robert is."

"And Marie?"

"By all reports, they've been at like two minks since he returned, which tells me he excels there, too. She's twenty-five, turning *every* man's head, Margaret. My only concern would be that he will confuse lust and release with love."

"We will introduce him to the respected judge's daughters on Sunday. This first one is from Monroe?"

"Judge Daniel Stanton Bacon of the County Courts. He served with me in the State House of Representatives. Do you remember him?"

"Yes, his wife Eleanor passed four years ago, and Daniel

married Rhoda Wells the following year." Mother kept up with all the deaths and marriages as a matter of social obligation and to find fodder for gossiping with others in our class.

My father continued, "Judge Bacon is desirous of serving on the federal bench, and because I am the presiding judge, he could use a word in the right ear. He understands how it works. A quiet word with the right people over lunch can change a man's career trajectory. I recall a daughter about Henry's age."

"Elizabeth, a year younger, has been closeted in an academy for girls to quell her adventurous spirit." Mother paused and said, "They *might* like each other."

"Horsefeathers, Margaret. It will be like water and a match. Henry will compare her to blonde and beautiful Marie DuPont. It's worth a try, but I hold out little hope."

My brother and sister had used the secret listening post before I discovered it from them. Mother and Father hashed things out in the sunroom, and we were much wiser.

I left through the kitchen, opened the outside door quietly, and had the groom saddle Glory, my black Andalusian stallion with two white rear stockings.

As soon as I mounted, I told Glory, "Well and good, boy. Let us gallop our fidgets out." I slackened the reins, gave a light tap of my heels, and felt the powerful muscles clench underneath me. After a quick mile, I saw another rider ahead of me, approaching from the opposite direction. I reined in, bringing Glory back to a walk, not wishing to startle the other, familiar palomino mare. Glory began to rack with his front feet. Splendid, Marie's mare, Cloud, must be coming into season. Our horses would spar with their courtship even as we did.

"Ah! Marie. How are you this morning, ma'am?"

She had a new place, a cottage that would be unoccupied for the hour or two we needed. We cantered together without speaking until she led the way down a garden path to a small slat wood building with flowers planted along the flagstones. Ivy crept up the cottage walls. Lilac bloomed abundantly and fragrantly along the wall of a small barn where she dismounted. I haltered Glory outside and led her mare, Cloud, inside the barn as they called to each other and stomped.

She gave me a mischievous grin and said, "Cloud and I have something in common." Then she gave me a long kiss. Our tongues met. Her breasts swelled out of her riding top, every terrain feature visible. Her hair was so blond it was almost white, and she played with it as she laughed at me. "Do you like what you see?"

"I confess that I'm in love."

She led me inside. The parlor was small and relaxed, with comfortable furniture and shelves lining the polished wood walls. The house was filled with the earthy smell of savory vegetable soup.

At a month shy of twenty-five years old, Marie regularly exercised her husband's horses on dry days. We had only a few afternoon showers this springtime, and once we met that first time, we met daily thereafter. Her husband, Amos, married her the year before and was well past twice her age. He spent his days at a counting house when he wasn't pressing the flesh and scheming in his political role.

WHEN WE MET BY CHANCE, I noticed she wore breeches and sat confidently astride her horse, not side-saddle. I didn't doubt that her style and flamboyance led to gossip among the local dames. She recognized me, "Mr. Hudson, are you back from studies in Georgetown for good?"

"Indeed, I have completed my studies and now must consider my future life."

We rode together for a few minutes and passed a patch of scrubland, a mixture of hazel, birch, and gorse bushes, tall enough to provide a little shelter. She dismounted and walked her animal into the shade of a grassy glen. "A chance for us both to cool down, Mr. Hudson."

"Henry, please."

"Call me Marie." She removed her riding hat and unbound her long blonde hair.

She sat on the grass, under the trees, out of sight of the open expanse of turf. She patted the ground, inviting me to join her. Joining became more than a metaphor.

I was not wholly inexperienced and judged that I had played my part to her satisfaction.

"We must do this again one day, Henry—maybe tomorrow."

When we completed our first assignation, Marie confessed that her portly old husband, Amos, had left for Chicago that morning. He paid her a courtesy farewell the previous evening – as always, he had put up a perfunctory performance, leaving her wholly unmoved. She explained that it was his fault, not hers, that she sought satisfaction elsewhere.

"Home, Henry! They will wonder what has become of me. Bye-bye!"

I thought it was all rather brusque and businesslike, but there were worse ways to spend a morning. I adjusted my clothing, brushed the grass and twigs off, and settled back into the saddle, turning Glory's head for home. I did not concern myself with possible repercussions from our enjoyable half an hour – Mrs. Cholmondeley was old enough to look after herself astride her horse. The Victorian age was not one to put an excessive value upon virtue, and a scandal had to be quite remarkable to smear any reputation. If my groom felt that Glory was not sufficiently exercised, he would draw whatever conclusions silently.

Our relationship grew more familiar and comfortable during the ensuing three weeks until the confrontation in the sunroom. I didn't think of what we shared as love exactly. She was too businesslike for that, absolutely demanding of what she preferred, and because I enjoyed the very same thing, it was like two spoons laid in a drawer. I didn't tell her that my father ordered us to stop. How could I? There had to be a solution allowing us to keep our morning exercises.

MY GIVEN name is Henry Laughton Hudson. I was born the youngest of three in Oakland County, Michigan, to Charles James Hudson and Margaret Louise Forsyth. My father, a lawyer, was elected to the Michigan State Assembly, and we moved to Detroit when I was eight years old. He was appointed to the Federal bench by President Franklin Pierce in 1856 and was promptly confirmed by the US Senate. Two years later, he was appointed presiding judge. I heard a rumor that the appointment coincided with a gift of railroad stock, but I never inquired of my father.

My father, Charles, was the only son of my paternal grandfather, Elijah Hudson, who established the Farmers' and Mechanics' Bank. He invested the profits in railroad construction, resulting in extensive ownership stakes. The publishing end of the Hudson family empire owned three newspapers with wide circulations in Michigan and Indiana, which added to our family's political clout.

My mother's family owns the majority interest in the Michigan Central Railroad and a small fleet of ships. Her father, my grandfather, is prominently involved in politics and was appointed minister to France. She spent some of her formative years in Paris.

My older brother, Robert, is at Dartmouth, preparing for the day that he will take over the Michigan Central Railroad. My older sister, Louise, married the son of a steel manufacturing fortune. They're partnered with an up-and-coming Scotsman named Andrew Carnegie, a Pennsylvania native.

That rounds things out. As the third son, you can say I've been indulged, and you wouldn't be wrong. The romantic situation with Marie Dupont Cholmondeley bothered my mother more than my father, and now they will introduce me to young ladies on Sundays, who will be paraded. I will be expected to reciprocate with a letter to the girl, composed by my mother, written by my hand. There may be heavily chaperoned meetings arranged. I'm a tall, fit, intelligent, financially stable suitor with a family-friendly budget. Though not the eldest son, it is common knowledge that I stand to inherit a more significant fortune than many of the smaller American States' annual budgets.

Although they didn't directly impact me, I was accustomed to seeing fortunes won and lost in my life. The 280-foot sidewheel steamer *SS Central America*, belonging to a family rival, sank in a hurricane last year in September 1857, taking 425 of her 578 passengers and crew to the bottom along with 30,000 pounds of gold, contributing to a national financial crisis. Their loss was our gain. The monetary gold-and-silver panic that has gripped the world in cold fingers also propelled our family fortunes forward because of the positions we took. The U.S. Mail Steamship Company, which owned the *SS Central America*, is poised to lose the mail contract next year. Cornelius Vanderbilt and the Forsyth shipping interests will then buy the ships owned by U.S. Mail Steamship for pennies on the dollar. I eavesdrop. So many things are planned well in advance. It is how fortunes are made and kept.

. . .

JUDGE DANIEL BACON and his sixteen-year-old, marriageable daughter, Elizabeth, arrived promptly on Sunday at 2 pm. The conversation began slowly between my father and Judge Bacon, who had taken rooms for himself, his daughter, and staff at the Biddle House on Jefferson Avenue and Randolph Street. Monroe is not more than twenty-five miles down the lakeshore from Detroit. Had they come that morning by steam carriage, they would not have arrived freshly coiffed. The summer train carriage between Monroe and Detroit is an open ash car, and people arrive black with coal dust and smoke. Better to take the train the day before and book a hotel to freshen up.

Elizabeth, prettier and better composed than I expected, wore a pink dress with rose accents and didn't say much at first. After supper, we were invited to stroll through the garden with her governess and my father's butler, an old German with prominent gray sidebushes and bald as a cueball named Bestian, who my father called Sabastian, walking five paces behind us.

"I have heard that you graduated from the Georgetown Academy, Henry," she said coquettishly as we walked.

"And you attend the Sacred Heart Academy?"

"Not willingly, but yes, my father intends that I be schooled to be presentable in polite society and that I learn to keep my opinions to myself."

I laughed, "Are your opinions radical?"

She stopped and turned to face me abruptly. "I favor women's suffrage, for one."

"As do I," I replied.

We continued walking through the garden. "Do you mock me, Henry?"

"No, I have been raised in a home and educated in a setting where it seems reasonable to me."

"I'm surprised."

"You don't know my mother. I think it's inevitable and just."

"Do you favor a young lady?"

The question caught me off guard. Elizabeth had a directness that I also found in Marie DuPont, though I had not expected it.

"No, not as such. As you can see, my parents would like me to make a proper match now that I'm out of school. Possibly before I can entangle myself with somebody unsuitable."

She had a robust laugh, and I looked over my shoulder at her governess, who began to close the distance. Bestian stopped and had a quiet word with her. I could tell that they both spoke German.

"And you, Elizabeth?"

"You can call me Libby."

"You can answer the question, Libby."

"I correspond with a young man currently enrolled at the Military Academy at West Point, New York, but his father is a blacksmith. My father hopes that I will achieve more than a soldier's wife. I'm the only one of my siblings who survived to adulthood. My young man asked me for a favor before he left for New York, and I gave him a square of embroidered silk—not as a promise but—."

"It's time that you young people return to the parlor," the governess said. Bestian looked as if he needed a stiff glass of schnapps.

"Of course," I replied, taking her tiny hand, twirling her as if on the dance floor, and heading in the opposite direction. She rewarded me with a mischievous smirk.

When the Bacons left for the Biddle House, my mother asked my opinion of Elizabeth. I told her that she seemed to be spoken for, even though her father disapproved of her favored suitor.

Two more Sundays followed with Judges, their wives, and an eligible daughter. None of them came up to Marie DuPont in my eyes, and my parents sensed it, expressing a sense of futility.

I sabotaged the Sundays as best I could. In the case of Millie Burns, I asked her if her corset was too tight. She looked at me sharply, trussed tightly like a suckling pig. "It's important for you to breathe, Millie."

Betina Sorensen, whose judicial family also prospered in timber, had a pronounced overbite, and I asked if it made eating corn from the cob easier.

Lucille O'Rourke, from a family not traditionally ensconced in law, came from a Northeast Mining consortium. Miss O'Rourke had an odd cast to one eye, and I wondered aloud if it was real or made of glass. When my mother scolded me later, I opined that the traits might be genetic and would be handed down to her grandchildren. That quieted her effectively.

My assignations with Marie ceased, and I felt restless. I hunted pheasants with Grandfather Hudson and fished the lake from his steam launch. I shot for prize money and won the purse at the gun club. There were horse races and a Cotillion where my mother paired me with a tall and homely blueblood banking heiress, but the formal dance, even with rum punch to take an edge off it, did not rise to a morning ride with Marie DuPont in my estimation. The banking heiress's hand was as cold as her personality, and her breath stank of onions. Her teeth were crooked, and she did not clean between them.

Finally, Father called me into his library for cigars and port as spring turned to summer. As we sat with the smoke from Larrañagas curling around our heads, he gave me his benediction, "I've decided that you need to be run out like a two-year-old stallion. It took some doing, and I called in

THE CONFEDERATE CIPHER

favors to wedge you in, but you will have an appointment with the United States Military Academy beginning at the end of summer."

The disclosure came as a complete surprise to me.

"You ride, you shoot, you are not sloppy with a blade, and word reached me that you've been bare-knuckle prize-fighting with other young men even though they have not marred your face by smashing your nose—yet."

"It was only the one time, Father."

"My point is that Dartmouth would bore you, and you need to be disciplined and tamed. The Academy's course of study is five years. I'm told it's challenging and will keep you occupied. You'll graduate with the Class of 1863. I've corresponded with Lieutenant Colonel Hardee, the Commandant of Cadets, responsible for discipline and good order there. We met in Washington, DC, when I was there last week. We were each there on other business but stayed at the Willard Hotel and had long conversations over whisky and billiards.

"He told me of a change of focus. West Point underwent curricular changes, implementing a five-year course of study in 1854. There has been a debate in the Army over what kind of education the school should offer. Army leaders expressed concern about prioritizing technical and scientific studies over professional military education and subjects such as history, languages, and ethics. Cadets take courses in those areas in the new curriculum, even though the overall emphasis remains mainly on technical fields, including mathematics and engineering. The present course of study is more to my liking. By the time you graduate at twenty-two, you will have a more rounded view of the world and, as an officer, *may* have learned to be a gentleman."

"May I speak?"

"No." He looked at me sharply. "Colonel Hardee had a storied career in the War with Mexico, the Campaign to pacify the Seminoles, and later, as a Captain of Texas Rangers, killing Comanches on the frontier before he returned to the Army. It is the sort of thing that may suit you, Henry."

I said sourly, "And it will take me under guard, far from Marie DuPont."

"It will do that too."

"Even though I have avoided her."

Father judicially scrutinized me, "Under protest. If you remain here, your discretion won't last."

A WEEK LATER, when I returned home with my grandfather after three days of fishing from his small tug steamer on the lake, my father stood on the corner looking at our house. I bid my grandpa farewell, and he snapped the buggy whip and turned his carriage toward home. Something happened that put him on bad terms with Father. I suspected that it was because I had been forced to select the Military Academy.

I walked over to where Father stood.

"Ah, Henry, my boy. Times are changing. I'm considering moving to a new home, a larger and grander place."

"What's wrong with this house?"

"It does not befit my position adequately. I've thought of running for governor or perhaps the United States Senate. This home is too small for the entertaining that I would need to do. I purchased a lovely lot on Adelaide Place, situated on the land that had once been the Brush Family plantation. The area was developed carefully: the land directly facing Woodward Avenue was subdivided into large and expensive lots. I engaged Martin Edwards, a famous architect in Detroit, to show Margaret some drawings of what I have in mind."

"I will miss this house."

"You'll be gone, campaigning somewhere with the Army.

The war with Mexico is over, but there is always another war to come. The nation must expand, and the West must be tamed. The red men shall be subdued or destroyed. We will build railroads and bring commerce to the vast expanse of land from here to the Pacific Ocean. The Army will go first as it must. If nothing else, the land needs to be surveyed, and surveyors will be scalped by the red men if there are no soldiers to protect them. Then will come miners, followed by ranchers and farmers, mainly from Europe. Good protestant stock to lay the cornerstones of what will be cities!"

I said, "Grandfather fears there will be unpleasantness over the issue of states' rights." Father looked at me closely, and I explained, "I have never been to the South."

Father lit a cigar and offered me one. I lit it with one of his cedar matches. "Let's go to the porch and continue this conversation."

As we walked, he said, "The Southern States are agricultural, and much of the population is augmented by negro slaves. In truth, there is little difference between those slaves and the servants in our home here. The new house I'm planning will have separate servants' quarters for black and white under different roofs. There are subtle differences between slaves in the South and servants in the North. I do not buy and sell the Irish, but they can't find other work if they're discharged without references. The system binds them here in the same way it does slaves in the South. It's better nuanced here."

"We don't beat our servants," I observed.

"Not in my house, but they're beaten in other homes or workhouses if they get out of line. White men of our class don't beat them; the head man, one of their own, handles the discipline. It's more sensationalized in the South by newspapers in the North. The role the abolitionists take on is one of self-righteousness. Immigrant workers from Ireland, Italy, or

Germany who work in our factories are every bit as badly treated as slaves. Suppose abolitionists turn their attention to that situation here. In that case, they can end up face down in the river, but nobody minds their inflammatory rhetoric if it's directed at the situation in Georgia, Louisiana, or the Carolinas."

We puffed on our cigars, and I thought about what he said.

"Perhaps it would be better to discharge the negroes and replace them with indentured servants from Ireland. Voluntary indentured servitude of poor, bog Irish seems to sit better with many of their betters here in Michigan than that of free negro servants. Your mother favors it—more fashionable in our modern era."

There was a difference, of course. The Irish were not free to leave under penalty of law for seven years, while *free* negroes could always try to find placement in another home if they were dissatisfied. Of course, in practice, an absence of references meant penury.

"Colonel Hardee, the Commandant of Cadets at West Point, is a Georgian. Most of the best officers in the army are Southern men. You'll meet them when you get to the military academy. They will be your instructors. They'll share their opinion of things, which will broaden your view of some of the problems we face as a nation."

My father perched his cigar on the edge of the ashtray, pulled out a pocket handkerchief, and blew his nose. Then he continued. "From 1854 to 1856, there were eight killings in Kansas Territory attributable to slavery politics. The issue was to be decided by the voters of Kansas, but who these voters were was not clear; there was widespread voting fraud in favor of the pro-slavery forces, as a Congressional investigation confirmed."

I shrugged. I didn't read the newspapers as closely as my father did. "How does that apply to me here in Michigan?"

"They didn't teach you much in that fancy Georgetown academy, did they?"

I shrugged again.

"You spent your time with swordplay and horsemanship rather than your letters, even though your grades were acceptable." He shifted focus. "This slavery situation in Missouri and Kansas is far from settled. When winter snows thawed in 1856, the pro-slavery activists began a campaign to seize Kansas on their terms. Lawrence, Kansas, was sacked; you can call it a local war. Two years ago, there was a massacre at Pottawatomie that led to twenty-nine people being killed in raids and counter-raids. A month or so later, General John W. Reid led three hundred Missouri men into Kansas to destroy Free State settlements, and they met at Osawatomie. Does the name John Brown mean anything to you?"

It did. I read something about him in a newspaper, but it was at least a year ago. "Didn't the governor of Kansas pardon him for something?"

"Yes, but the federal government didn't. He remains wanted and continues to cause trouble. The Army became directly involved with Brown and his army of abolitionists and runaway slaves. As an officer in that army, I don't see how this slavery issue wouldn't directly impact you, if only because so many of our officers are from pro-slavery states."

"Do you favor Abraham Lincoln or Stephen Douglas, Father?"

"Douglas believes in popular sovereignty. In short, as long as the people in a territory or state support it, slavery should be allowed. Lincoln takes the opposite view. Douglas believes Lincoln is trying to make abolitionism an issue among the Whigs and Democrats to poison the well. He does not consider slavery to be a moral issue. There will be debates between the two in a few months. As a Michigan man at the Military Academy, they will surely try to force you to take sides, and if it comes to that, you must support your state, which is free soil."

"I don't think that slavery is right."

"Neither do I, but the law allows it; the Constitution approves of the institution, and the Southerners would not have supported the Constitution's creation if it had not. I preside on the federal bench here and rule according to the law, where conscience is not a factor. I would return a runaway slave to its owners as a matter of law in the same way as I would return a stolen horse. As an army officer, you must also follow the law. Do you understand what I'm saying? That is your oath and obligation."

I drained the fiery drink from my crystal glass rather than engage him.

"In the case of Dred Scott v. Stanford last year, Chief Justice of the Supreme Court Roger Brooke Taney, a Maryland man and a good Catholic, held that a black man had no rights that a white man was bound to respect. Chief Justice Taney emancipated his slaves and gave pensions to those who were too old to work, but was outraged by Northern attacks on the institution and sought to use his Dred Scott decision to end the slavery debate permanently."

"But it's not over, is it, Father?"

"Abraham Lincoln and Stephen Douglas don't believe it's over. Neither do the Southern Democrats."

MY GOING-AWAY PARTY, which started as a small family gathering, developed momentum as my mother did what she did best: dipping boldly into the family funds, spending lavishly, and inviting everyone who mattered in Michigan.

THE CONFEDERATE CIPHER

Servants had been borrowed, bowers had been erected and adorned with flowers, and food had arrived in wagons, some of which had been prepared elsewhere. In contrast, others were delivered to the seldom-used cookhouse, located behind the extensive larder and the icehouse.

The train of deliveries boggled my mind: beer by the barrel, expensive single malt and blended whiskies, brandy, bourbon, bottles of champagne, oysters buried in ice, and aged beef loins delivered chilled in the summer heat to be carved into steaks on the premises. The seldom-used ballroom had been opened and pelted with doo-dads of lavender flowers and red roses that hung from the walls.

A majordomo was introduced to me as Pierre, overdressed in black tails, in his early forties. He was paunchy and nearly bald, with an elegant black mustache. He perpetually perspired, dabbed it from his florid face with a silk pocket cloth, and began fussing over details.

When the day arrived, a long line of carriages with matched teams pulled around the circular driveway. Women in gowns were helped out of the back seats. Men stepped out, some wearing tails and white ties. Others wore uniforms.

Inside, the rooms gleamed with fresh polish, as if the maids had just finished, the hum of conversation bouncing off the shiny surfaces.

Quietly bidden, I climbed the stairs to my room, sweltering in the summer heat and humidity, awaiting my moment.

Father's butler brought clothes to my room for the occasion, and I dressed on command in a suit cut to fit militarily with a suggestion of cadet gray martial glory without announcing that I was pretending at something not yet achieved. Once clothed as directed, I came down.

Mother sent me back upstairs, suggesting I join them only when they specifically bid me. It would not do for me to make an early entrance. When I finally descended at her suggestion, it was into a cloud of cigar smoke and perfume and to a crowd of assembled grandees who clapped for my honored departure. Their congratulations were augmented by the chamber strings playing martial tunes that lacked the brass and percussion needed to drive the beat.

Side by side, the women's tresses were elegant and glossy, begging for a forbidden touch. Detroit's and Dearborn's elegant wives took mythological pride in their hair. Some traveled by luxury train coaches along the line my family owned from Lancing, ninety miles distant. The competition between them seemed fierce. They nurtured their manes as though they held the secret to everlasting life. Hues of auburn, gold, and ebony cascaded across the entry hall, eclipsing their husbands and parading on display like stampedes of vainglorious ponies. There were spots of dowager gray here, but they were the exceptions. What they lost with advancing age, they compensated for with gems, ribbons, and gold.

I made my way among them, kissing this offered silk-encased hand and that ungloved and bejeweled claw.

Nails exacted equal devotion; I had yet to press my lips to a hand that was not perfectly finished. It was part of the package. Detroit was the first city in Michigan, no matter how other cities tried to rival its glory. The city's women inhabited a world far removed from tiny box houses, where their lesser gender's hands were often rubbed raw from dishwashing, housework, gardening, and other forms of petty labor.

Among Detroit's glory, fashionable women could sip from pyrite spoons and talk of Michelangelo. A tuxedoed waiter entered the room carrying a polished silver tray of stemware filled with bubbling champagne. He worked the crowd with it as they lifted the contents from its luster to their lips. Another liveried retainer circulated with a large gold bowl filled with caviar, surrounded by an engraved silver platter with crackers piled around the edges. Yet another platter of half-shell oysters was served to the men, resting on mounds of ice. A young lady clad in white with an apron of French lace followed, holding a silver bucket containing discarded shells.

The governor stood next to an army officer in full dress uniform. Another lean man, well known as a hero of the Mexican War, in civilian garb, stood in attendance, lighting cigars distributed by the governor's hand. Alderman Amos Cholmondeley looked like a stuffed turkey inside a gray suit two sizes too small, working to wedge himself into the governor's conversation that excluded him.

Marie Dupont Cholmondeley chatted amiably with the governor's wife, whom I recognized. Then Marie turned her soft, large blue eyes on me, and I almost tripped on my feet.

My father joined the governor, who had a full head of salt-and-pepper hair and the kind of fundamental muscular build that only gets leaner and more sculpted with time. His face, pleasantly aged, was tinged coppery red with sunburn. I shook his large, soft, and sweaty hand, of the sort that hadn't ever known labor.

The governor raised a glass and called my name. The patrician class, crowding the large room, offered and gave me a toast. The governor asked me to join Father and him in a corner of the parlor.

Father excused himself from Alderman Cholmondeley, who had been clinging like a lamprey.

The governor said, "We should have kept you for our state militia, Henry. I had no idea you were interested in a military career. At the same time, the Academy will do you good, and you can return and still rise in the ranks here in Michigan when you've served your eight years. I don't think a major's oak leaves are out of the question as a start."

"I'd be honored, Governor," I spoke to him, but looked over his shoulder at Marie, wearing a powder blue dress that stood on the very point of nearly revealing too much. Of course, I knew what else was there, having sampled the wares. She pointedly ignored me as decorum required, while flirting obliquely and shamelessly in her way.

The governor introduced the military men: Major Thadius Kidd of the Michigan State Militia and Captain Thornton Fleming Brodhead, who traveled from his home on Grosse Isle to attend my going-away party. Brodhead, a native of New Hampshire, a Harvard-trained attorney, and an officer in the regular infantry, won two brevets in Mexico, served with my father in the state legislature, and had most recently been postmaster of Detroit.

We shook hands. "What say you, young Henry?" Brodhead asked me, "D'ye think there will be a war in the South when we bring those scoundrels to heel?"

I shrugged.

"I'll wager a silver dollar that you graduate early to put them straight," Brodhead said, "And the rest of us will be put back into uniform to help. Oh, it will be a grand volunteer army of the North. The Southern boys can fight. Those states claim the best of our officer corps, and they proved their mettle in sharp conflict. They saw the elephant at the gates of Chapultepec, and they didn't run by God. They stood and gave better than they got."

I asked, "Given that valor, would they prevail?"

Major Kidd said, "The war will be over before you are fitted with your new blue uniform, Thornton. Oh, I agree there will be a war of words, and maybe a few hotheads like John Brown will stir up the darkies, but it will be a tempest in a teapot."

"Marcus Tullius Cicero, 52 BC, wrote it first." My Father added, in "De Legibus, 'Excitabat enim fluctus *ut dicitur Gratidius.*"

Broadhead bowed and said, "I defer to your knowledge and understanding of Cicero's writings, Charles. You will be our Chief Justice one day."

My Father said, "I was telling Major Kidd of your proficiency with the Düsack and your gold medal." Father liked to brag.

I clarified, "I have competed with saber and épée and won with both edge and tip. I did not favor the cavalry saber, but I used a purpose-forged Düsack with a thinner, quicker, and lighter Damascene blade. The competitions allowed it."

"Blooded once," Major Kidd gestured to a pink scar along my jawline.

"Only once, sir."

"And your choice?" Captain Brodhead seemed interested.

"Yes, foil, saber, or épée?" Major Kid asked.

I went over the basics. "Foil competition can only score by hitting your opponent's torso with the blade's tip. With épée, scores are counted by touching or striking any part of the opponent's body, including the head and limbs. Many competitors who had practiced with foil found themselves developing bad habits in épée. Foilers outwitting their opponents using feints or misdirections. Épée emphasizes defense, as you're obliged to protect a larger target area. It's more like actual combat than a game, so that was my preference with the tip. Saber requires focusing on the edge, as you are undoubtedly well-versed. I prefer the aggressive nature of the saber over all, and it holds an overwhelming advantage on horseback."

Brodhead looked at my father, "He looks quick. I doubt anyone would want to challenge him." He glanced at me,

"You'll have plenty of time swinging the pattern cavalry saber at West Point in practice."

Marie edged our conversation to distract me. When I looked in her direction, she turned away. At that exact moment, dinner was called by the string quartet enthusiastically pumping out Vivaldi's *Four Seasons*.

Marie's short, fat, old husband waddled to her side and took her arm. She arched an eyebrow, stuck out half an inch of pink tongue in my direction, and strutted beside him.

Captain Brodhead looked at her and said quietly, "You don't *need* to tell *me* the story, Henry." He jabbed me gently in the ribs. "Let's go eat."

The tuxedoed waiters carried their trays, topped with flutes of champagne and platters featuring golden bowls of caviar and crackers, back into the kitchen.

Our banquet was anticlimactic. I had been seated at the head of the table between my grandfathers, Hudson and Forsythe. Grandfather Forsythe presented me with a gold railroad pocket watch, and Grandfather Hudson presented me with German binoculars in a waterproof case covered in fine leather. My name was engraved on both the instrument and the case. I opened the watch cover, and a daguerreotype of my Grandfather and grandmother had been inserted. I would have preferred a photograph of Marie, but my impending departure to New York would forever put her beyond my reach.

I looked down at the long table where she had been seated twenty people distant, happily chatting with other guests. My heart ached, as did my loins.

Withdrawing my binoculars from their case, I lifted them to my eyes, and she filled the lenses. As quickly as I could, I replaced them in the case and responded to the offered toast by emptying my wine glass. A servant standing behind me promptly recharged it.

CHAPTER 2

US Military Academy, West Point
Fall 1858

Colonel Hardee, the Commandant of Cadets at West Point in 1858, as the ranking officer in charge of the Corps of Cadets, held significant responsibilities for the administration, discipline, and military training of cadets at the United States Military Academy. Much is written of him in my account, and I have written very little of Colonel Richard Delafield (Engineers), Superintendent of the US Military Academy during my education there. I had almost no interaction with the Superintendent, but significant contact with the Commandant, whose duties included serving as the Head of the Department of Tactics. This role positioned the Commandant as the primary authority on tactical instruction and implementation for the cadets.

Colonel Hardee oversaw the daily administration of the Cadet Corps, including enforcing rules and regulations and maintaining discipline among the cadets. A central part of the Commandant's duties was to ensure that the cadets received thorough and systematic military training, preparing them for service as officers in the United States Army.

The Commandant acted as a role model, embodying the ideals of a soldier, officer, and gentleman, and was expected to instill soldierly honor and discourage any dishonesty or prevarication among the cadets.

The Commandant of Cadets played a crucial role in shaping the character and military competence of future officers by supervising their training, upholding discipline, and fostering a strong sense of honor and duty under the authority of the Superintendent, Richard Delafield.

The plebes of Class 1863 gathered at the Academy to sign their admission warrants formally by way of contract and swear loyalty to our respective states—in my case, Michigan. In exchange for five years of education, provided free of charge by the federal government, I obligated myself to eight years of service—thirteen years in total. Once signed, they duly notarized and sealed the warrant with a large wax instrument, inserting a blue ribbon through a brass grommet in the warrant, which was written on vellum. It might as well have been written in blood, for it bound me by my honor.

Following that, they handed out oaths printed on sheets of paper. Colonel Hardee administered the oath. We read it in unison after raising our right hands and inserting our names.

"I, Henry Hudson, do solemnly swear that I will bear true faith and allegiance to the United States of America; and that I will serve

them honestly and faithfully against their enemies or opposers whomsoever; and that I will observe and obey the orders of the President of the United States, and the orders of the officers appointed over me, according to the rules and articles of war."

It was later changed, but in that first affirmation, our duty was to the United States and the thirty-two states, individually, in my case, the state of Michigan.

Commandant Hardee gave us a stern lecture on our place as plebes in the Corps of Cadets, two hundred seventy-eight strong. We were the lowest of life forms on the entire planet. We were to learn and immediately begin reciting the names and terms of service of those who served as superintendents or commandants to any upperclassman who requested the information. We needed to know the ranks associated with the chevrons worn by upperclassmen. They were unique to the Corps of Cadets and bore no relation to regular army ranks. Answering a cadet first sergeant or sergeant major by acknowledging his rank was life or death, and demerits would be awarded for lapses after a short period of instruction. Upperclassmen were honored to carry an ivory-headed cane, and any plebe seen holding one would be severely disciplined.

I asked about carrying a sword. I received an icy stare in return, so no.

Regulations detailing even the most minute positioning of buckles and buttons complicated the uniform situation. We had summer uniforms, winter uniforms, parade uniforms, dress uniforms, shell jackets, foul-weather uniforms, and riding uniforms, including a riding jacket. I rarely wore waistcoats as a part of my civilian dress, but that would change. We had kepi caps, forage caps, shakos, and foul-weather headgear, which consisted of oil cap covers. All buttons were brass and required constant attention, as did the leather belts and rigging, which had to be polished or pipe-clayed as needed.

Hair on a cadet's face was as closely regulated as the shine on his buttons, but hair length had relaxed by 1858. I resolved to keep mine trimmed short by the post's barber, who also served as the dentist.

The cadet's choice of military branch would be based on his final standing after graduation. There were only a limited number of openings in each branch. Those first in standing would naturally become engineers, the next artillerists, and so forth, with the anchor man at the bottom of the class taking what remained. Good marks in cavalry drill and practice were expected of engineer and artillery officers in the same way that they'd naturally be expected of cavalry officers. Dragoons, or heavy cavalry, designated by orange piping on the uniform as opposed to cavalry yellow, usually fought dismounted, carrying carbines as opposed to pistols. Though they were still in service, the superintendent projected an end to their utility as a separate mounted branch.

With the advice given, we were marched out, carrying a broad armful of issued equipment and uniforms, to the barrack dormitories that would be our home for the next five years. As I walked, unable to see the ground in front of me, an unseen foot tripped me, and I fell ass over teakettle to the ground with my army possessions spreading out before me on the floor.

Forgetting the code of conduct completely, I stood and looked at an upperclassman laughing at me. He was about my height, with golden-tinted hair under his shako. "Stand at attention, plebe. What is your name?"

"Damn it all, you cur!" I replied hotly.

He looked surprised and smiled even more broadly. "Maybe you'll demand satisfaction, plebe?"

One of the upperclassmen said, "Autie will go through that plebe like a dose of salts through a widow woman."

I slapped him on his cheek as hard as possible, knocking him down. "That's a splendid idea. My choice of weapon is the épée. I will act as my second since I don't know anyone here. Pick your time and place to die. I'm in no mood to nick your ear."

The legs of his white trousers were scuffed and dirty, and when he stood, his eyes spat ice-blue fire. One of the men behind him, an upperclassman with a chevron on his sleeve, took his arm and whispered in his ear. I knew the man with the chevron, Alonzo Cushing of Virginia. I attended the Georgetown Academy with him. His large, brown doe eyes were mirthful rather than angry.

He said, "George, meet Henry Hudson, who won the gold medal for saber at Georgetown three years running, beat our fencing master, and even bested an Austrian in competition."

"Henry," Alonzo said, with a nod of his head.

"It's nice to see you, Alonzo."

He pointed at his stripe, "Sergeant Cushing."

"Sergeant, this man tripped me."

"I saw no such thing," Alonzo said, shaking his head *no*. "I did see Mister Custer tumble over his own big feet."

"You saw him strike me," the golden-haired cadet replied. "It's an honor violation."

"If you push it, Audie, he will kill you with his épée over a matter of your hazing. You're both Michigan men. You have too much in common to push this thing either way."

The cadet asked, "You're from Michigan?"

"Detroit," I replied. "You?"

"Monroe."

Racking my brain, I said, "The only person I know in Monroe is Judge Daniel Bacon."

"How do you know him?"

"He came to my father's house for dinner a few months ago."

"Henry Hudson. They call you Hud, don't they?"

"You have me at a disadvantage, sir."

He held out his hand, and I reluctantly took it. "My name is George Custer, and my friends call me Autie. You paid court to Libby Bacon."

"You're the blacksmith's son, she writes to."

He smiled broadly, "Can we put this unpleasantness behind us? Let me help you gather your belongings. Libby told me of your Spanish horses, bred for combat."

"She only saw them from a distance."

We picked up my uniforms and kit, and he helped me carry them all to my room. A few upperclassmen looked on, with Custer and Alonzo Cushing warding them off. "They'll trip you unless we let them know it's all right," Custer said warmly. "I don't want you booted out and gutting them before I've had a chance to show Judge Bacon my new best friend."

We walked up the stairs. Custer asked me, "How do you shoot?"

Alonzo answered for me, "He decapitates turkeys at a hundred paces with his rifle. I've seen it."

"It's good that we're friends, Hud. If there's a war, you can stand before me, deflecting bullets with your Christ-like presence and vanquish all comers. You can walk across the surface with me mounted on your back if we must cross a river."

"I'll tell you where the rocks are, George."

"That will do."

After I deposited my military equipment and personal goods on a bunk with a name tag assigning ownership, I followed the two upperclassmen to the cadets' mess wearing my civilian clothes. We weren't expected to form in uniform until the following morning. The time would allow us to sort out everything we had been issued, and those tailored uniforms we brought from home.

They cautioned me that we had to arrive separately, so I took a longer route at their suggestion. As I walked, I overtook a softly bulging, shorter plebe who had sworn his oath to South Carolina earlier at the time as I swore to Michigan. His kind gray eyes, framed by girlish lashes, sat eagerly in a round, freckled face. Curly brown hair had been cemented to his head by palmade.

"I'm Henry Hudson — Hud."

"The famous explorer?" He flashed me a gap-tooth smile. "When his men mutinied and set him adrift in a longboat, he wasn't heard from again."

"No, I'm a different one. That was two hundred and fifty-some years ago."

He offered me a fleshy hand, sweaty and a size too small, "I'm Nate Beaufort of the Port Royal Beauforts."

"A pleasure, sir. Are you heading to the dinner mess?"

"I am, but I have not heard the bugle call us."

"Bugle?"

"There is a bugle call for every activity at the Academy." A bugle called from a short distance away. "That is dinner call. We are expected to know and differentiate between 132 bugle calls. You are not fully informed of the details of our Tactics of Artillery, Cavalry, Infantry, and Equitation texts, Hud. Napoleon had only forty bugle calls; one might say we are even more advanced because we have over three times that number to recall.

"No, Nate, I'm as green as grass when it comes to

soldiering."

We entered the mess somewhat informally. As it was our first day, we were ushered toward a sepulchral corner without windows, ordered to take seats, sit at the position of attention, and wait for our betters to dine first. I sat beside Nate of the Port Royal Beauforts because he knew more than I did about how things at West Point were to be done.

Nate whispered, "From here on out, we'll assemble on the parade field and march to meals together as a class."

I stood when directed to stand and followed Nathaniel Green Beaufort III to the tin platters as he clarified his full name. The dinner meal featured stew meat, a potato, a slimy, oddly textured glop that a corporal chef had slapped on the platter, a green pear, and a roll. When we sat and were cautioned not to speak while eating, I whispered to Nate that I didn't know what the off-white glop was. He informed me that it was grits, a staple of Southern cuisine. "Some say that it is the very marrow of Southern culture." I tasted them, and they didn't taste like much of anything.

The smell of Nate's pomade, blended with his body sweat, which was poorly masked by scented powder, turned my stomach. It put me off my food. I could only pick at it and eat a few forkfuls, avoiding the grits after the first bite.

Nate tore through his food like a starving man and waited, sitting at attention, for the command to stand. Once we stood and cleaned our tin plates into a wheeled bin, I noted that Nate's belt struggled to circle his rotund waist like a snake clinging to its tree. On the walk back to the plebe barracks, Nate told me that he had served as a captain in the volunteer infantry militia at Port Royal in Beaufort County, where his father had also served as the colonel in command.

"You have a county named for your family?"

"It is not a large county, but I do."

I asked, "Tell me more of your duties as an infantry

officer in the militia."

"We are on call in the event of slave uprisings and drill for that eventuality every Sunday after church services. We work up a considerable appetite by marching, target practice, bayonet practice, and our cavalry conducts coon hunts on horseback to simulate riding down runaways."

He waited for me to offer my bonafides, but I had none. I didn't even know one bugle call from another.

A bugle called. I looked at him, "Assembly." We walked to the grinder like a herd of recently fed beeves, and they lined us up and told us what was expected.

Over the next week, our training took the entire day but evolved slowly. The bugle calls were not as challenging to learn as I feared. The Plebe class broke into its platoons, stood at the position of attention, and the bugler would bugle a call. Some calls were more complicated, involving a call, and a second signal of execution would follow. The designated sacrificial goat would be given temporary authority as the acting platoon corporal and would issue the verbal command associated with the call, after which the platoon would execute it. An upperclassman stood ready to chew on the ear of the Goat Corporal if he got it wrong. Sometimes, the bugler was instructed to mix the calls, at which time we remained unmoving at the position of attention.

Then they combined the platoons with different buglers, each giving a distinct call, and we were instructed to respond only to our assigned bugler. On the battlefield, we were told, it was common to have many buglers giving different calls to different formations within a division.

When my lot was called, I assumed command of the platoon, unsure but determined to make decisive decisions. I watched the staff climb all over Cadet Nate Beaufort, who was the soul of indecision on the parade ground but stood first in the early engineering exams designed to ferret out those who would be given remedial instruction.

The call, *by the right flank*. I remained still —the next call, a *common step*. I remained still. The call to execute the maneuver. "Platoon, at the common step, forward, march!" The platoon marched forward until the next call, *charge as foragers, disburse*. Then, the call to *execute*.

I shouted, "The platoon will charge in loose order; charge!" We charged across the parade ground in loose order, howling like banshees until the bugle called *assembly*, which required no additional call of execution, and I formed them up into two ranks. We stood at attention and waited. I was dismissed as Goat Corporal and was replaced by Cadet Beaufort, who lumbered forward and saluted. My first command was relinquished and assumed with proper etiquette and solemn decorum.

Having barely managed formations and orders afoot, we mounted in the newly constructed indoor riding arena, where, as the training cadre expected, things quickly went wrong. The Southern plebes all handled their mounts well except for Nate. I didn't shame Michigan, but the rest of the northerners had trouble controlling their horses. We had been given green mounts, barely broken, newly acquired by the Academy at the beginning of the class year. The mounts fussed continually.

Cadet Nathaniel Green Beaufort III's quarters were two rooms down from mine, and he arranged to swap so that we were closer. I had been sharing my room with Cadet Hector Mitchell, a Florida man who slept soundly and snored. Nate Beaufort was barely a step up.

Our first class in *The Manly Art of Self-Defense* had been scheduled for the following day. As we both lay in our bunks after lights out, he asked, "Have you been in a fight before, Hud?"

I didn't want to brag. "One or two."

"Did you win?"

"I hurt my hands on their faces, so no, not really. I soaked them for several days until the swelling went down."

"How about you?"

"No, even though I was in the militia, I never touched anyone with my fists. I never shot anyone either. When the hounds chased the coon to a tree, we usually didn't kill it."

"That might change tomorrow. They're big on doing here at this Academy."

"My hands are soft."

"When I was at Georgetown Academy, I had a dancing master, a euphemism for a swordsmanship instructor. We had a fraternity that engaged in Mensurfechten, and we were very active in the practice. We carried our Schlagers with us when we went out as a group."

"He once took us to the harbor to introduce us to the ways of seamen and stevedores. He said we were lucky because we witnessed a fight between a French sailor and a bouncer outside a pub. The sailor fought with his feet. Jürgen Oomkens von Esens, my dancing master, said that combat is known as savate. It originated in France but was learned by sailors on their trips to the countries of the Indian Ocean and the China Sea. The sailors called it Chausson, referring to the shoes French seamen typically wore on board. They fought with shoes to protect their hands and knuckles, delivering kicks instead of punches."

Nate said, "Kicking violates the Queensberry Rules. It's ungentlemanly."

I smiled, "We asked Herr Oomkens to teach us the basics of Savate, and it's helpful. It uses savage kicks and open-hand blows in thrusting *la baffe*, smashing palm strikes, and stunning slaps targeting facial nerves. I favored the *chassé italien*, an Italian kick. He combined it with boxing."

"Would you teach me, Hud?"

"Sure, when we have time. You need to focus on scored things like saber and horsemanship first."

"Is that scar on your cheek from dueling?"

"Yes. My ears are not puffed from grappling, my nose has not been broken from boxing, and I have all my teeth in place. There is only one mark, but I received it honorably."

One of our classmates broke Nate's nose the next day while boxing. He learned to keep his guard up the hard way. Using one's feet in fighting was considered brawling, and gentlemen did not engage in such behavior. We were to become officers. The rules were inviolate.

NOT EVERYTHING WENT SMOOTHLY for me. I ran afoul of the battalion quartermaster sergeant, a Mississippi man, in my second month. Jubal Hay was a wiry redhead with wide red mutton chops and piggish blue eyes. Unbeknownst to me, he regularly observed my habit of scraping the grits from my metal mess plate into the hog barrel. He reported me to the Quartermaster officer, Captain Timothy Jefferson Buell, also from Mississippi.

Perhaps a better understanding of the role of quartermaster sergeants would be in order. The rank of company quartermaster sergeant was not a command position, although he was required to know the drills, the duties, and responsibilities of the line non-commissioned officers. He was the second-most-senior NCO in the company, after the first sergeant. During combat, his role was to safeguard the company wagon and its supplies. He was generally required to fight only in defense of the company property. In an extreme emergency, he could be used to replace a fallen line sergeant, but this was extremely rare. Each cavalry company was authorized to have a wagoneer, a corporal who assisted the quartermaster sergeant. As a plebe, I ranked well below a

THE CONFEDERATE CIPHER

quartermaster sergeant, and even junior to the cook's cat, but was considered by the Army to be senior to all the Admirals in the Navy while at the Academy. The cadre looked down on the Navy, where officers were trained through apprenticeship as midshipmen and advanced by passing difficult examinations. In their academy, it was said that the midshipmen were senior to all the generals in the Army.

Following consultation between the captain and the QM, which I observed but did not link to my refusal to eat grits, I was served nothing but grits three times daily for breakfast, dinner, and supper for ten days. Having had the implications explained to me by my friend and upperclassman, George Custer, I ate the entire plate of grits with enthusiasm that I did not feel. The matter passed, and I was again served the full academy menu. I ate grits after that, but did not enjoy them. You may say that grits and I developed an adversarial relationship.

Our barracks had lockable "light prison" rooms for cadets in trouble. Autie knew the rooms well. They were located in the corner section and were off limits to cadets except the cadet officer of the day, who would let prisoners out for class and other duties.

There were bathing rooms in the basement, used only for bathing; there were no toilets. Cadets were required to bathe and were charged for the service. I was assessed 40¢ for baths and 85¢ for cleaning of the barracks. Bentz, the bugler, lived in the basement. We called him Lucifer because he lived in the underground and had a proprietary and pecuniary interest in everything that went on there.

I NEVER FULLY EMBRACED THE theodolite in artillery and engineering, and my scores reflected that deficiency.

Sketching defensive works and general geometry became more effortless for me with practice.

I stood first in my horsemanship class. Then they brought out lances. There were no lancer units in the United States Army, but some cavalry officers had enough sway to include them in training in the event they needed to come into everyday use.

The American Army revered Napoleonic tactics above all others, and we were instructed to replicate his strategies in detail, as he had achieved almost universal victory until the end of his career.

During the Napoleonic Wars, lancers were highly valued for their use in shock tactics. More recently, they were employed during the Crimean War from October 1853 to February 1856, between the Russian Empire and an ultimately victorious alliance of the Ottoman Empire, France, the United Kingdom, and Sardinia-Piedmont. American Army Officers served as observers with the French and British armies, watching lancers in combat. Those officers returned, full of martial zeal, urging our army to follow suit.

Major Geoffrey Clark Randall (Cavalry) stood before us in class. He explained that he petitioned the War Department to create a battalion of US Light Cavalry armed with lances, modeled after the order of Napoleon's French Imperial Guard, the 1er Régiment de Chevau-Légers-*Lanciers de la Garde Impériale.*

He recounted the charge of the British 16th Lancers at Aliwal on January 28, 1846, during the Anglo-Sikh War, complete with diagrams, and wished on our behalf that we could do as well in our careers in the US Army.

French lances with which we were to train were ten feet long, weighed around six and a half pounds, and had a blunted steel point on an ash wood staff. In near-peer-to-peer cavalry engagements, lances trumped swords because of their reach. I thought those French troopers must not have had revolvers, but I didn't say anything.

Major Randall admitted that lancers were more vulnerable to other cavalry units in mêlée situations, where the lance proved a clumsy and easily deflected weapon when employed against sabers. In accordance with French military doctrine, his solution was to post lancers in the front rank of the charging formation. Cavalry, with our sabers drawn, would follow to defend the lancers. That was what we practiced.

The use of break-breech shotguns in close-range cavalry engagements was considered to be barbaric and beneath gentlemanly conduct. To me, it meant that they were effective.

Our sword drills against opposing cavalry stressed the use of the arm as a pivot. The wrist wheels the sword independently of any other action. Neither incline the hand to the right nor left of the given position nor sink it below the level of the antagonist's left ear, but above all, we were not to bend the elbow: these were faults that beginners are apt to commit and which expose the sword arm to be completely disabled.

The necessity of keeping the sword aimed at the left ear of opposing cavalry, with the shoulder only being used to take the hand to the start position of the cut, which is then executed by the wrist alone, was taught with many repetitions. Cadet Beaufort's wrist was too limp to perform these maneuvers properly, and he fell behind the class, dropping his saber repeatedly.

His work with a lance was barely better.

I took him aside and offered to work with him on mounted and dismounted sabers after hours if he'd help me with the finer engineering points. We agreed to meet at the riding arena after supper twice weekly before taps.

The Academy was justifiably proud of its new riding stable. Its design was based on the famed École de cavalerie in Saumur, France. The same design, with some modifications to the size and roof, was the one approved and built. It is similar to the Manège des Écuyers in Saumur.

The building was stone and essentially one large open area for riding. Stone from the 1817 North Barracks may have been used. The interior riding area was 210' x 70' with a height of 58'. The overall footprint was 218'x78' with walls that measured about 3 feet thick. Balconies were built on both sides of the hall for observers. The roof was curved. Given that the building in Saumur lacked a curved roof, the design element may have been modeled after the Providence Railroad Depot at Park Place in Boston.

George Custer became a legend for his practical jokes. Late at night, he rolled a cannonball down the hallway where we plebes slept to wake us up and kept up his campaign of tripping lower-classmen. He and the other upperclassmen spared me because of my reputation as a duelist, spread by Custer himself.

Balls mitigated the rigors of military etiquette for all but us plebes. We were prohibited from joining in the hops at Cozzens's Hotel. I stayed in quarters and studied. George Custer invariably drank too much and received disciplinary demerits when he presented himself drunk and hungover as we stood at attention at morning colors. I witnessed varying degrees of debauchery throughout my time with him at the Academy, but we had become friends by then.

OF THE BOYS who entered the class with me, few had received either social or educational advantages of a very high order. Having been schooled at the Georgetown Academy, I enjoyed an advantage, and after the first examination,

Nate Beaufort and I were placed toward the head of the class because of our prior educational experiences.

One young man, Isaiah Hamilton, was awkward and uncultured in manner and appearance, but there was an earnest purpose in his aspect which impressed all who saw him. He was placed in quarters with Nate and me to help him improve.

When I first saw him, he was clad in gray homespun and wore a coarse felt hat, such as wagoners or constables usually wore, and bore a pair of weather-stained saddlebags across his shoulders. I commented to Nate, "This fellow looks as if he had come to stay."

Every night just before taps, he would pile our grate high with anthracite coal, so that by the time the lamps were out, a ruddy glow came from the fire, by which, prone upon the bare floor, he would "bone" his lesson for the next day, until it was literally burned into his brain.

Hamilton was as clumsy in his horsemanship and with his sword as Nate, and we were painfully anxious as we watched him leaping the bar and cutting at heads. He would do it, but at the risk of his life.

Autie's pranks went too far when he greased the stairs in our barracks, and poor Hamilton slipped, tumbled, and broke his left leg and right arm. He was discharged from service, and none of us implicated Custer in the incident, though we all knew his mischief caused it. The honor code did not require that we speculate.

CHAPTER 3

US Military Academy, West Point
Winter 1858

*A*nything to do with the matter of slavery was a hot topic. George Custer, whose friends were all Southerners, was pro-slavery to the chagrin of his Northern countrymen. Some considered him a traitor of sorts, and he made enemies, which led to more demerits for even minor infractions.

The Utah Insurrection Campaign was a topic in our Science of War class because it had been underway for a year and had become an embarrassment for the Army and President Buchanan. While the matter of slavery was being hotly contested in Missouri and Kansas, with the Army assuming the role of peacekeeper, Mormons in Utah, abolitionists all, were said to be in rebellion against the United States.

Colonel Joseph Hooker, an artillery officer newly raised

to the rank in the California Militia, prepared to depart his home in Massachusetts for his new post. Before he left, he agreed to serve as a guest lecturer on the Utah War at the behest of Colonel Hardee, our commandant. Colonel Hooker served in the Seminole Wars and the Mexican–American War, receiving three brevet promotions before resigning from the Regular Army. A reputation with the ladies and a trail of gambling debts followed him.

He looked resplendent as he stood before us wearing his militia colonel's dress uniform. I didn't see the reputation reflected in his demeanor or in his lecture. Hooker seemed to have a clear understanding of how the Army's business should be conducted. He brought maps, charts, and a solid understanding of what happened and possibly why. Given that the campaign undertaken to bring the abolitionist Mormons to heel was managed by pro-slavery officers, Col. Hooker may have been more keen to cast blame than if that had not been the case.

"An army division consisting of the Fifth and Tenth Infantry Regiments supported by a battery from the Fourth Artillery left Fort Leavenworth, Kansas, in July for Salt Lake City in the Utah Territory. They were obliged to leave the Second Dragoons behind to manage the insurrections in Kansas and Missouri, so they marched without scouts or a cavalry screen. Who among you can point out the problems with that campaign?"

I raised my hand, was called on, stood, and asked, "Wouldn't it have been prudent to have sent men forward before the main body to understand better what they faced, like Joshua in the Bible?"

"It would have been, but the Army has no mechanism to accomplish that activity beyond the word of civilian scouts, and Jim Bridger was known for telling tall tales. You have pointed out a weakness in our structure, Cadet Hudson, that we may live to regret. The Mormons, who were mounted, burned our supply train and scorched the Earth before them. They ran off the Army's cattle, and the division was starving and completely bogged down during the winter. Newspapers reported on the progress—or lack thereof. Eventually, the Mormons *sold* the stolen cattle with their Army brands back to the quartermaster a few at a time to prevent starvation at triple the going rate for beef."

"This past summer, the matter was resolved. Brigham Young, the Mormon prophet and territorial governor, was replaced by an appointee from President Buchanan, and the Army built a fort to house troops in the Great Salt Lake Valley, obliged to rely on the Mormons to supply them at prices the Mormons set."

Colonel Hooker quizzed us on lessons the Army should have learned from the debacle. "How could 2,500 soldiers have been stymied by fewer than half that number of irregular militia, none of whom fired a shot in anger?"

After being invited to stand again, he asked, "Cadet Hudson, what do you think?"

"They had no cavalry screen, no spies among the Mormons?"

"None, Cadet Hudson?"

"Why was that not undertaken?"

"The Mormon settlers were all well known to one another. Their watchwords were from their particular scripture and were not known to us. Strangers arriving from any direction would be put to the question and likely have failed to remain with a hidden purpose."

I sat.

Colonel Hooker continued, "Colonel Alexander expressed frustration that he would be like the Persians at

Thermopylae in the narrow mountain passes he had to navigate to get through the rocky mountains. A few marksmen could take the high ground and pick off his slowly moving concentrated infantry command below in detail."

One of the cadets asked if the artillery regiment couldn't have supported infantry advances through steep canyons.

Colonel Hooker replied, "The U.S. Army's field artillery, and in this case, the Fourth Regiment, utilized the Model 1841 12-pound mountain howitzer. The 1841 12-pound mountain howitzer is a bronze smoothbore weapon that can fire explosive shells, spherical case, and canister. It is designed to be lightweight and portable, capable of being broken down and transported by pack animals, making it well-suited to mountainous or rough terrain characteristic of Utah. This portability enabled these small howitzers to provide artillery support to mobile military forces in areas with limited road networks. Can anyone point out a potential problem with these weapons?"

Nobody answered. "Cadet Hudson?"

I stood and said, "They lacked range, having short barrels and being smoothbores."

He smiled, "They do indeed. They're effective in defense, particularly when loaded with cannister, but the longest-ranged projectile, the exploding shell, has a maximum effective range on a flat plain at 5-degree elevation of 1,072 yards. Shooting at opponents in high canyons, they'd be lucky to reach out one-third that distance with any degree of accuracy. Exploding shells, while effective against infantry on an open field, are not useful in rocky terrain where the landscape absorbs the shrapnel."

Hooker turned to his map, pointing. "A thrust of steamships loaded with troops to support the northern route had been undertaken, coming up the Colorado River, but it got bogged down because of narrow canyons with swiftly flowing shallow water, which frustrated the navigation of the steamships.

"Mojave Indians paid to massacre Mormon settlements in the south likewise proved generally ineffective. The Mormons treated them humanely, and they betrayed our trust in them. So you see, Cadet Hudson, the Army was not completely derelict in its duty. Only incompetent.

"I foresee that a commanding general in the field might direct his provost marshal to undertake the function you correctly specified. I am informed that the British established a service a few years ago, before the Crimean War, to undertake such efforts systematically. Their Great Game with the Russians over control of Central Asia demanded it. Does our manifest destiny to expand the nation from ocean to ocean not do the same?

"The institution of slavery colors much of what we do in our nation at present. It taints our actions and humiliates us as happened in Utah." Colonel Hooker, a militia officer now, could speak his mind in a way that a serving regular Army officer might not.

Cadet Jubal Pickens from Alabama raised his hand, was recognized, stood, and said defiantly, "State-sponsored slavery has existed for thousands of years after the Old and New Testaments. It seems that if God intended to end slavery, he might have been a lot more specific in *His Bible* about ending it. I can only conclude that God understands the lack of equality between his chosen people and negroes and guides the hand of nations to ensure that miscegenation does not take place, so that if it does, that mulattos and octoons know they are lesser." He sat.

Colonel Hooker, now astride a powder keg among the majority of cadets and faculty who were from the South, navigated his way out of the quagmire admirably. After class,

I waited to speak with him and helped him roll and pack his maps.

"I know your grandfather and his brother, Samuel Hudson, who lives in Boston. Samuel and I met across a *Lansquenet* table where he acted as the banker more than once."

"Will there be a war over the matter of slavery?"

Colonel Hooker smiled and said, "I can't predict the future beyond my current engagement in California. I will travel around the Horn of South America in *the City of Baltimore*, Glasgow-built and owned by the Peninsular and Oriental Steam Navigation Company. Samuel Hudson owns a respectable stake. Your dear uncle gifted me a first-class stateroom."

"Uncle Samuel grips every penny tightly as if it were his last," I said, knowing his character.

"You have me there. I won it at Faro—but from him. I'll tell you, Cadet Hudson, I look forward to living at the Presidio in California, where these slavery matters are not so constantly pressing. *You* only need to study Euclid, memorize bugle calls, and keep your uniform pressed. Stay as far from the matter as you are able."

I replied, "Yet, Stephen Douglas, not a span taller than Napoleon, would separate the nation and lead us into war. The talk of the Academy between young men of conscience is unending on this matter."

Hooker smiled, "I will be in the California Militia, a free state, far from the bear baiting. Slavery may be a moral wrong, but it is not now a legal wrong. I'll leave it to the legislature to argue the matter and the courts to interpret it. I shall sit on my porch, sip ardent spirits as the sun sets until I'm stiff as a galvanized corpse, and will my duty to oversee drilling the troops at sunrise without another thought to this disaster."

"If there is a war, California may be called upon to support the federal claim," I said.

"It is a very long march from San Francisco to Washington, D.C., without forage to sustain such reinforcements in the field. No, Henry, distance has its own political opinion. By the time California politicians decided whether to send their only line of defense to aid the federal government, and the federal government decided to send ships around the Horn to collect the troops, the contest would have been resolved one way or the other. There are not many men in the free states who feel that negro emancipation is worth fighting over. I will ask you personally, would you shed your blood so that a negro may own a mule?"

"No, I am not inclined that way, nor does the law require it."

"And that, Cadet Hudson, is why any contest over the matter will be short-lived and bloodless."

I walked Colonel Hooker to his coach and bade him farewell, envying him his posting far from the swell of harsh opinions. I disagreed with him. The officers and cadets from slave states were more than willing to fight, and *they* had the spirit and elan to carry those intentions forward if pressed.

As 1858 turned into 1859, the political situation at the Military Academy mirrored the country's overall state. The polarization between a full two-thirds of the 278 cadets from Southern States and the remainder from Northern States was catalyzed by Commandant Hardee, a Georgian, and more than half of the instructional and institutional staff who were also sympathetic to the Southern Cause. The upperclassmen from both factions left me alone because I kept my opinions to myself and ended the term ranked fifth in my class. George Custer, ahead of me at the Academy, struggled to maintain good grades and suffered from excessive demerits. He faced the possibility of expulsion for cause.

THE CONFEDERATE CIPHER

Nathaniel and I returned from the riding arena one evening and were challenged by a sentry. He was ghostly white, his lips curled back, shaking like a bird dog shittin' peach pit. I thought, 'This idiot is either going to shoot me, skewer me on his bayonet, or pass out.' George Custer, corporal of the guard, appeared when summoned and calmed the sentry who had an unreasonable fear of spirits from the great beyond. Whatever George was or wasn't, he had leadership skills that often went unappreciated.

At the conclusion of the annual summer encampment, we were furloughed for one month. Autie Custer and I traveled back to Michigan together, wearing cadet gray. I was no longer a plebe and could be seen in polite company with other cadets.

I took a room at Monroe for a week at Sally Gibbon's boarding house. He introduced me to his father, Emanuel, who spent long hours over the forge. The coal dust under his skin on his face and arms had darkened them. He said that his mother, Mary, named him Armstrong after a Bible thumper in Ohio, hoping he'd find God and become a man of the cloth in adulthood. George Armstrong Custer was not inclined to a preacher's soft and pious life of rhetoric.

George's parents were ordinary people with little to say. His brothers, Tom and Boston, were both lively and mischievous, unlike their serious, hardworking parents.

We went by Libby Bacon's house, and since Judge Bacon was home, I paid my respects with Autie tagging along. The Judge was surprised that Cadet Custer and I were friends. Autie told me later that I helped him score a few points with the man he hoped would become his father-in-law.

I believed Judge Bacon was unlikely to relent and take George into the family as his son-in-law. You could see an almost seething arrogance to the notion that he'd allow George any opportunity. There was a gap in their classes, even though George and I attended the US Military Academy together. Judge Bacon viewed us differently.

George and I spent two days in Monroe drinking and shooting grouse, but I had to go home to see my parents and, with any luck, impress Marie Cholmondeley enough with my dashing uniform to go riding.

I boarded the Detroit, Monroe & Toledo Railroad, which my father's family owned outright now, for the final leg of my journey home. On the trip, there was gossip between conductors that the Michigan Southern & Northern Indiana Railroad planned on purchasing the line. My mother's family owned that one. I sensed my brother Robert's hand in the maneuver. The stock would be traded, my family would come out ahead, and others would lose.

I replaced my cadet's straight sword with the model 1840 heavy dragoon saber manufactured by N. P. Ames of Springfield to wear with my gray uniform. The saber, known as a wrist breaker, gave me a more serious appearance. If I hadn't been out of uniform to wear it, I would have also worn my Colt M-1851 Navy Revolver. It seemed important to me to make a good impression on Marie when I saw her.

I hired a gig carriage at the station to transport me home and arranged for my luggage to be delivered. I paid the driver extra to pass Alderman Cholmondeley's house. I didn't see anyone outside, so we continued to Adelaide Place, where the Brush Plantation once stood. A home my father described to me almost a year earlier was still under construction. The driver stopped. I unlinked my saber and left it in the gig while I walked the lot. It reminded me of the most elegant homes in New York City. No expense had been spared. The house, which had a copper roof and was weathered in, still had a long way to go inside.

After exhausting all other options, I went home, clanked up the steps to the front door, and pulled the chain with bells on the other end. Bet, the downstairs maid, answered the door and gave me an inappropriate but most welcome hug. "You've grown three inches, Master Henry!"

Mother came from the kitchen to give me another hug and a peck on the cheek.

"Your father is at court but expected home for dinner. Let me look at you. Oh, you are so dashing. I won't be able to keep the young ladies away from you now." She gave me a sly look, "There is news in the community. Old Amos Cholmondeley, who now sits with the City Regents, is the father of twins." She judged my reaction as only a mother can. "They are adorable, healthy twin boys now three months of age. Who would have thought the fat old man had it in him?"

I muttered, "I'm sure that congratulations are in order. I'm surprised that you took note of the event."

"Charles took a greater interest in Amos recently after he crowed that his young wife was with child. He remarked that they are robust young lads, much like you were at that age."

Changing the subject, I said, "I have three weeks of leave remaining and wonder if it would be possible to ride to hounds at Grosse Point while I'm home?"

Mother said, "I'll telegraph father. I'm sure that he'd be thrilled to see you."

"I'd like to bring another cadet who is home on leave. He's from Monroe."

"I don't think that would pose a problem. The groom has been exercising Bayard and Glory regularly in your absence."

Father arrived home and wasted no time informing me of my likely lads in Amos Cholmondeley's household. Because I had been inside the new house on Adelaide Place, I was able to change the focus of our discussion before it became even more tedious. There was other news. Grandfather Hudson had another steam launch built. This one was docked on Lake St. Claire, and he'd enjoyed good luck with the catch.

Robert, now a graduate and practicing lawyer, played games with the railroads, reaping significant profits, and my sister was expecting her first child to arrive in two months.

Dinner—a beef Wellington with Yorkshire pudding, broiled potatoes, greens, and apple pie with clotted cream—was an extraordinary departure from the mess hall at West Point.

After dinner, my father said, "Please join me in the library."

I didn't know what to make of it. Past meetings in the library were mixed bags. He poured two single malt Scotch whiskeys into crystal glasses and raised his, "To a successful plebe year!"

I clinked glasses and sipped the amber liquid —a complex blend of smoky and cherry notes with a mild burn. "Delicious."

"I have a surprise for you, son." He withdrew a flat mahogany box from a drawer in his desk and put it on top. "Open it."

The oiled hinges glided open, and a handgun of a sort I had never seen lay within the box. "May I?"

"It's yours."

The weapon was heavy but balanced. I lifted it and aimed out the window.

"It's a Grape Shot Revolver, developed in New Orleans in 1856 by Jean Alexandre Le Mat, whose manufacturing effort was backed financially by an engineer, Colonel P. G. T. Beauregard. John Krider of Philadelphia made this revolver under license. It fires a forty-two caliber ball; the shot option is sixteen gauge."

"It's the perfect horse pistol."

Father said, "My thoughts exactly. I fear we are headed for conflict with the Southern States, and wanted you to be properly armed, no matter what your role might be."

I hefted the pistol again, loving the weapon's lethality and overall feel. The cylinder carried nine shots; the second barrel could deliver a devastating point-blank charge.

"I'm speechless."

"I bought two spare cylinders so you can reload the weapon quickly without taking the time to pack more powder and ball."

I hugged my father, and he held me tightly. "I fear that I might have set you on the path to injury or even death by securing your appointment."

"No, it's the right fit for me. I don't know if the South will pick a shooting war to solve the problems and disagreements we have, but they will have fine officers to lead their rebellion if they take that course."

He released me from his embrace.

"You will be set against your new friends."

"Some of them, not all of them. Many remain loyal to their states in the North. I will not turn my back on Michigan. Besides, we have Crazy Autie Custer. He's a friend of mine from Monroe. I want to take him to ride with hounds at Grosse Pointe."

My father smiled, "Will you take an old man with you on your fox hunt?"

I replied, "You and I can ride the Spanish stallions. George Custer can ride one of Grandfather Forsyth's Morgans. George talks about the benefits of Kentucky thoroughbreds, but he hasn't ridden a Morgan to hounds yet. We ride Army remounts at the Academy, which are primarily tired geldings purchased at a low cost. I'm out of practice riding real horses."

* * *

SPITTLE FLEW through Elijah's crooked brown teeth. "Git down, Bobby, get down, Chinny." His dark, pockmarked, youngish skin was framed by greasy, long brown hair that hung lankly in the humidity, dripping with sweat. The two dogs bayed as they worked the scent to determine the direction of travel. Elijah, Grandfather Forsyth's Waldvogel and forest marshal, lost his two favorite dogs to a panther the week before, and he hoped that we'd be able to pick up the scent and run the cat to the ground. He looked leaner than usual, dirtier than I recalled, and chewed from a thick plug of tobacco that distended his unshaven cheek. Elijah Crowfoot, half-white and half-red, spoke English learned at the Brethren's Normal School for Indians, and was about the same age as George Custer and me. Flies swarmed around him.

George smoked a pipe, and Father and I smoked cigars to ward off the insects.

Father rode Glory and kept him on a tight rein, making him rack occasionally with his front hooves. Nobody could tell Judge Charles James Hudson how to ride, and every time Autie Custer began to open his mouth, I silenced him with a glance. Custer rode Lancer, a stocky, powerful black Morgan stallion from the stables. I rode Bayard, black with a white star on his forehead, taller by two hands and prone to bite Lancer when he got in his way, despite my best efforts to have him behave. My absence hadn't been good for either of my horses' discipline, who trailed the coach on a halter lead as Father and I rode to Boroughfield, the family hunting lodge on Lake St. Clair. They would have been more disciplined if we'd ridden the entire twenty-five miles.

"There now, Chinny!" The timber of the hound's bay changed as the redbone bitch determined the direction that the quarry had taken under and through a blackberry thicket. Chinny ran low, followed by Bobby, the get of a litter two years previous, and Father spurred Glory, who jumped a deadfall, intent on following the general path taken by the dogs. Elijah held his pony back, deferring to George, and I went first.

"Is it the panther?"

"Only the Most High God knows, Hud. It could be a coon or a fox as much as the panther."

I spurred after my father, followed by Custer, who gave a war whoop as his straw hat flew off his head, restrained by a loose chinstrap that kept it linked to his neck.

Elijah stopped us when the track ended in a wide bramble bisected by a meandering creek. He called in the baying hounds and put them on a leash. "I baited and trapped the bramble. I daren't let the hounds in there for fear they'd meet the traps."

"I'm not going to ride my horse aimlessly through there without knowing the precise location of the traps," I said.

My father suggested we retire to the hunting lodge for a hot buttered rum and consider the situation.

"Bully!" George Custer said, turned his mount, and cantered back. We followed him, electing for the consolation prize.

So much for the great adventure, but something equally interesting awaited us at my Grandfather Leslie Forsythe's drawing room. The old man unwrapped a large ship's model on his expansive desk. Near it, he placed a book of plans on a pedestal.

"Ah, Henry, Charles, and a friend."

"Cadet George Armstrong Custer, Upperclassman, at your service, sir."

"You've arrived to witness the unveiling of my most recent acquisition; meet *SS Seraphim*."

My Father said, "A boat model."

"Not just a boat, Charles. You have a judge's talent for

understatement. This is a steam-powered, armed screw trader that is under construction in Liverpool."

"Where are the paddle wheels?"

Grandfather looked at me as if I were my father's son. "There are no paddles. It is pushed through the sea by two screw propellers at the stern of the ship." He pointed to an appendage immediately before a respectably large rudder. "That's what pushes it through the mighty deep."

"It only has one cannon, sir?" George asked.

"I've been convinced that it only needs one. It can be rotated on its gun platform to fire in any direction, propelled by a gear and a small steam engine driven by the main steam engines, then locked into place. It's a nine-inch Dahlgren gun that can fire either shot or shell."

George asked, "What are those barriers around the gun?"

Grandfather said, "They're steel barbettes. They protect the crew and don't turn with the revolving gear. If they were on the rotating platform, it would only add unnecessary weight to a very heavy gun."

He left the room and returned a minute later with a scale model of the gun system. It incorporated gears that moved. "Obviously, this is only a representation of the actual works, but I'm told that it's a faithful recreation."

My father said, "That's most impressive, Leslie."

Grandfather proudly told us, "There are twenty-six patentable inventions, including the engines, which work on Fulton's basic design with some radical innovations. The compound engine, which uses steam in multiple stages, was developed by Alfred Holt. It will significantly improve fuel economy. We believe she will steam at 10 knots while burning only 20 long tons of coal per day, which is half the consumption of a conventional engine. We have also incorporated surface condensers so the boilers use fresh water. Most steam ships feed saltwater into their boilers, limiting boiler pressure, wasting heat, contributing to poor fuel efficiency—around four pounds of coal per horsepower-hour."

"Your ship, the *Seraphim*, seems longer than I would have expected it to be for a cargo hauler." I tried to sound smarter than I was.

"Bright boy," He replied. "Larger ships are generally more efficient for long voyages. Carrying capacity increases with the cube of their dimensions, while water resistance increases with the square, a principle that favored larger vessels on long trips."

The mathematics eluded me, but I nodded as if that was specifically what I meant to say.

"*Seraphim* is 233.2 feet in length, 29 feet in breadth, drawing 14 feet, 629 gross tons. She is designed to carry high-value cargo rather than bulk. The rigging is necessary because the ship can only carry a limited amount of coal for the steam engine. She draws very little water. More than a side-wheeler, but she should be able to navigate significant rivers instead of being confined to major ports."

"Arthur Bradford designed it, and it was laid down at John Laird Sons & Co's - Birkenhead Iron Works. It has a strong steel hull resistant to worms and weather. Two smaller, more efficient steam engines and twin screws for reliability."

"You built a smuggler, Leslie," my father pronounced. "My father-in-law, the pirate."

"Steel sinks, wood floats, Grandfather," I observed.

"The water is displaced. The ship doesn't have to be made of buoyant material. Its first cargo will be an opium tincture —Laudanum—made in England. There is a high demand everywhere, and I have cornered the market on its manufacture in Suffolk, including the opium harvest brought by my clippers from China to England. It's important to diversify beyond railroads and steel. Bulk haulers have their place, but the market is fast-delivering high-value goods anywhere in the world. Steam engines enable delivery schedules to be met even without considering wind conditions. Tides must be considered when crossing a bar at a harbor mouth, but they are no longer critical to departures or arrivals."

"And the cannon, Leslie?"

"Because there are both pirates and rivals."

CHAPTER 4

US Military Academy, West Point
Fall 1859

Autie Custer and I made the trip back to the Academy on the Michigan, Ohio, and Pennsylvania Railroad, with few diversions. I secured first-class tickets for us, which gave us access to the dining car. They'd be the last meals served on China plates, resting on white linen tablecloths, which I'd have for some time.

Custer would have been content with cheap roadhouses with ticky mattresses for lodging and meals, but I covered the cost of more improved situations, that included maid service, and properly laundered rooms. We took lodging in Cleveland at the Excelsior on the first night of our travel. The chicken and dumpling soup had real chicken rather than only flour, grease, and thin broth available at the poorer locations. Breakfasts were hearty, not just a stale biscuit, a boiled egg, and coffee. Our military pay of $30 per month would resume once we passed back through the gate. Custer left what he had with his parents. My purse was always filled.

George would gamble on horse races or even something so mundane as which fly would crawl up the wall faster. I didn't indulge him by fronting him money he would inevitably lose at games of chance. The poker table at the Excelsior called to him, but I remained firm. Autie Custer gambled poorly. In a way, I felt as if I had become his older brother, even though he, an upperclassman, was my superior in rank.

Much of our discussion on the trip was prompted by newspapers announcing the discovery of the Comstock Lode in the Utah Territory. Prospectors flooded west at the news that silver nuggets could be found lying on the ground and were there for the taking. "Henry," he said, "We could go West and make our fortune in a month rather than drilling, reading rhetoric, and trying to make heads from tails in Greek."

"It will be more complicated than walking around with a sack picking up nuggets, Autie. Once you have found your fortune, you must also keep your fortune."

"Henry," he said, "you're good with a rifle, pistol, and sword. As good as any of us, you know I'm a master of warfare and tactics. Together, we can subdue any prospector or claim jumper intent on mischief."

"You only recognize one tactic, Autie," I replied, "Draw sabers, bugler sound charge, and head straight at 'em."

"Napoleon, Hud."

I said, "He lost."

"—gloriously. He lost, but he lost gloriously, and usually he won."

I gave my benediction, "You're only as good as your last game."

He spent the time he would have spent gambling working

out the trip west to Utah on paper. The news had been out for two months, and he collected newspapers to help organize his expedition by extracting facts from each.

I quizzed him. "What do you know of mining?"

"I don't have to know much, Hud. It's a matter of collecting enough silver to make me as rich as Croesus and then buying a steamship to bring me home from California."

The other news in the papers concerned the so-called Pig War, a border dispute between the United States and the United Kingdom over the San Juan Islands in the Canadian Pacific. It began with the shooting of a beloved pig, and the conflict was still underway as we rode the rails.

Abolitionists were always sensationalized or demonized in the papers, depending on the political bent of the particular publication. George predicted, "The abolitionists are going to go too far, and then the sword will be drawn and not sheathed until the business is settled." He mostly ran around with Southerners at the Academy, and his feelings toward talk of secession were very sympathetic toward them. I tried to avoid it by being as non-committal as possible while being polite. As a result, the Southerners felt I had an affinity for their cause, while the Northerners knew I was committed to the Michigan country and that I had signed an oath to Michigan when I entered West Point.

"What about Libby Bacon?" I asked. "What will she do when you go West to seek your fortune? If you're gone too long, she'll offer her hand to another."

George looked at me narrowly, "I'd demand satisfaction from her suitor or her husband and then marry the widow."

And so it went.

I told him that if he went West to seek his fortune, his yellow-blonde hair would make a magnificent scalp on a warrior's lance.

"Maybe that's how I'll be remembered."

I advised, "Cut your hair short, make your scalp undesirable to the barbarian hoards."

After presenting travel orders, we spent our last night on the road at the visiting officer's barracks at Fort Lee, New York. Four other cadets were waiting for contract space on a paddle steamer to take them up the Hudson to West Point. I fronted Autie five dollars for a card game. Gambling was frowned upon if we had been officially on duty. The fact that we were in transit made a difference. He doubled his money at poker for once, and I came out a dollar ahead. He paid me back the loan and gloated over his winnings.

I asked, "What will you do with all that money?"

"Buy a few drinks and find me a sporting girl."

"What about Libby?" I asked.

"She's understanding."

"The way most women are," I added dryly.

He never found a bar or a soiled dove. The paddle wheeler *President Tyler* rounded a bend in the river, belching smoke from both stacks as it toiled upstream, machinery chunking loudly, the steam whistle blowing.

Looking at the other cadets, Armstrong ordered me, "Get my bag."

I stood there and scrutinized him.

He thought twice and said, "Never mind, Cadet Hudson, you'd probably drop it," for the benefit of the others.

I had returned.

Major Robert Anderson (USMA 1825), our mathematics instructor, crossed the gangway shortly after we did, wearing his full major's uniform. Although he did not instruct full-time, the Army regarded him highly for his skill as an artillerist. In 1854, the Army put him on various board and inspection duties, and he saw himself as clear to teach when he had a slack schedule. It wasn't something pushed on him. He fought in the War with Mexico and was severely

THE CONFEDERATE CIPHER

wounded in a heroic assault on the enemy's works at Molino del Rey. They gave him a brevet majority for gallant and meritorious conduct, and he had only recently been raised to permanent rank a decade later. Seniority ruled almost everything in the Army. Competence was a distant fourth or fifth in order of importance.

I waved, "Welcome aboard, Major Anderson."

He waved back at me, "Cadet Hudson, it's good to see you." He also acknowledged Autie Custer, "And Custer, you're still here. I'm sure you'll find a way to finish your career soon."

Custer was notoriously bad at mathematics and the artillery course and had not endeared himself to Major Anderson. He continually talked of how cavalry could easily ride down the artillery from a flanking attack more quickly than the artillerists could redirect their guns. Autie would have taken on the Pope over the size of the nails pounded through Jesus' hands on the Old Rugged Cross. Whatever position the Pope would have taken, Autie would have argued the matter regardless of whether either of them had been there.

"You'll join me in the salon for a mug of punch, Cadet Hudson?"

"Thank you, sir."

Custer made a loud pig grunt and then an authentic-sounding pig squeal.

Once in the salon, Major Anderson removed his hat and set it on a table. I likewise removed my shako. "I'm still the inspector of iron-work manufactured at Trenton, New Jersey, and for public buildings constructed under the Treasury Department contracts, but that will end soon. There is nothing to do until November 15th, so I will be here teaching you lads for some months. While I'm here instructing, I'm to arrange an instruction program for artillery officers at the Artillery School for Practice at Fortress Monroe. My orders to the school take effect on December first." He paused with gravitas. "I hope you will select artillery as your chosen branch of service, Henry."

A waiter delivered fruit punch in tall glass cups and sweet biscuits covered in honey.

I explained, "E. Porter Alexander has been my Practical Military Engineering instructor, and he says the same about being an engineer."

"Pfft, he's a Georgia man. He has openly expressed Southern sentiments. They shipped him off to the Pacific a few months ago. Let him employ his engineering skills there. He's a favorite of that little black Frenchman, Pierre Gustave Toutant-Beauregard."

Major Anderson's antipathy for both engineers Alexander and Beauregard was well known, even though, in the case of Beauregard, he may have been punching above his weight. He downed half his punch in one and savagely bit into a biscuit. Beckoning to the waiter, he demanded a full beaker of punch to refill our glasses. "Travel is a thirsty business, Henry."

His voice became sad and heavy, "I am from Kentucky with all that means, but I am an Army officer before a Kentuckian. It's a claim that Alexander can't make." Major Anderson continued, "They will bring back old General Totten, Chief Engineer of the United States Army, to oversee instruction from a distance, and he will assign his hand-picked pets. You should do your best at engineering studies, but save your heart for the artillery. They play with mud bricks, and we blow them to pieces and reduce them to rubble."

"Yes, sir."

"Major George Cullum will likely take charge of the Engineering Department. He served as director of the

Sappers, Miners, and Pontoniers at West Point and acting superintendent. He's skilled, though not very imaginative, as engineers tend to be, but clever in the arts of war. He will woo you toward the Corps of Engineers as he is able."

The steamship was not the only way to get to the Academy. The Hudson River Railroad line had been completed in December 1849. The Army improved the dock in the river. Having a better dock allowed West Point to connect to the station by large ferries and gave Academy personnel and visitors a range of options for getting to and from with easier transfers. Cadets guarded the ferry landing on the West Point side of the river. A ferry named the *Putnam* was in service. Putnam County resident John Garrison was granted a legal right under New York law to operate the ferry, as he explained to every person who rode it.

The *President Tyler* docked, and I carried Major Anderson's bags as well as my own from the Hudson River up the hill. Autie secretly hoped I'd take his as a symbol of his seniority, but as things worked out, I carried the bags of someone far more important.

Meals were still taken in the Mess Hall during the summer, but the summer encampment was still underway. When we arrived, the summer rules were still in effect. Cadets could buy oysters or sweets, such as pie or ice cream, from Joe Simpson, the barber. Crackers and cheese could be purchased at the post store. It all changed with the onset of the academic year when discipline increased.

Commandant Hardee's chief aim during the weeks of encampment seemed to be keeping the cadets' hair cropped close. When Autie presented himself before him on our return from this leave of absence, the Commandant looked at him disapprovingly and said, "Go and get your yellow hair cut, sir, and report back to me."

Joe, the barber, put his shears around Custer's head,

nearly scalping him. The barber could cut hair quickly and short than any living man. Custer stepped into his tent, was there for no more than a minute, returned, and stood at attention.

"Well, sir," said the commandant, "what's the matter now?"

"You ordered me to have my hair cut and report to you, sir."

"Ah! That's very well indeed, sir."

ONE OF THE more challenging courses we had to face in our second class was Bartlett's "Optics," which was a fearful book, and the most formidable discussion in it was that called "optical images. I made myself master of the course. The "optical images" received my undivided attention, for if that was well demonstrated I should be safe. Professor Bartlett of the Ordnance Corps, who was our instructor, ordered, "Mr. Hudson will go to the board." The week before the examinations. It was a complete success, a perfect demonstration.

Now ask me whether I'll ever use it professionally. Doubtful.

CADET UPPERCLASSMAN GEORGE ARMSTRONG CUSTER approached me while I was on guard duty at the Guard House. I don't know if it was ever used as a guardhouse. I can only share my experiences. When I stood guard, it stored equipment used for practical engineering instruction. Guarding it placed grave responsibilities on us. Anyway, while standing my post, Autie walked up officially because there were other cadets in the general area and demanded to know my general orders. "I will guard everything within the limits of my post and quit my post only when properly relieved. I will obey my special orders and militarily perform all of my duties. I will report all violations of my special orders, emergencies, and anything not covered in my instructions to the commander of the relief."

While I chanted off my general orders, he whispered to me, "I'm being sent to Fortress Monroe for practical artillery remedial education, and we have a day in town in New York on the way. I'm out of money; I need the loan of twenty dollars, Hud."

I spoke quietly so nobody else could hear. "The Upperclass Cadet knows that it is an honor violation, and this cadet could receive demerits for loaning an upperclassman money."

"It's not like you haven't done it before, and I paid you back."

"If you brace me and reach into my right pocket, there is a double eagle."

He retrieved the coin, thanked me, and left with a wink.

"Is there something in your eye, Cadet Custer?"

On October 16, while Autie was on the Peninsula in Virginia, shooting cannons, an armed band of abolitionists led by John Brown assaulted the federal armory located at Harpers Ferry. We heard about it after the fighting was over on October 18th, when an account appeared in the newspapers. The buzz throughout the Academy among both instructors and cadets was electric.

Brown and his men captured prominent citizens and seized the federal armory and arsenal. The insurrectionist had hopes that the local slave population would join the attack and hoped that, following the assault's success, weapons would be supplied to slaves and freedom fighters throughout the country; this was not to be.

First held down by the local militia in the late morning of the 17th, Brown took refuge in the arsenal's engine house. He held out until the late afternoon when eighty-eight US

Marines under Colonel Robert E. Lee arrived and stormed the engine house, killing many of the raiders and capturing Brown. There would be a trial, and Brown's execution was inevitable.

The news accounts went from factual to sensational. The United States Armory was a large complex of buildings that manufactured small arms for the U.S. Army. The press reported that the arsenal contained 100,000 muskets and rifles. Instructors at the Academy confirmed that as many as one hundred thousand firearms and millions of rounds could be in storage.

We cadets were outraged that the assault was carried out by the Navy's infantry and not the Army, but we were given an audience with Commandant Hardee, who set the record straight. Late in the afternoon, when the attack occurred, President Buchanan called out a detachment of U.S. Marines from the Washington Navy Yard, the only federal troops in the immediate area: 81 privates, 11 sergeants, 13 corporals, and a lieutenant, armed with seven howitzers. The Marines left for Harper's Ferry on the regular 3:30 train, arriving about 10 PM that night under the command of Marine Lieutenant Israel Greene.

President Buchanan ordered Brevet Colonel Robert E. Lee, an army officer and engineer with a considerable reputation who was conveniently on leave at his home, just across the Potomac in Arlington, to repair to Harpers Ferry, where he arrived about 10 PM, on a special train. Lee had no uniform readily available and wore civilian clothes.

Colonel Lee's father-in-law, George Washington Parke Custis, died at Arlington. The colonel had been on extended leave from the US Second Cavalry in Texas to deal with family affairs as the Custis will's executor and manage the plantation. That explained the absence of a readily available uniform.

An additional lecture from the Superintendent didn't settle anything among the cadets.

I was walking my guard post in front of the central barracks in the late afternoon when the upperclassmen returned from remedial practical artillery education. By all indications, they stopped at Benny Havens' tavern for a wee dram before continuing to the Academy. Benny Havens first opened an establishment on the military reservation in the early 1820s to offer refreshments, but the superintendent ran him off. Undeterred, he opened a larger roadhouse in Highland Falls.

As I walked in step, I sang softly, *"Come fill your glasses, fellows, and stand up in a row. To singing sentimentally, we're going to go. In the Army, there's sobriety, and promotion is very slow. So we'll sing our reminiscences of Benny Haven's, Oh!"*

Autie Custer caught my attention and waved to me. He looked miserable. His pallor was gray, and his yellow curls were lank. I thought that he must have laid one on. He saw that I acknowledged him even though my pace and direction of sight didn't waver.

When I had been relieved, I had been standing in front of the sallyport, so it wasn't much of a trip to stop by Autie's quarters. He was the only one of the two there, lying on his bed, groaning.

His room was notoriously cold. During the coldest weather of winter, some rooms could not be occupied; others were so warm as to be oppressive, and required the windows to be opened on the most inclement nights. The building was heated by a boiler in the basement that circulated air, which was then distributed through flues to each floor. The design of the heating system left much to be desired, but since eminent Army engineers had laid it out, we could not comment on it.

"What's wrong? Benny poured from the bottle under the bar instead of the shelf?"

"No, Hud, it's worse than that. I am in agony when I piss."

"When you piss?"

"I fear that I have contracted the Venus' Curse?"

"What is a Venus' Curse?"

"The French Pox!"

I said, "Oh," now that I understood. "You have hundreds of demerits. I don't know how many they'll give you for voluntarily damaging US Army property."

"What are you talking about?"

"That's how they'll write it. You'll take the big bounce."

"You have to help me; there must be doctors. But don't ask at the dispensary."

"There will be doctors in New York."

"I don't have any money, Hud."

"Secrecy is our concern, not money. I'll stand you the medical treatment. A detail leaves in the morning by wagon to pick up vegetables from a greengrocer in the city. I'm owed favors. I'll get us assigned. You will need to wear a clean uniform and not look so sick, or the sergeant of the guard will put you on the medical report list."

"Thanks, Hud."

"We're both from Michigan; we stick together. But if I'm caught aiding and abetting, they'll bounce me too."

He looked at me frankly, "No, they won't. Your father is a judge and is well-connected. They'll only give you demerits."

Autie had a point.

It took a gold eagle in the right hand to get us put on grocery detail. The dodge allowed cadets to leave Academy grounds for the better part of a day. It wouldn't work if we were on a duty roster, but neither of us had the duty, and the instruction was light. I'd miss a saber class, but since I was

THE CONFEDERATE CIPHER

number one in saber, there wouldn't be a hue and cry over an authorized absence.

When dawn broke, reveille played, drums rattled, and the National Flag was raised as we stood, our backs ramrod straight in formation. Autie's face was tight, but he walked without faltering, and we made our way to the Commissary with the written authorization to leave the Academy on a work detail.

The wily old commissary sergeant looked at us both, shook his head, knowing we were up to something, and said, "Be back before taps. I'll have to report you if you're out after that."

Autie stiffly thanked him as the superior officer in charge of the detail. As soon as we cleared the gate and presented our pass, he crawled into the back, assuming a boiled shrimp's posture. He removed his uniform and put on civilian clothing, and I draped a black riding cloak over my uniform once we entered the Northern portion of New York City.

I asked for a doctor at a dry goods store and was directed to Dr. Mortimer Collins's office, a few blocks away. I spoke with the doctor's assistant, who was reluctant until I counted out three times what any doctor would charge. Dr. Collins was in, and he examined Autie. Collins, a stoop-shouldered, balding man with a severe comb-over and a droopy mustache, came out of the office with Autie.

"He has the pox. Syphilis. This is not the first case of a cadet with this condition. I understand that it is a measure of some sensitivity."

I counted out two double eagles in addition.

"It's early in the first stage, but there are secondary and tertiary stages which can lead to disability or death. I use a mercury and potassium iodide-based treatment, which is the same he'd receive from a specialist. The cure is almost as bad as the disease because the medicine has a certain toxicity, but it usually halts the infection."

Autie asked, "What about a cure?"

The doctor raised his hands and said, "We can treat it, but we can't cure it." Speaking to me as the man with the money, he said, "He must return for treatment if it is to be effective. You've paid me enough to cover the regimen, but we must see him. I understand it can be challenging to leave Academy grounds, but we can meet at the Bugle and Drum Boarding house if you take a room. He will be ill when treated, so you must allow for a day or two in recovery. I didn't know how to arrange it, but the doctor would have his secretary write to me at the academy, as if I were her nephew, to organize the examination and treatment.

George put on his uniform, and we drove the wagon to the grocer who had the commissary contract. Pushing the horses, we returned a few minutes before taps, and Autie went to bed. The next day, he reported on sick call, and the Academy doctor was none the wiser.

Out of George's earshot, the doctor informed me that the treatment, although usually effective in halting the disease's progress, often caused sterility in patients. Thinking of Libby, I asked him if he would pass it on to other romantic partners. He believed that it wouldn't be spread after completing the months-long treatment.

* * *

I ACCEPTED Cadet Nathaniel Green Beaufort III's invitation to spend Christmas furlough at his family's plantation estate in Port Royal, South Carolina. No invitation was proffered to Cadet Custer, who was below his social class. Autie would remain at the Academy during the holiday season and visit the doctor.

Nate and I boarded the paddle steamer *SS Virtue,* which made port calls at Norfolk, Wilmington, and Charleston. His mood darkened as the ship passed Fort Sumter, strategically positioned in the harbor.

As we stood on deck, he said, "I tell you, Hud, the fort's presence is odious to us of South Carolina. They rub our noses in it continually."

"How can you say that, Nate? You are positioned to be an officer in the United States Army. What will you do if that is your post? Would you disobey orders if you were sent there?"

He remained sullen. "You don't understand, Hud. Its presence is a smear on our honor, on the honor of my country, on the honor of Carolina. In 1832, South Carolina passed an ordinance of nullification, which could be used to repeal a Federal law. It was directed against the most recent tariff acts designed to punish us. The Tariff of 1828, the Tariff of Abominations, was enacted to protect the Northern economy at the South's expense, with a specific target on agricultural production. Duties on us were as high as forty-five percent. To enforce the act, the Army sent troops to our forts and began collecting tariffs at the point of a bayonet. We found a species of rapprochement, and the tariffs were reduced gradually, but the Army remained."

"You're in the Army, Nate."

He gave me a dark look and mumbled, "The Northern Army."

Changing the subject, I offered him the finest steak in Charleston when we landed. He had a dining establishment in mind, sparing no expense.

"I could do with a bowl of she-crab soup, Hud. I purely could. Shrimp and grits—real shrimp and grits, too. A steak is fine, but I can get a decent beef steak anywhere."

I asked about the she-crab soup, curious but not necessarily wanting to know all the details.

Nate licked his fleshy lips. "It's a delicious traditional crab bisque made with heavy cream, sherry, and crab eggs, roe if you will."

Given that my family served caviar at formal functions, I could give it a try. Nate's food preferences always revolved around heavy cream and butter as the main attractions. He'd lost weight at West Point, and I was confident we'd both put a few pounds on during the Port Royal Christmas festivities.

We had rooms booked at the Bible and Sword Boarding House for the night. The schedule called for boarding the *SS Virtue* in the morning and continuing for 60 sea miles to Port Royal. Sailing on a steamship meant we didn't wait on the tide, and there was no significant bar to cross at Charleston. The captain told us he intended to get underway at a civilized 9 am and hoped to dock in the early afternoon.

The weather closed in as we docked: fog, damp cold, and a sun that dimly peeked through. The purser checked with us and said our luggage would be delivered to the Bible and Sword and should be available for retrieval by 7:30 p.m. "Our man who handles drayage is reliable. We haven't had any problems with him, Mr. Beaufort," he assured Nate, who looked skeptical.

Both of us traveled light, wearing white over gray summer uniforms because of the South's climate, and carried our long gray overcoats against the possibility of a chill. We packed our India white and full dress uniforms, as well as our gray parade dress. I wore my LeMat pistol in a military-style flap holster belt and the Düssack saber. Nate wore his cadet's sword. He kept a small pocket pistol on his person. We discussed arming ourselves before we set out on the trip. As the *SS Virtue* would make port in several locations and we were not confident of the waterfronts, we opted to travel heavy.

Before we went to dinner, Nate sent a telegram ahead to Port Royal informing his family of our estimated time of arrival. "You're a celebrity, Hud. They will want to put on the dog for you."

Nate brought up South Carolina's militia as the focus of our dinner conversation. I didn't mind. It interested me.

"As with other states, South Carolina's militia system compels able-bodied, free white males between 18 and 45 years to serve. The militia is organized into regiments and battalions, similar to the Army, with both elected and appointed officers. Some minutemen are specially equipped and trained for quick mobilization in the event of an uprising."

The She-Crab soup was as good as advertised, and the claret was of a fine vintage. We took a break from our conversation while we ate.

"South Carolina levied many of the able-bodied men to fight in the Second Seminole War. The Act allowed for uniformity in managing volunteer efforts within the State and to reinforce the compulsory service requirements for state defense."

The rural component of South Carolina needed the ability to call up regiments from other parts of the state to come to its aid if the hostiles or slaves threatened decent people. Having the rules in place only made sense.

We retired to the boarding house after supper, and the porter from the ship beat on our doors early to wake us.

Coming into his home on the steamship, Nate took on the mantle of tour guide. We passed Hilton Head and then continued into the sound, where Fort Fremont stood on the right, and the Parris Island swamp lay on the left. As we approached the old town, also known as Beaufort, an infantry battalion dressed smartly in cadet gray, not unlike our uniform, was arrayed on the green. A band struck up *Camptown Races* and then *Dixie Land*. Ten six-pound Napoleon guns fired a salute as the *SS Virtue* belched smoke from her stacks, blew its whistle, and approached the dock.

A plump officer with protruding eyes, who had a red plume in his smart, gray hat, sat astride a large horse that seemed to handle his girth. "That's Daddy," Nate pointed out proudly, "the colonel."

We disembarked to the tune of *Home of My Youth* and then *Angelina Baker*. "The band is excellent," I told Nate, who beamed. "I've never heard better."

The homecoming unfolding around me was like nothing I had ever experienced before. We rode in a carriage decorated with bunting next to Nate's mother and two eligible teenage sisters, Martha and Belle. Both were pretty and wore green hoop dresses, awkward in the carriage. It was more like a triumphant Napoleon riding through the streets of Paris with the battalion and now limbered artillery marching behind us, the band playing *Old Dan Tucker* and then *Dixie Land*.

The parade was joined by the town's children holding whirligigs that spun in the breeze and led through the Beaufort neighborhood of Port Royal to the long tree-lined drive up to the plantation house.

The honor guard posted the regimental flag, a white crescent with the horns upward on a dark blue field, flanked by two men with muskets and fixed bayonets.

We were ushered into the mansion while the town's residents enjoyed a free meal outside under canopies on the green. The reception line was headed by Lieutenant Governor William Henry Gist, his wife, and an eligible teenage daughter wearing a fancy white hoop dress that cinched at the waist, somewhere around eighteen inches. Her face, slightly flushed, smiled brightly at Nate and then at me as he introduced me by first listing many of my family's rail and shipping interests. There were uniformed militia officers and their ladies, businessmen from the town, and a Doctor named Shrewsberry who fought with General Winfield Scott in Mexico.

Colonel Nathaniel Green Beaufort II, Nate's father, and Governor Gist quizzed me on secession as soon as it was polite to bring the topic up.

"Will the cadets and officers side with their country or the federal government?" Governor Gist was most curious.

"Is a division of the nation a foregone conclusion?" I asked. "Slavery is legal. The Army put down a slave revolt at Harper's Ferry, and the ringleaders were either shot or hanged, not a few months ago. The Army and, in the case of Harper's Ferry, the Navy, will follow the law."

"So says the son of a presiding federal judge," Big Nathaniel said. I thought of the colonel, Nate's father, in those terms.

"The abolitionists are pining for a division of the nation based on the institution of slavery, but should we separate, it is likely that Great Britain would recognize our new country as free and sovereign from the old one," Governor Gist said.

His words took me by surprise. "I had not heard that."

"Yet it is the case," Governor Gist assured me. "Where is Baron Langford? He was there in line; you shook his hand. Owain Rowley-Conway, eleventh Baron Langford, and the newly raised Baron Fermoy, Edmond Roche, an Irish Peer created by letters patent by the Queen three years past. My Lords Fermoy and Langford are part of an embassy that arrived a fortnight past to secure cotton futures on behalf of Her Britannic Majesty's Government. They are both acquainted with your grandfather, Forsythe, and wanted to speak to you while you are here."

"Me?"

"You are heir to the Forsythe and Hudson fortunes."

"The second son-heir and a spare - I'm the spare."

"Hardly."

I turned to face Edmond Roche, tall, athletic, and wearing a uniform that I presumed was of the Royal Horse Guards Regiment. "I missed the line; apologies." He held a beaker of punch and sipped from it.

Roche smiled broadly, "Call me Edmond or Ed, and I know your friends call you Hud. Can we proceed that way?"

I smiled back and took his hand. "That works for me, Edmond."

"Splendid, we have a distant family connection, fourth cousins once removed or something like that. I know your grandfather. We have some shipbuilding interests in common in addition to distant blood."

"As to secession," Governor Gist redirected the conversation as a string quartet began a Viennese Waltz - the precise name escaped me. Nate's Mother and his Sister, Belle, took me by each arm and carried me backward onto the dance floor.

His mother said, "You will not monopolize the most eligible bachelor in Port Royal this Christmas season, Nathaniel!"

So I danced, changed partners, danced, changed partners, stopped for a drink of spiked punch, and continued dancing. The evening fogged over as the festivities progressed.

CHAPTER 5

Christmas 1859
The Beaufort Mansion, Port Royal, South Carolina

From my current perspective, perhaps our first meeting was not nearly as momentous as I thought at the time. Maybe it was far more ordinary: an American boy meets the ward of a British Army officer and diplomat in his bedroom in the morning as he recovers from a wicked hangover. How often did that sort of thing happen? I have no way of knowing.

The curtains had been opened, and the morning sun beat down on me through the window - God's light, burning through my painful headache. My mouth tasted much the way a mule's butt must. I've never actually tasted a mule's butt, for the record. It's all speculation on my part.

In the corner of the room, near the door, she sat on a high-backed chair wearing a simple white dress with a matching embroidered apron. Not a maid's apron, the sort of apron a lady would wear when she didn't want to have her dress soiled. She was not exactly beautiful, at least not in the way most men I know would term beautiful. Her face was feminine but sharp, her nose narrow and conspicuous, her chin less pronounced. Her eyes were almond-shaped and translucent green, the color of the leaves and ferns when the late afternoon sun shines through them. She wore a morning cap that matched everything else down to the embroidery. From beneath it, a honey colored curl peeked out, just enough to begin a mental picture. She had a slender, birdlike neck that gracefully curved into her dress. Her features were so delicate, so finely angled, they had the perverse effect of amplifying any proximate bluntness.

She stood, and I had a better view of her clothes. They weren't as simple as I first thought. It was as though she had tried to strike a suitable balance between modesty and glamor in an everyday dress.

I recalled her name. We had danced much of the night together as she monopolized me fiercely against all comers, flattering me.

"Victoria."

Her Scottish lilt captivated me last night at the ball, just as it had in the morning, with my head waiting to explode. "The maid waits outside with a pot of hot coffee and French patsies. Let me know when you're ready for it, or if you'd prefer a chamber pot."

I used the chamber pot during the night; when I looked over, it had been emptied.

"I'm ready for coffee and a biscuit."

She opened the door, and a short, plump negro maid entered, pushing a small cart with a coffee service on it. She curtsied and left.

"Do ye have any recollection of last night?"

I touched a tender point on my jaw. "Did I get in a fight?"

"Oh yes, with a brevet captain from Colonel Beaufort's Carolina Panthers' Militia. He punched you, and it didn't rock you. Then, you slapped him — hard, and he challenged you to a duel, and young Nate, whose place he took in the militia when Nate went off to school, accepted as your self-appointed second."

I groaned, my foggy memory of events returning. *My second.*

"Nate bragged about your use of the saber and pointed to the Düsack in your scabbard, so Captain Pervis chose pistols, and Nate selected Christmas morning at the Beaufort Family Cemetery at dawn."

Ezra Pervis, chubby as Nate had been, but six inches taller, belligerent, entitled, cocky, and a bully. He had a cupidic and at the same time pugnacious face with fleshy lips and porcine eyes. It came back. We'd both had too much to drink.

"Pistols?"

"Edmond Roche, the Baron Fermoy, offered to serve as the Overseer of Satisfaction. He wagered twenty gold guineas you'd prevail. The Pervis family, who were present at the ball, had to match the wager, but then others wagered on you. The Pervis clan has money and, from what I am given to understand, a zeal at the cockpit or track, and the numbers became more significant as the men argued well into the hundreds of gold guineas."

I suddenly realized that I was naked beneath the covers as Victoria McKay (pronounced in the Scottish way) handed me a china cup filled with rich, aromatic coffee. It scalded my mouth and tongue as I drank it, but it seemed to help the headache.

"It may sound rude to ask, but why are you in my room?"

"You insisted that I come to your room last night. Nate helped you to your room, and I waited outside, preserving my honor while he tucked you in. I came this morning because you'd asked."

"Oh."

"My Uncle Iain will return from inspecting cotton and tobacco plantations in the Carolina interior by Christmas Eve. He will want to meet you."

"Refresh my memory."

"He is a military aide to Her Majesty's ambassador to your government. We live next to Richard Bickerton Pemell Lyons, 1st Earl Lyons, the Queen's Ambassador in Washington City. Major Sir Iain McKay of the Second Battalion, Coldstream Guards, is my uncle. He is here as part of Her Majesty's delegation of cotton buyers. You danced with my aunt, Maude, last night, too. Do you recall that?" She maneuvered you under the mistletoe and demanded a kiss. A long, passionate, and wholly inappropriate kiss, as it turns out."

My memory was foggy, but I recalled the kiss with tongues and a prolonged grope of my tumescent manhood. "She is your aunt?"

"My natural father, Sir Iain's brother, and my mother died of a fever within days of each other five years ago. Since then, I've been my uncle's ward."

I recalled the woman's kiss. Too deep, too serious. She tasted champagne and cinnamon—the aunt—the girl—and a major from the Coldstream Guards Regiment. What had I gotten myself into?

One duel at a time. "I need to get dressed."

"And you want me to leave?"

"Would you prefer me to dress in front of you?"

She paused, mulling over the question. "Yes, but given that we just met, perhaps not yet. It would be best if you also washed, and I could scrub your back, but we can leave that for another day."

She opened the door, called for a maid, and demanded

that hot water be brought up for a bath immediately. Then she returned to my bedside.

"My aunt pointed you out when you and the younger Nathaniel disembarked from the ship and recommended that I speak with you to determine your character. She knows the Hudsons and the Forsythes by reputation."

"That seems impulsive."

"Both my aunt, The Lady of Primrose, and I are Royal Scots women descended from the Bruce. We have the gift of sight beyond sight. It's how I know you have a small birthmark high on your thigh." With that, she turned and left the room.

The birthmark she referred to was small and very high on my thigh. I blushed. Did Nate tuck me in, or did she? And did we do anything? I doubted that I'd have been capable. And what of Ezra Pervis? What led to the altercation? The matter of a small fortune in gold guineas wagered on the outcome of a duel meant we'd both be pushed into fighting rather than reasoning. The formalized rules of duelling stipulated that we had twenty-four hours to resolve our differences. I didn't want to fight him over a drunken argument and a point of honor that I could not recall.

Pistols. It would likely be a matched set of dueling pieces, flintlock, large bore, possibly half an inch. I was familiar with the typical pieces. Their accuracy was far less than the LeMat my father gave me, resting in the flap holster on my belt, even then within my view.

Sabers to the first cut would have been preferable, retaining honor without murder. I practiced with sabers daily at the Academy. It took physical conditioning, strength, stamina, and agility, which Pervis didn't seem to possess if I recalled the man adequately. He appeared to be a large, florid-faced, oafish man with a family pedigree from a rival gentry who didn't get along with Nate's family.

Anyone could take up a pistol, aim, and pull a trigger. A large caliber bullet burying itself in the flesh anywhere in the body proved instantly fatal or from later infection due to the ball or embedded patch. A saber cut was easier to mend with catgut and a poultice.

Since the Irish Baron interposed himself, we would likely be guided by the *Code Duello*, written by an Irishman in 1777. The rules were created to make pistol dueling more civilized, but they also included notes about swordplay and how varying degrees of insults should be addressed. I studied it with my dancing master during my time at Georgetown, but during my last year of Academy studies, my focus shifted to other areas of learning. Countless variations to pistol duels could be worked out by the seconds: standing and firing at the drop of a handkerchief, striding towards each other and firing at will, marching to a beat away from each other, then turning and firing. How it happened was a matter of negotiation, which decorum required that I not have a voice in.

Ultimately, it came down to us, combatants, shooting at one another at close range, usually once. The duel would be declared over if neither man was hit and the challenger felt honor had been served. If the offended party was not satisfied, a pistol duel could continue until one man was shot, but the seconds and witnesses would often try to prevent further combat. Having more than three exchanges of fire was frowned upon as ungentlemanly and an embarrassment to both parties. The pistols commonly used were notoriously prone to misfiring. Loading could be awkward if multiple rounds were discharged unless paper cartridges were used.

I took my LeMat revolver out of its holster, oiled it, and cleaned it as I sat naked on the bed.

It took time for the hot water to be delivered in buckets.

After washing and dressing, I walked downstairs to the dining room for breakfast to find Nate, his family, the Baron,

Lord Owain Rowley-Conway, and the Christmas company busily working out the details of the duel to be fought as they ate from platters of food spread along the table. Ham, eggs, freshly baked bread, sliced fruit, the ubiquitous grits on warming plates (because even they didn't like a cold grit), and tea and coffee were present.

Everyone cheered as I walked into the room wearing civilian clothing.

The amount wagered staggered me, having increased based on Nate's assertion that I'd slaughter Ezra Pervis easily.

Nate said of me, "I've seen him shoot turkeys in the head at considerable range with a cadet's short-barreled musket."

I replied to the group, "With a *rifled* musket and one of Claude-Étienne Minié's conical projectiles," I replied. The Minie ball provided greater accuracy than a patched round ball. "Nate, what if he gets lucky and hits me?"

I could tell by his reaction that it never occurred to him.

"He won't."

"But what if he does?"

"We have a doctor in town."

"Who will bleed me with leeches to cure me as I'm leaking profusely from the gunshot wound?"

"It's a matter of honor now," Nate said, folding a small slab of ham into his mouth, chased by a buttered biscuit and washed down with a mug of hot coffee.

"And several purses," the Baron, who insisted that I call him Ed, added. "It will be dawn in the Beaufort family graveyard. Nate will serve as your second, and Ezra Pervis' father, Gordon, will be his. We've worked on the details of the match that I will courier to them shortly."

I asked, "Can you share them with *me*?"

He smiled, "Of course. Your seconds will choose your pistols from a set belonging to the Beaufort family. They've been in the family for fifty years. Half-inch bore, seven-inch barrel. The seconds will load and prime the pieces. You will each step off four paces, turn, and fire, which will put you close enough to have the possibility of a hit. Too far and a hit is a matter of probability rather than skill."

"I hope he's not an expert with a dueling piece."

Nate said confidently, "He's challenged several people, but the matter was resolved before it came down to a final solution."

I nodded, feeling some relief.

"He serves in my battalion; he's a puffin, all talk and bluster—a bully with the yellow heart of a coward."

Nate's father, the colonel, said. "You kill him, Hud, on the morning of Christmas, and then we'll all gather for the traditional festivities of worship and frivolity, counting our money."

"Or he kills me, and the Pervis clan celebrates."

The Baron intervened, saying, "It will work out satisfactorily," as Nate prepared a plate of breakfast for me, omitting grits.

Victoria McKay looked on from the far wall with a smirk. I didn't know what that meant, but she was a tawny little vixen if ever there was one.

After we finished breakfast, bottles of port were opened —the hair of the dog from the night before. I took my glass, then a second draught, walked out to the covered porch behind the kitchen, and stepped down onto a cobbled path lined with small shrubs that hadn't lost their leaves in winter.

From where I stood, I could see the broad river that snaked to the Sea in the distance.

"The cemetery is over there." Victoria's voice came from behind me.

I turned to her, "You're looking forward to this contest."

"My uncle sent word that he would be back by nightfall, so that he will be present. He's a keen judge of character."

"I thought you relied on some magical Scotts curse to auger such things."

"Maude and I both do, but my uncle has more experience with the metal of young officers."

"This sounds like a test."

"I wouldn't be so bold as to suggest—."

"No, not so bold."

"Come, Hud, we haven't had that chance to see whether she or I is the better kisser."

I shook my head.

Nate called me, "Hud, we're going to play cards. It will rain most of the day, and we must profitably pass the time to tomorrow by besting the Baron and Lord Owain at whist."

"In a minute." I took Victoria in my arms and kissed her gently. She put her arms around my shoulders, and I drew her in. Her soft, full lips were sweet, and her mouth tasted like fresh citrus. The kiss lingered as we both took our time. When we separated, I told her, "You win."

She smiled mysteriously.

Our discussion over cards revolved around whether the weather would cause the powder in the pan to fail. Colonel Nate offered to send for matched percussion lock pistols with caps to ensure proper ignition. The Baron forbade it as the Overseer. Weapons had been agreed upon. They would be flintlocks with fresh flints, and the plan would have to proceed as scheduled.

Since Christmas Day would feature a large banquet, Christmas Eve was more subdued. Hot buttered rum by a roaring fire, two men played string instruments well, and we wished each other Merry Christmas.

. . .

I WOKE TO A QUIET HOUSE. When I retired to bed, Sir Iain had not returned, and I wondered whether he would be present for the duel.

Taking my time, I dressed in light clothing and shaved closely. The weather from my bedroom window had cleared, but the air was very humid, and a fog rolled in. It's not at all ideal weather for a pan that would flash.

When I arrived downstairs, the Beaufort portion of the dueling delegation was present and subdued. A large man with broad shoulders dressed in a dark blue British patrol uniform turned when I entered the room. "This must be Hud." His statement lacked emotion, but he grabbed my hand in a meaty grip that was not a squeezing contest. "A day of days, though I'm told you've crossed blades before."

"Sir Iain, it's an honor."

"The honor is mine. I'm well acquainted with the Forsythes and have heard of your father. Your bloodline is renowned, and if what Young Nates tells us is true, you'll be an honor graduate of the West Point Academy."

"Nate is too kind, and he exaggerates."

Nate, as if on cue, asked, "Are you ready, Hud?"

I nodded. Knowing how the Academy felt about dueling, I didn't wear my uniform. Civilian dress would have to suffice. I decided against wearing a hat.

Nate led the way to the cemetery where half a dozen Pervis men, dressed in the cadet gray uniforms of the militia, waited. Victoria stood at a distance, and I couldn't see the expression on her face. Ezra wore his gray militia captain's dress uniform with two rows of brass buttons, gold epaulets, and an aiguillette over his shoulder. His officer's trousers were medium blue with a light blue infantry stripe. His gut overhung his belt inappropriately. He had a dyed red ostrich plume in his cocked gray hat. He looked terrified under that gray, brim.

"We still have a chance to resolve this without bloodshed, Ezra," I said.

He looked around at his disapproving family and said, "No, it will go forward."

I walked to a table brought out for the occasion and watched as Nate and Gordon Pervis loaded and primed the pistols they chose for the duel.

Nate handed mine to me, and I took the weight in my hand, lifted it, and sighted along the barrel that did not have a sighting blade. I nodded at Nate. "I am satisfied."

The Baron said, "It will happen as discussed. Both men will behave honorably. They will begin back-to-back. I shall count four paces; each will turn and fire at will. There will be no reloads. Let God decide this matter. He nodded to Nate and Gordon Pervis.

Ezra had sweated through his uniform, leaving dark rings under his arms. I could feel the moisture from the fog, pushed back toward the ocean by a gentle morning breeze on my back, as we stood on the field of honor.

The Baron counted, and in a sense, time stood still. When I stepped the fourth pace and turned, a bee seemed to hover near Ezra's face. He panicked and discharged his pistol in my direction. I heard the ball buzz past my ear.

As I lifted my pistol, he squealed, let out a sob, and turned to run. He stepped a pace away in flight when I squeezed the trigger, and the gun discharged. The half-inch soft lead ball struck him high in the back of his neck above his shoulder blades. The Pervis family saw the ball emerge far more dramatically than I did as it blew out his throat, splattering them with a fountain of squirting blood. He fell face forward onto the lawn of the graveyard.

The Baron stepped forward, looking down at the large hole in the back of the Pervis boy's neck with blood pulsing out onto the turf. "Honor is satisfied. God decided the contest."

I handed Nate my pistol numbly.

"Good shot, Hud," he said quietly.

"The priming was not an issue this morning," I replied, looking for Victoria and seeing her uncle, Sir Iain, Knight Companion, beaming.

He said, "Well played, Hud. You saved the honor of the Pervis family and accounted yourself well."

"I shot a bully in the back."

"Not a bully, a coward, gunned down as he ran. One does not flee from a field of honor."

Gordon Pervis approached me, "Sir Iain is correct, Henry, you saved my name from shame even though it cost me a son. I won't shake your hand, but there is no hostility."

I may have nodded.

I turned and walked away, and they all let me go. As I stepped out, I wasn't sure why we had fought the duel in the first place. I was drunk when the offense was given, which caused the demand for satisfaction. The day before, Christmas Eve, I tried to get a moment to quiz Nate, but there were too many people around.

Victoria walked at right angles to me, closing on me, and she took my arm in hers. "That was horrible."

"I think you had a better view of the exit wound than I did."

"I've never seen a duel."

"Do you want to see another one?"

"No, that was quite enough. Uncle said that you had nerves of steel."

"If his ball had been four inches to the right, you wouldn't have had to worry about kissing me again."

She said, "He seemed distracted."

"A bee or some flying insect, perhaps."

"Sight beyond sight. I told you."
"Seventh son of a seventh son?"
"Something like that."

CHRISTMAS DAY FEATURED A BANQUET. The guest of honor, forty-year-old Admiral Sir Owain Rowley-Conway, who held the rank of Rear Admiral of the White, wore his ceremonial uniform, including a straight sword. Our host, Colonel Nathaniel Green Beaufort II, sat beside him wearing his cadet gray militia colonel's double-breasted uniform with gleaming brass buttons, gold braid at the collar and the cuffs, and a blood red sash circling his ample middle. Victoria sat next to the Admiral, and her aunt Maude sat at Colonel Beaufort's arm.

On the right of the table, next to his wife, sat Major Sir Iain McKay, Second Battalion, Coldstream Guards, wearing scarlet mess dress; then me in my cadet dress uniform, which consisted of a single-breasted, dark blue coat with a standing collar and eight gilt eagle buttons. I wore winter blue cloth trousers. I left my sword and revolver in my room. Nate was dressed the same as I was.

Lord Major Edmond Roche, Baron Fermoy, sat on my other side, wearing his Royal Horse Guards Regiment uniform. The Blues and Royals wore a dark blue tunic with scarlet facings, piped in scarlet cloth. His tunic had gold lace on the collar and cuffs, and the skirts had a three-cornered flap edged in scarlet.

Ed Roche asked me, "What do you think an Admiral of the White is doing here, sitting at this table at this time, young Hud?"

I went with my impression. "He appears to be the Queen's plenipotentiary here in the South."

The Baron Furmoy raised his wine glass, smiling. "I have

not underestimated you, Cadet Hudson. He is indeed a diplomat, an envoy authorized to represent the Queen with full power to conduct business and make decisions on her behalf. Of course, his presence here in all his finery, along with that of myself and Sir Iain, is a secret."

"Not a well-crafted one."

"No, Cadet Hudson, not well crafted at all—a brazen secret."

Their first toast was to the Queen, offered by Governor Gist, who sat between Nate's mother and his wife at the foot of the table. He said, "The Queen!"

Admiral Sir Owain Rowley-Conway toasted a free and independent American South. "The inherent and inalienable right of a people to govern themselves", emphasizing popular sovereignty and the right to withdraw from a government they felt no longer served their interests.

Colonel Beaufort then raised his glass and toasted, "Southern honor and the defense of our sacred institutions."

Ed Roche looked at me closely. I responded to all three toasts, which, given in that order, should not have been joined by a completely loyal American officer familiar with protocols. As presented, they were toasts to rebellion.

Throughout the various courses of the meal, I couldn't take my eyes off Victoria. Nate Junior, my friend and classmate, kept trying to hold my attention from his seat directly across from me. I humored him as best I could without being rude, but at that moment, Victoria was lovely and desirable. She had an intoxicating haughtiness that complemented her features, making her the most unique among the women I had met.

I hadn't forgotten Marie Cholmondeley. I didn't disregard our physical romps. There was a time when I thought we might be in love, but I didn't understand love. Yes, I had consummated my feelings with Marie again and again, with the utmost athleticism. Our touching was never tender. In my fantasy, at the Christmas banquet crowd, I mused that, should we join, it would be different from what it had been with Marie.

After dinner, the men retired to the drawing room for port and cigars, and the women went to the great room to make whatever preparations were necessary for Boxing Day to follow.

When the drinks were poured, the conversation drifted to the duel I fought that morning, the cowardice of Ezra Pervis, and my steadfastness, followed by the killing shot. Nate reenacted the mortally wounded Pervis as he fell over and over. Each time it was more dramatically acted. At the same time, Admiral Sir Owain Rowley-Conway and Baron Fermoy recited the large purses they collected from betting on my victory. As the consumption of port continued, the idea of provoking another duel, wherein even more could be wagered and won, emerged. Nate mocked a sword lunge, "Hud will run them through."

Eventually, the conversation slowed, and merry makers drifted off to their various rooms or the couches there in the drawing room.

I climbed the stairs, loaded with guilt for killing Pervis, field of honor or not. His pistol discharged, he turned to run, and he was no longer a threat when I killed him. I opened the door to the room and shed my uniform on a wooden chair in a heap.

My head remained in a haze as I sat on the bed, and then twisted under the sheets, only to discover abruptly that I was not alone. I felt the warmth of her skin, the scent of her, and our mouths met gently and tenderly.

"Victoria."

"Merry Christmas, Hud."

Our ardor lasted through most of the night, but eventually, exhaustion from the long day and evening caught up to us.

A servant woke me with a coffee service, a whole pot, and a plate of sweet rolls. He reminded me that the guests and the Beauforts would all attend the Boxing Day post-Christmas Mass together at midday. I noticed that my uniform had been pressed and was hanging, ready to wear.

CHAPTER 6

US Military Academy, West Point
Spring 1860

He couldn't contain himself despite my firm instructions that Nate should not discuss the Christmas duel. Suddenly, he became the center of attention as he recounted the events, adding details that were absent on the day. Wooing Victoria McKay, the duel, the grand ball, when the grave offense to my honor was given, and my pistol accuracy became a legend as the gossip widened the story at the Military Academy. Four paces distant suddenly became ten.

Autie Custer, who had undergone treatment for his affliction during the Christmas season, looked much better, and he embellished the story far past what Nate had done. He had me shooting it out with the entire Pervis Family on Christmas Day from horseback with both my saber slashing down and revolver blazing.

As one would expect, I was ordered to report to the commandant's office and explain myself to Colonel Hardee. I waited outside his office for one hour before being summoned in.

William Joseph Hardee, Commandant of Cadets, Colonel (Dragoons), returned my salute from a seated position. "Sit, cadet Hudson."

I sat in a chair conveniently placed in front of his desk.

"You are midway through your second year." He flipped pages assembled on his desk. "Your grades are excellent, and you are on the path to becoming a competent officer." He looked up, "Possibly an engineer or an artillerist?" He looked down at the file of paperwork. "Word reached me of a duel at the home of Colonel Nathaniel Beaufort in Port Royal. As it happens, I am acquainted with Nate Beaufort, the elder. We served in the Army of Occupation under General Zachary Taylor. We were both officers in the Second Dragoons when we were ambushed and captured by Mexican troops on April 25, 1846, at Carricitos Ranch in Texas. The Thornton Affair. You've heard of it?"

"Yes, Commandant, in class. It led to President Polk declaring war on Mexico."

"We were captured and exchanged a month later. The month in captivity gave us time to get to know one another. When I heard rumors of this duel, I telegraphed Nathaniel. He explained that he was present, that you had grave cause, and that you acquitted yourself honorably without bringing a stain on this institution or the Army."

I didn't respond.

"He said that you were an honored guest in his home and that the duel was conducted under British peers' supervision and by Major Sir Ian McKay of the honorable and venerable Coldstream Guards."

He looked up at me.

"Yes, Commandant."

"You are well acquainted with Major McKay?"

"He is the military advisor to Minister Lyons, who reports to the Queen of England."

"Quite. I telegraphed him at the Beaufort plantation, too. We are socially acquainted previously, but are not friends in any meaningful way."

I didn't say anything.

He picked up a piece of paper, "He responded by claiming that if we didn't commission you in the American Army, there would be a lieutenancy waiting for you in the Coldstream that he would purchase on your behalf himself."

I must have blushed.

"Going on, he said that there would likely be fisticuffs involved with Major Lord Fermoy of Her Majesty's Royal Horse Guards Regiment, who would sponsor you for a purchase into *his* command."

"Yes, sir." I didn't know what else to say.

"So let me summarize, if I may. You go to Port Royal with young Nate Junior, whom I have been informed you've tutored after hours on your own. During this Christmas romp, you go crossways with another young gentleman, and you two shoot it out on the Beaufort estate with representatives of Her Majesty's Government egging the matter on? Several hundred were wagered in gold guineas on the outcome?"

"I tried to have him agree to sabers —the first cut, but it went to pistols."

"And you killed him with a shot through the throat as he fled the field of honor, as Cadet Beaufort tells it?"

"Yes, Commandant."

"There are laws against dueling in many states, but not in South Carolina, so you skirted criminal difficulties. If you'd declined, you'd have been called out for cowardice, tarnishing this institution and the United States Army in front of British royalty. Therefore, honor is satisfied: you shot accurately, his shot missed you, he's dead, and you're back at school. Is that how you see it?"

"It is, sir."

"Do you intend to renounce your American Citizenship and citizenship of the State of Michigan and take a commission in the Coldstream or Royal Horse Guards Regiments?"

The telegraphic response was the first that I'd heard of this. "No, Commandant."

"Then you are dismissed. There is no need to bother the Superintendent with this. The incident will be noted in your official record. Return to class."

I stood and saluted.

"Get out of my office, Henry. Let this be the last duel you fight while under my command at this academy."

"Yes, sir."

As I walked back to class, I consulted my pocket watch. My mathematics class would end soon, and I had an hour of study before the midday dinner. As I walked across the grinder, the bugle called the hour. I saluted an upperclassman I passed, sweating from my encounter with Colonel Hardee despite the winter weather.

"Cadet Hudson!" I recognized the voice of my cadet commander. I stopped, turned smartly to face the direction of his voice, and saluted Cadet Sergeant Major James Harrison Wilson, Class of 1860, my company commander, who strode up to me. "You've been to see the Commandant of Cadets?"

"Yes, Cadet Sergeant Major Wilson."

"Over the duel you fought in South Carolina last month?"

"Yes, Cadet Sergeant Major Wilson."

"You killed a captain of the South Carolina militia?"

"A *brevet* captain, yes, sir."

"Do you like killing captains, Cadet Hudson?"

"If there is a war with the Southern States, there will be one fewer enemy captain to plant, Sergeant Major Wilson." I knew that James Wilson, an Illinois man and an outspoken, virulent abolitionist, expected a war over states' rights to occur and that the enemy would include the significant militia presence in South Carolina and elsewhere. We never discussed the matter personally, but his feelings were not a secret.

"Hmmpf." He looked me up and down for a uniform violation. "Carry on, Cadet Hudson."

"Thank you, sir."

And so it went. Those who preferred the northern states believed that removing a militia officer from South Carolina was a service to the Federal Government. Those from southern states understood that a duel on the field of honor, fought within established rules between gentlemen, was a matter of honor, decided honorably, before God, and was settled once and for all.

The question of what Sir Iain McKay, a serving British officer, had been doing in South Carolina under the pretext of securing cotton and tobacco contracts continued to perplex me. I didn't raise the issue with anyone. Still, I felt he'd been inspecting militia groups and gauging the local intentions and strength—the matter of collecting intelligence brought back memories of the class with Colonel Hooker. Our Army should have been doing it before we sent infantry forward into hostile territory on the approach to Utah without a cavalry screen or adequate scouting. An inferior militia unit, well-mounted and prepared, ran off the Army's beef herd, captured the supply train, and left the infantry immobile and starving during the winter.

The politics of the Utah War and the potential secession of Utah from the Union were distinct from those in the

South. Still, I'd seen the tension in Charleston and Port Royal for myself, and I had seen the militia preparing, fully armed, training with cavalry and artillery supporting well-drilled infantry. The English Queen's economy required the cotton trade to continue. Tobacco and sugar may have been of secondary interest, but they were equally vital in the symbiosis between Birmingham factories and Southern farms.

If the Beauforts, Governor Gist, and those like them had their way, they'd separate from the United States and form a new nation. Would Great Britain recognize that new nation? Would they send red coats to support the Southern militias in the field if the American Army intervened and stopped secession?

The presence of Lord Rear Admiral Owain Rowley-Conway, eleventh Baron Langford, the Queen's plenipotentiary, sealed the matter. He didn't skulk about like a thief in the night. He was present with other peers of the British realm, personally treating with Lieutenant Governor Gist in full regalia.

Our Army had few men under arms. Sixteen thousand officers and men were organized into 198 companies across 79 posts. If the South left, how many of the 1,080 active army officers and cadets at the academy would find their greater loyalty required them to support their states? After all, we cadets swore loyalty to our states and signed those warrants of obligation.

As I walked, I also reflected on my grandfather, Leslie Forsythe, and the *SS Seraphim*, an armed, steam-powered screw packet under construction in a Liverpool shipyard. How many ships of that type had my family constructed, and what role might they play in a war? The Forsythe family had deep ties to the Crown, including kinship to peers of the realm. It was not only the Forsythe Family, but their business partners and Cornelius Vanderbilt, arguably one of the wealthiest men in America, who would be involved to some extent. I knew from speaking with my grandfather that, even then, Vanderbilt had shifted his focus from steamships to railroads and was currently negotiating to purchase the New York and Harlem Railroad.

The answer came about two weeks later in the form of a letter wrapped in another piece of paper in an ornate envelope with a waxed indented crest of the Coldstream Guards:

Miss Victoria McKay
    Locknoir Estate
    London, England

February 24, 1860

Cadet Henry Hudson
    US Military Academy, West Point,
    New York, United States of America

My dearest friend:

    I am writing to you, having returned first to Washington City and thence to England, following your departure from South Carolina, and am accompanying my Uncle and Aunt, who are known to you. Enclosed is a favor that I hope you will take and keep close to your heart as a token of our shared Christmas past.

    I expect to return to Washington City in the late Spring and would like to visit with you, appropriately chaperoned. You warm my heart.

I am your devoted servant,
    Victoria

A white square of fine, embroidered linen had been enclosed. I smelled it, and it smelled like the perfume she wore, immediately reminding me of our night together. I placed it in my pocket while I reread the letter.

There was something odd about the blank paper that enclosed the letter. I looked closely at it in the light, and it had slight stains. I put that into my pocket next to the favor. After keeping it close for a day, I took the letter, paper, and favor out of my pocket to re-read it; the empty page wasn't entirely blank.

You warm my heart. Somehow, that phrase didn't fit. I placed the blank page over the chimney of a coal oil lamp, and the writing became clear.

> Dear Hud, I used lemon juice as ink, and I hope you can warm this letter so the invisible becomes visible. You must meet with me when I return to the United States. My uncle will formally invite you to visit us at Ambassador Lyon's residence. - Victoria

On Monday, March 12, Colonel Hardee summoned me to his office after the assembly had been dismissed with a smart bugle call just after sunrise. I arrived in parade uniform. His aide, an artillery sergeant major named Arlund Bisbee, looked me over before allowing me into the office. Bisbee, my height but twice as broad with a high forehead and a lantern jaw, followed me in. Bisbee wore an immaculately tailored uniform, riding boots, and polished stub spurs.

"Cadet Hudson, it is my privilege to promote you to cadet corporal with immediate effect. See to it that the appropriate badges of rank are applied. Sergeant Bisbee, please direct your people to assist the Cadet Corporal as necessary, forthwith."

Bisbee said, "Sir!" and remained standing where he had been next to the door.

"Once appropriately uniformed, you will deliver this dispatch to Major Arnold B. Strauss of the Sixth Artillery Regiment, Batteries C, D, and F at Fort Schuyler, some sixty miles distant. Do you know Fort Schuyler, Cadet Corporal Hudson?" He pointed to a polished leather dispatch case on his desk.

"I do not, sir."

"Construction began in 1833 and was dedicated in 1856. The fort is located on Throggs Neck in the Bronx. Its small garrison protects New York City from naval attack. I suspect that even if I gave you a map, you'd be lost after nightfall and might not arrive for a week. Therefore, Sergeant Major Bisbee will accompany you as your aide-de-camp. He knows the way. Even though you are only a cadet, you will be assigned the temporary rank of officer-on-parade, granting you limited official status. At the same time, you are off-post and on this mission. Is that clear?"

It wasn't the least bit clear, but I had no intention to ask for clarification in front of Sergeant Major Bisbee. I looked over at his face, which seemed to be carved from stone. I didn't want to do anything that would embarrass me, the Corps of Cadets, or the Army. "Yes, sir."

"Repeat your instructions to me, Cadet Corporal."

"Once in complete uniform and in the company of Sergeant Major Bisbee, I will travel with all possible haste to Fort Schuyler at Throggs Neck in the Bronx and deliver that dispatch to Major Arnold B. Strauss, Artillery."

Colonel Hardee looked at Sergeant Major Bisbee and said, "I told you he's a bright lad, Arlund. Good with a saber, quick and accurate with a pistol, rides a horse like a Comanche."

Sergeant Major Bisbee looked as if he had swallowed a wasp. "Sir!"

"See to it. You're burning daylight."

I selected our mounts from the stable, drew field rations for a day, picked up my newly tailored uniform jackets, and set off. Sergeant Bisbee rode quietly. "We could have arrived sooner if a steamer had been scheduled, Sergeant."

"I expect so, sir, but we're in the Army, not the Navy."

"Have you ever met Major Strauss?"

"No, Cadet Corporal Hudson."

"When were you last at Fort Schuyler?"

"I was at its dedication four years ago, Cadet Corporal."

I could tell that he didn't like being assigned to nursemaid me.

I led the way, making excellent time —maybe forty miles — to the Fifth Avenue Hotel in Manhattan, which had opened a few months earlier. I read about the opening in the newspapers. It occupied an entire frontage block between 23rd and 24th Street at the southwest corner of Madison Square. We didn't speak much during the ride. The Sergeant Major said that, as officer-on-parade, I was responsible for getting us to quarters. He was present to keep me from getting lost, a task often relegated to senior non-commissioned officers.

Sergeant Bisbee looked up at the fancy hotel and said, "Cadet Corporal Hudson, the Army warrant you carry for *our* quarters and rations will not cover this location."

I dismounted, handed my reins to the groom, and tipped him. "Henry Hudson and Arlund Bisbee, US Army." Then I turned to the Sergeant Major and said, "Please dismount." He balked. "Officer-on-parade, Sergeant Bisbee. He lunged off his horse and handed the reins to the groom.

"Please curry, brush, oats, and alfalfa."

"Yes, sir," the groom said, taking the horses.

I approached the doorman, who tipped his hat and opened the front door for us. Sergeant Bisbee followed me, carrying our luggage, which consisted of a carpet bag and saddle wallets. Rather than walk to the front desk clerk, I steered to the concierge.

He took us in with slight skepticism but wore a habitual smile. I said, "Henry Hudson," presenting a card. My sergeant and I will stay on my account at the Farmers' and Mechanics' Bank if you will send a messenger or confirm by cable. I'll need a suite with an adjoining room for Sergeant Major Bisbee, and our uniforms should be cleaned using the Stoddard process of white spirits, pressed, and ready by first light. We will be attending to the Army's business here throughout the day, staying for this and at least one additional night. I want a personal valet assigned during my visit."

The concierge may not have been impressed by our uniforms, but he knew money and those accustomed to spending it. He took notes.

"Your name, sir?"

"Jennings," the concierge said.

I tipped him a double-eagle. The twenty-dollar gold piece vanished into the watch pocket of his red vest like magic.

He snapped his fingers for the bellman, who tugged our saddle bags and the carpet bags from the grasp of Sergeant Bisbee.

"The Presidential Suite for Colonel Hudson and his sergeant, please." He handed the keys to the bellman. Turning to me, "I'll have the valet for you in a few minutes." He snapped another bellman over and said, "Fetch Flexman to the Presidential Suite if you please."

We followed the bellman up a grand staircase and down a polished-wood hall with a red-and-blue Persian runner down the center. Gaslight richly illuminated the hallway. The bellman opened the door, and Sergeant Major Bisbee snatched our bags back. I tipped him a silver dollar, and he doffed his red pillbox cap.

"Your valet, Flexman, will attend you shortly."

"Thank you. Your name?"

"Carlo Severino."

"Carlo. Very good."

I closed the door, and as soon as it shut, Sergeant Bisbee said, "Cadet Corporal Hudson, that was well managed."

"I've watched my father and grandfathers. I just copied them."

"And the Farmers' and Mechanics' Bank?"

"Was founded by my grandfather. The account will be verified."

"Why the Army, if I may be so bold, Cadet Corporal? Aren't there other things you could be doing? I realize I'm crossing a line by asking. I've been in the Army most of my life and am accustomed to some familiarity with officers I serve in a senior non-commissioned capacity."

"My family wanted me separated from a woman who would have become a problem. Indenturing me to the Army and having me in New York while she remained in Detroit, worked for them, and retained the family honor. I'm the second son, not the first."

"Ah." I saw a light in his eyes.

"And, Sergeant, I have more aptitude for the army than I do for counting and cheating, which would have been my lot as a belching civilian."

"I heard you were a dead shot."

"He turned to flee. I back-shot him through the neck, and it came out through his throat, making a mess."

"Back-shot. I hadn't heard that."

"Now you know."

"Cold."

"Sad. It was a challenge given and received while we were in our cups. Others involved themselves, and influential people wagered on the outcome."

Bisbee said, "You could have been killed."

"Odd as it sounds, that thought never seriously entered my mind. Not in the sense that I gave it much thought then or now. I had some confidence that I could best him." I rubbed my chin, which bore a white scar. "I was only nicked once, and that was years ago."

A knock at the door, and Sergeant Bisbee answered it. He opened it wider.

"Flexman, sir, your valet."

"Come in," I beckoned. He stood slightly over five and a half feet tall, wearing a tailored black broadcloth jacket and trousers, and a strikingly yellow silk waistcoat with Oriental designs. His face was florid and closely shaved. Brown hair had been carefully combed, parted down the middle, and pasted down with pomade. He looked through close-set eyes, his nose long and pointed. He was as flashy as a rat with a gold tooth. Likely just as honest.

"Take notes, please, Flexman."

He produced a small notepad and a pencil.

I opened a gold pocket watch and wound it absently as I consulted the time.

I will require the papers for today and tomorrow morning. Both Sergeant Major Bisbee and I will need hot baths drawn. Are there bathing tubs close?"

"The bathing rooms are down the hallway."

"Have a humidor with a dozen of the best Cubans delivered before the baths and a large pail of mild beer to clear the dust of the road."

He scratched on his pad.

"We will require a coach at seven and a half; send a messenger to Delmonicos. We will dine there at eight. The coach, driver, and footman can wait on us. Instruct the majordomo and sommelier that we will use my grandfather's private liquor cabinet. Elijah Hudson, President of the Farmers' and Merchants' Bank."

"I have a maid coming to take your dusty clothing for dry process cleaning as instructed." Flexman's voice was precise and measured. He knew the game.

"This is your best suite?"

"It is, sir. It's the Presidential Suite."

"The cut flowers are not fresh; see to it that the oversight will be remedied."

He nodded wordlessly and glanced at the colorful spray on the table.

"We'll require a nightcap in the room, a bottle of suitably aged Macallan with crystal tumblers, and a collection of sweets; I'll leave it to your discretion."

"Indeed, Mr. Hudson."

"You need not tarry until our return from Delmonico's, but please have maids available should we need them."

"Of course."

"Young, clean, and pretty."

"Naturally, Mr. Hudson."

"Off with you. You have your chores." I handed him two double eagles.

Arlund Bisbee looked at me with new eyes. I had never done this before, but being a keen observer of my father and family, I knew how it was done.

I motioned to the center table and chairs, "They'll see to the flowers."

"What is wrong with the flowers?"

"Nothing, but they're yesterday's blooms. Recognizing that will be mentioned, and it won't happen again. Very well, your room is through that door. Please remove your uniform so it can be cleaned, and we'll dress in our spares for dinner once we've bathed. You'll have a robe until you're ready to dress."

When the Sergeant left, I noticed yesterday's newspaper on the table. The Virginia House of Delegates rejected South Carolina's proposal to organize a convention of southern states. Lieutenant Governor Gist had been quoted in his outrage. The first Japanese ambassador arrived in San Francisco en route to Washington the previous week and was expected to dock the following month. Dion Boucicault's stage melodrama "The Colleen Bawn, or The Brides of Garryowen" had been scheduled to open at Laura Keene's Theatre on the 29th.

A knock on the door.

"Enter."

Flexman poked his head in the door. "Your baths will be ready in fifteen minutes. They're hauling up buckets from the boiler room."

"Very good."

THE CARRIAGE RIDE from the hotel to Delmonicos was managed well.

I sat in the back of the coach, facing the Sergeant Major. "I realize that decorum and discipline are important, but when we're in private discussions, I call you Arlund. You can call me Henry or Hud?"

He thought a moment and nodded. "I don't know what to think of all this, Henry."

"We're traveling on orders with dispatches to Fort Schuyler; it doesn't mean we can't do it comfortably."

"It's just that I expected a rope bed in a boarding house with a shallow bowl of thin soup and possibly a hard biscuit to dip so I wouldn't chip a tooth at dinner, Henry. Maybe I'd get lucky, and there would be fewer than three or four other snoring, farting men in the room. I've never slept on a feather mattress."

"Sleep soundly, and we can continue our journey and then return here for morrow's eve. If you like Delmonico's, we can return it tomorrow. They're known for their steaks but also offer a decent variety of entrées. Or we can go somewhere else. The Albemarle is as new as our hotel; we can walk to it, and it is said to have a French chef specializing in the rare and exotic if you tire of oysters and steaks. We should enjoy it now because, after this, we're both back to the Academy's routine."

"It's too much."

"I'm enjoying shaking out the cobwebs, Arlund, and I'm glad you're along to enjoy it too. A serial was published in a French newspaper called *Le Journal des débats* a few years back—*The Count of Monte-Cristo*."

Arlund smiled. "I know it. There were old newspapers in Mexico when I was on campaign. Edmond Dantès, a young, promising sailor from Marseille, was betrayed by friends jealous of his success."

"You read French?"

"*Oui.*"

"It told of the wealth of the Spada family, hidden on the Island of Monte Cristo. That's roughly how much money my extended family has. When they read the invoices, if they ever get past a clerk's scrutiny, to my grandfather, he'll laugh and ask what the young scallywag is up to, hoping that I'm barricaded behind the suite's walls with an expensive French woman named Monique or something. The woman who got me sent out of state was a married woman with French blood, named Marie DuPont. The family knows that I have a fondness for a slender ankle."

Arlund said, "It's better than being poor."

"What's your story, Arlund? Who are your people? How

did you enter the Army and find the artillery?" I motioned toward his red stripes and piping, indicating his branch of service."

He breathed in, "There isn't much to tell. My family was middling, not poor. I was born in Fort Smith, Arkansas, and am the youngest of nine children. I attended Saint Mark's Normal School for Boys at Fort Smith and learned to read, write, and cipher under the strict gaze of the Holy Fathers. Studies came naturally to me, and mathematics did, too, which led to my transfer from infantry to artillery, but I'm getting ahead of myself.

"My oldest brother, named Baptist, after he who dunked Jesus, is eighteen years my senior. He took up with a grass widow whose husband died at the hands of outlaws at the cockpit. Baptist left my father's employ and took over the late husband's interest in the Arkansas Northern Coal Company. I went to work for him when I was sixteen, shoveling coal and then, as a teamster, hauling drayage. I was skilled with numbers and learned that the Arkansas Northern was shorted on deliveries on their Little Rock to Helena line. I suspected the receiving clerk of collusion and took my concerns to Baptist. I should have known better, but being young and looking up to him, I deluded myself. A fortnight later, a rich man accused me of stealing a gold watch. Baptist told me that he'd save me from the charges and enrolled me in the army, attesting to my age falsely, claiming he was my father. I was big for my age and strong from shoveling. Baptist took the enlistment bounty for himself, and off I went. I never returned, fearing that I'd kill my brother if I confronted him.

"I found myself billeted to the construction garrison at Fort Pulaski in Savannah, attached to the engineers as an enlisted private laborer. The fort was located on Cockspur Island at the mouth of the Savannah River. The Seminole

War was underway, and more soldiers died of fever than died from arrows or scalping. Losses required replacements to be sent out, and I was relieved of my digging and marched with a company to provide replacements for the First Infantry. When we arrived in Florida, an officer from the Fourth Artillery Regiment tested those who could read and knew numbers, and I was taken from the replacements to serve in B Battery. Because I could write legibly, I became the scribe for the Battery First Sergeant, who could only make his mark. I was promoted to corporal. I received the attention of Lt. Colonel Matthew M. Payne, who transferred me to the headquarters section. During the Mexican War, I was promoted to sergeant and then to sergeant major when the sergeant major died from a fever after the Battle of Palo Alto, where he broke his leg."

"After the war, I was transferred to Army Headquarters, where I met Colonel Hardee, who asked me to serve with him at West Point, bringing me here with you."

"You didn't tell me how you learned French."

"I took up with a Creole schoolmarm who lived outside the fort in Florida, and the language came naturally to me.

I observed, "You advanced because you could think."

"Thinking got me into more trouble than it got me out of, taken as a whole. Artillery was always a better duty. Our officers ensured we had adequate food, and we were more likely to be stationed as garrison troops or in coastal defense artillery units than to march endlessly. Since caissons drew light artillery, we rode the trace horses or on an ammunition wagon. Because I could write well, I usually scribed orders for the officers, managed invoices and ledgers, and led the team. Though I was responsible for shot and shell fired at Mexicans, I can't tell if they killed anyone. I never put a pistol ball through somebody's throat at close range."

"I'm not proud of it, Arlund."

THE CONFEDERATE CIPHER

When we arrived at Delmonico's, we were ushered into a private booth. Invoking my grandfather's name led to exceptional service.

On the return carriage ride, I asked the Sergeant Major, "Arlund, why are we here?"

"Do you mean in your hired carriage?"

"No, why are you and I taking a dispatch to Fort Schuyler? Why you, why me?"

He lit a Cuban and puffed thoughtfully. "I expect that Colonel Hardee wishes to take your measure, Henry."

"What do you mean?"

"You read the newspapers like a man consumed by the news. You have recently visited South Carolina. You must know that the matter of States' Rights is coming to a head."

I said, "The Virginia House of Delegates rejected South Carolina's proposal to organize a convention of southern states. It was in yesterday's paper. It will antagonize South Carolina, firming their resolve to leave and form a new government. They can not do it alone, no matter how much they want to. They must organize a group of states, or they'll be smashed no matter how well-drilled their militias are. There is a strength in both numbers and territory."

Arlund nodded, "I'm not an officer, Henry. The Army does not pay me to think deep thoughts, but as the Romans used to say, 'the ram is against the wall.' You're a leader in your class. You are close to Southerners, with friends like Nate Beaufort and Armstrong Custer, a clown from the North who is also friendly with the South. If a side is to be chosen, which will you take?"

"Slavery is legal, Arlund. It is the law," I sounded like my father.

"Many believe that the law could change against the South, that their rights could be threatened, forcing secession." Arlund puffed his cigar, scrutinizing me narrowly.

"I do not oppose slavery. It is a matter to be taken up in the courts. And it has been, with slavery affirmed. The fate of the negro was decided, but the abolitionists chewed it like a bone. Colonel Hardee wants to know my feelings on secession. I am a cadet, not an officer."

Arlund laughed, "Look around you, Henry; your family is wealthy; therefore, *you* are rich. Cadets listen to you. Even the staff respects you. Anderson rode a paddle wheeler up the Hudson with you and told Colonel Hardee you'd be one of his artillery proteges. You could be another Colonel Robert Lee."

"I have demerits. Lee was not awarded one."

"The point is the same. People are taking notice of who will do what. After the duel, telegrams arrived offering you Queen's commissions in the most elite units in the British Empire."

"They were covering me because of the duel. Men of influence didn't want to see me broken."

"And you don't think that counts for something? The Coldstream Guards, Henry."

"Posturing."

"You're the only one anyone has ever heard of they postured toward in this way — in the memory of old men. *Only you.*"

"What will I find at Fort Schuyler?"

"More scrutiny, I'd expect."

"How's your cigar?"

"Like the meal, the best I've ever had."

Major Arnold B. Strauss of the Sixth Artillery Regiment was a man without guns. The Corps of Engineers built the fort and turned it over to the Artillery Corps, which accepted it. The promised batteries had not yet arrived, and the extensive star fort was a hollow shell. Major Strauss accepted the dispatch case, opened it in another room, and then returned to his office, where we waited. Hailing from New Orleans originally, he neared the end of an ordinary artillery officer's career. Standing maybe eight inches over five feet, he had thinning gray hair with reddish gray sidebolts and a double chin. His hands had a slight palsy. Having gained weight, he took to waddling as he walked. Such was the case during my interview. Bisbee was dismissed to the Enlisted Mess, and Major Strauss took me on a tour.

The major spoke slowly and deliberately with a pronounced basso regional accent. "This will be a premier fortification for the defense of New York, Cadet Corporal Hudson. Once fully equipped, we will boast over three hundred cannon and mortars and a garrison of over a thousand. From our position on Throggs Neck, four of our five sides will cover the water approach to New York City. Each of the four seacoast fronts has embrasures for three tiers of cannon, ten guns per tier, except on the north front, which will emplace fourteen guns per tier. The bottom two tiers inside the fort are casemated, while the third tier on the roof has barbette mounts. Behind the fort is an extensive hornwork with two bastions and a ravelin that will break up a land attack."

I couldn't imagine assaulting the fort once it had been garrisoned and armed. A chicken couldn't run across those crossed fields of fire without being plucked.

After wandering through the fort, which took decades to complete, Major Strauss suggested that we retire to the Officers' Mess for lunch before I began my return trip to West Point. It could have qualified as elegant by any Army standard, with a French chef, Major Strauss, brought from New Orleans, and a staff of well-trained messmen wearing white. Seabass was served with pepper sauce, potatoes, and carrots basted in brown sugar, along with a long loaf of freshly baked, crusty bread. French vintage wine was served, with Major Strauss consuming the better part of two bottles, which calmed his shaking hands.

"You are acquainted with the British military aristocracy, I am told."

"A passing acquaintance."

He moved on without hearing my reply, "And I am told that they reviewed South and North Carolina's militias recently while in your company."

"I was told they secured contracts for cotton deliveries at a negotiated price."

"They may have done that, too, but what, Cadet Corporal Hudson, was your opinion of their assessment? You have been schooled in these matters, taking in these facts."

"I'm in my second year."

"But well regarded and from a fine judicial and commercial family, and a duelist with both saber and pistol of some renown."

"Thank you, Major, but I do not boast of these things."

He slapped the table, "Others carry the word for you, Mister Hudson! And what are your feelings on the secession issue of states leaving the United States and forming another Union, equally bound by the rule of law but one more favorable to an agrarian society?"

"Some might call it treason?"

"Some might," he conceded, "but when they formed the Articles of Confederation at the commencement of the rebellion against the crown, nothing bound them. Gentlemen agreed to work together for the common good, connected by agreed-upon values."

He drank another swallow of wine. "If this separation occurs, cadets at the United States Military Academy will likely be offered commissions at advantageous rank in the

THE CONFEDERATE CIPHER

newly organized country in the South if they are the right sort, with suitable families and the correct leadership qualities. I cannot offer such a thing, but I wanted to give you a proper lunch and something to think about, entirely off the record. You would not need to complete your studies to become a serving officer in the new country with the rank of captain, possibly artillery, for the sake of argument."

"Or as an engineer?" I baited him.

"Engineers. If you bought one for what he's worth and sold him for what he thought he was worth, you'd make a fortune."

I laughed, and the major called for his steward to bring our dessert.

As Arlund and I rode back to the Fifth Avenue Hotel, I confirmed what he knew would happen.

"May I know what you said when an offer was presented?"

"It was a hypothetical captaincy in a hypothetical country under circumstances that may or may not occur. We are indeed living in perilous times. I fear that the wrong spark could set the nation ablaze."

We passed the evening at the restaurant in the Fifth Avenue Hotel, eating pheasant. After dinner, as with the previous night, significant noise came from Arlund's room. I didn't engage in sport because I thought about Victoria and unfolding events.

I contented myself with the newspapers, excellent, well-cured Scotch whiskey, and a cigar. I continued to wonder how I had become involved in such a mess.

A tap at the door to the room. I opened it with my pistol in my hand, cocked and behind my leg. The other maid looked at me through large blue eyes, and I invited her in, tucking my pistol into the front of my trousers.

"So, what's this business?"

"My name is Adeline Stone, Colonel Hudson."

"I'm a *cadet corporal* at the military academy at West Point, Miss. Stone, not a colonel in the army."

"Beg pardon, Colonel Hudson, but Flexman sent me to see to your needs—*any* needs you may have. Any at all."

"Would you share a drink with me?"

"I do not partake in ardent spirits, sir."

"I see." The noise coming from Bisbee's room indicated that things were reaching a climactic moment. I motioned toward his room.

"If I am dismissed, it will go badly for me. Your pleasure and satisfaction are matters of some interest to the hotel that employs me."

"I see, Adeline, there is also a large glass jar of lemon water. Can I pour you a glass?"

She smiled and nodded.

As I poured the lemon water into a glass for her and added two spoons full of sugar, I felt my resolve weakening. "Do you perform this service for all the hotel's guests?"

"No, not ever before."

"What is your age?"

"I'm seventeen, came to the city for employment from north of Albany, where my parents lost their acres."

"Sit and tell me how that came to be."

She sat demurely and edged her chair closer to mine. I took her hand.

"We lost the farm through foreclosure when crop prices declined following a series of unfortunate incidents. Hail destroyed the early crop, an insect plague took the second, and by last winter, we ate our seed corn. My father said that the railroads dictated prices and policies for shipping and storing grain. He blames them as well. My mother died that winter of influenza. So we came to the city. He is now a farrier at the large stables at Washington Mews and the West

Side Livery on 38th Street. My brother is a groom at the stables. I came to work at the hotel after it opened and interviewed for positions just a month ago."

She untied a small pink bow at her throat, "Flexman said that there were ways for —."

"And he would share what you earned with you?"

She nodded.

I took a gold single eagle from my pocket and pressed it into her hand. Then I gave her five silver dollars. The silver is for you to share with Flexman, and the gold is for your purse. Do not tell your father about the gold coin, for he may think you have become a low woman, and I wouldn't want that."

I poured the rest of the lemon water into her glass and sipped my scotch. "A farrier, you say? Is he a good one?"

"Oh yes, he's very good with horses, but he's not a lucky farmer."

"What is his name?"

"Allister Martin Stone."

"Your brother?"

"Allister junior, we call Bud."

I took a quill, dipped it in the inkwell on the table, and then wrote on a sheet of paper.

> To Judge Charles James Hudson, Presiding Judge, United States Circuit Court for the District of Michigan, The Federal Building, Detroit, Michigan
>
> Father, this letter will introduce my friend, Allister Martin Stone, his daughter, Adeline, and his son, Allister Junior, also known as Bud.
>
> It would be a great favor to me if you would find them employment in our household or among our family companies. Allister is a farrier of some renown in New York City, and his son and daughter are intelligent and diligent.

As I have not written to you about others in the past, you may take this to be an exceptional request of people who need a new beginning. Please pay them generously.

Your dutiful son,

Cadet Corporal Henry Hudson, Army of the United States, at the M. A., West Point

"The Federal Building is quite large. It took seven years to build, and it fairly dominates the area. It occupies the northwestern corner of Shelby and West Fort streets. You can't miss it. It opened on January 30th of this year. My father's office and courtroom are there. Please take this to the clerk of the court and ask to speak to my father in chambers."

I forgot to ask, "Can you or your father read?"

She nodded quickly.

I handed her the letter, and she read it slowly, looking up at me.

"This is what will happen. You will sleep in my bed in my room tonight, alone. I will sleep here in the sitting room on the floor planks. In the morning, you will have breakfast here with me, and Sergeant Bisbee and I will give Flexman notice. I will order up a carriage, and you and I will ride to the stables. I need to make your father's acquaintance before I can call him my friend. Once we are introduced, I will give him the letter and silver to travel to Detroit."

"Why are you doing this, Colonel?"

"Call the favor me, trying to be a good man, and leave it at that. If you stay here, working at the hotel and favoring guests, you will be ruined, and I don't want to see that happen. Eventually, you will be poxed by a guest and turned out because that is how it happens. You will become a woman of the town. I would like to see a more promising future for you."

She handed the letter back. I folded it and put it into an envelope, which I addressed and sealed with wax.

I wrote a separate cover letter addressed to the Clerk of the United States Circuit Court in Michigan, with an individual introduction to help them meet my father, and then placed it in an unsealed envelope.

"Off to bed with you, Adeline, and don't tempt me with an offer to join you."

She slowly walked into the adjoining room and looked over her shoulder at me. I almost lost my resolve at that moment.

The next morning, Sergeant Major Bisbee joined me for breakfast, wearing his freshly cleaned and pressed uniform. He was surprised to see Adeline by my side, eating eggs and ham.

"This is a development, Henry."

"We can talk about it on the road to West Point. For now, enjoy breakfast. I've ordered a one-horse shay. We will visit the New York Central Railroad office, where my cousin Albert Forsythe serves as managing director, to ask for a favor. Adeline and I will then take the shay to Washington Mews to meet her father. I will tie my mount to the rear, and you can escort us. When we've completed our business, we can finish the trip to the Academy."

Allister Martin Stone was roughly the size of Sergeant Major Bisbee, with a face that could be a bookend of the sergeant major's. Unlike the sergeant major, who was clean-shaven, Stone had a coal black beard, and an old, worn leather apron covered his clothes. He had been surprised to see his daughter escorted to meet him, and he asked her where she had been all night.

I said, "Her honor is intact, sir."

He gave me a penetrating gaze and a slow nod.

"She has documents to be presented to the Presiding

Judge of the United States Circuit Court in Detroit, who will oversee your employment. I have heard about your farm and know that you will do better in Detroit than you can here. You have blamed the railroad for part of your misfortune, and for that, I am sorry. Although I am not responsible for those events, my grandfather owned significant shares in the New York Central Railroad from its formation in 1853 through the consolidation of several smaller railroads, including the Albany and Schenectady Railroad, which was initially the Mohawk and Hudson Railroad. I do not offer you charity, sir, but a reckoning in good faith if you will accept it."

"This is extraordinary and sudden, Mr. Hudson. You have me at a significant disadvantage."

"Your daughter has no future at the hotel, or none that you would desire for her. She's a young woman with potential, and with a turn of luck, it may be that you all can find a brighter future. If you take the letters she has to Michigan, you can decide for yourselves. I will cover the expense of travel associated with your journey of exploration."

I handed the Railroad Script from the New York Central Railroad. "It is a voucher for three first-class tickets, including a Pullman sleeping car, meals, and lodging at railroad-owned hotels between here and Detroit. You'll change to the Michigan Central Railroad, but they will honor the script. If you decide to return to New York, the script will work in reverse."

"How much—?"

"$136 each way plus lodging and meals for each of the three of you."

"You're taking one hell of a financial risk on us, young man. I'm paid $8 per week, and my son, Bud, makes half of that. You're paying a year's wages to send us to Detroit."

"What price do you place on Adeline's virtue?"

THE CONFEDERATE CIPHER

He looked at the girl who dropped her head.

"As I said, her honor is intact."

"I did not know this situation—"

"Take my hand, take my thanks, and allow me to remove your rancor toward the railroad and whatever wrong it may have done to you."

He offered a big, rough, thorny, calloused hand, and I took it. He then took Sergeant Major Bisbee's hand. "I would never have imagined that such integrity had its repose in the Army."

"You will need to return the shay and the horse to the Fifth Avenue Hotel. We must be about the Army's business, sir. I wish your family a turn of fortune and the best of health."

Sergeant Bisbee and I mounted for the long ride back to West Point.

"There is more to you than meets the eye, Hud." It came as high praise from the sergeant major.

CHAPTER 7

*US Military Academy, West Point
and Washington DC
Early Summer 1860*

As we concluded the year at the Military Academy, the Republican nominating convention took place May 16 - 18 in Chicago, and Abraham Lincoln, an abolitionist, received their nomination on the third ballot. Honest Abe, the Rail Splitter, promised not to interfere with slavery in the South but opposed the extension of slavery into the territories. Based on the partisan mood among cadets, those from southern states did not believe his intentions stopped short of abolition. Factionalism divided the Corps of Cadets *and* the faculty into different camps.

The nominating process for the Democrat Party was more involved because the Northern Democrats nominated Stephen A. Douglas, whom the Southerners found unacceptable. They were regrouping to hold their own convention, and John C. Breckinridge was the only candidate under consideration. Everyone expected that he would be nominated within the month.

The Constitutional Union Party nominated John Bell, who hoped to avoid any discussion of slavery *or* Southern rights.

It would be a four-way race.

I quietly surveyed the graduating class and felt that many of them would support secession if it came to that, even though they were being commissioned into the Federal Army of the United States. The majority seemed to reject such behavior as inherently treasonous and an act of oath-breaking, despite having sworn oaths to their respective states, some of which favored separation.

There was still time to stop the momentum, but I had no way of doing anything other than keeping my head down. It took considerable effort to avoid being swayed by one faction or another. Duty to the task prevailed.

My father wrote me from Detroit.

Dear Henry,

I received the Stone family and am reporting on the events surrounding their arrival and appointment.

I arranged for Allistair Stone to work at a steel fabrication factory owned by Baldwin Locomotive Works of Philadelphia, which opened here in Detroit a mere fortnight ago. He is doing well in his new occupation and is paid $15.00 per week, more than the prevailing wage of $13.50. His son works with him as an apprentice for half that amount. Their employer is satisfied with their work and commends me for the referral. I placed them at Bitty Sorenson's Boarding House at my expense for three months so they can save while they settle in.

Adeline Stone now works as a governess in the home of

Judge Hezekiah G. Wells, whom you know, who works under me in the Circuit Court. He is a good Republican and a Lutheran, and he introduced Abraham Lincoln at a major rally in Kalamazoo in 1856. She will be safe there, and I'm certain she will offer commendable service to his eight children.

I am not sure of your specific interest, but I trust that I have carried out your expressed wishes.

I am your servant and your loving father,
Charles James Hudson

And then I was summoned to the commandant's office. Sergeant Major Bisbee met me with a mouth stretched into a thin, straight line.

"Knock and go in. Colonel Hardee is waiting for you."

I entered, closed the door behind me, and saluted. Colonel Hardee returned my salute. "It's good to see you, Cadet Corporal. We have great hopes for your leadership in the next term."

"Thank you, Commandant. I will do my utmost."

He waved the air with one hand while holding a sheet of paper in the other. "I have a telegram from Washington, D.C. British Minister Lyons is holding a reception and has expressly requested your presence. He routed his request through the Secretary of War. Naturally, I will endorse your orders and grant you leave to travel and attend, with leeway for any extension you may require to fulfill the Army's needs."

"I was not aware of this, Colonel Hardee."

"No, I don't expect that you were, and you'll miss the encampment, but you've been promoted from pawn to knight on the chessboard, whether or not you wish to be. You're excused from final examinations at the request of the Secretary of War, which means that he knows more than we do. He has the power to make the adjudication of your grades to date, and so, without explicitly saying so, you are dismissed from the Academy until the commencement of next year. Your furlough orders allow for that."

I didn't know what to say.

"You may take Sergeant Major Bisbee with you if you wish. I wouldn't like to see him go, but you may need him more than I do. You certainly won him over on your little jaunt to New York, and not with prime steaks and oysters."

"From what you say, sir, I'm only invited to a party."

"That's what Lord Lyons *said*. And Secretary of War John B. Floyd *said* you didn't need to sit for your upcoming exams, which I take to mean that you won't be returning from the party, possibly until the end of the Summer. I am forced to read between the lines almost perpetually these days, Henry. We live in turbulent times, and the water of life is as muddy as the Mississip."

"Then yes, sir, I'll take Sergeant Bisbee along with me under flexible orders."

"I've already drafted them, Bisbee has them, good luck, and get out of my office before I throw you out, Cadet Corporal." He smiled as he said it.

In the outer office, Sergeant Major Bisbee said, "I heard it all through the wall."

"Yes, Arlund, Colonel Hardee is not a man of soft words. I need to say goodbye to my friends before we leave for the District of Columbia."

He smiled and nodded. "I'll be here."

Both Nate and Autie pumped me for information I didn't have. I explained that I had orders to travel to Washington, D.C., and that Sergeant Major Bisbee would accompany me.

"Today is Thursday, I should return by Monday," I lied.

. . .

I BOUGHT FIRST-CLASS tickets for Sergeant Major Bisbee and me on the *Herald*. The journey from New York City to Washington, D.C. by paddle steamer would take 12 hours. My family didn't have an ownership interest in the Baltimore Steam Packet Company, which operated a steamship route, including the *Herald*. Still, the captain knew my family name and joined us in the first-class salon before getting underway. He expressed an interest in obtaining a position commanding one of the ships in the fleet owned by the Peninsular and Oriental Steam Navigation Company. Would I put in a word with my uncle? Naturally, I said I would when we next met.

Arlund Bisbee asked, "Is there anywhere you're not known?"

"He doesn't know me, Arlund. The captain wants a better-paying job as master of a larger ship. I've never met the man. Perhaps he runs down the list of first-class passengers to see what he can do for himself with them. There were only two other passengers in the first-class salon. They were both older German men, and we didn't speak beyond a brief hello and a toast to a safe voyage. The captain didn't bother with them.

"When we dock, we'll take transportation from the Navy Yard to the Willard Hotel. Both the railroad and the steamship company keep perpetual rooms there, and if they're empty, we can use them. If not, we'll find rooms elsewhere." The invitation from Minister Lyons had the name and address of the Ringgold House, 1801 F Street NW, Washington, D.C. The Willard Hotel was located at 1401 Pennsylvania Avenue Northwest. I knew the area. The White House lay midway between the two locations, and I should be able to walk there in twenty minutes. It would not do to arrive on foot, though, so less than half that time by carriage. The nation's capital had many victualling houses, but I didn't know exactly where to get a good meal. That's why they had a concierge.

"We must have you fitted out in civilian finery, Arlund. My father's haberdasher is Redmayne. We're arriving early so we can get you at least one suit for the reception. Thereafter, you might best remain out of uniform unless directed otherwise."

Sergeant Bisbee began to object. "A sergeant major will not be as welcome as Mister Arlund Bisbee, unspecified cotton broker or coal magnate and friend of my family from New Orleans, wearing the latest men's fashion."

"It's not right."

"You're to watch over me, so stand there with a gill of gin, make small talk with the swells, find an assignation with the Danish Ambassador's wife or something, and do your political duty. There will be loose women at these receptions. It's one of the reasons they have them. I've never been to one, but oh, have I heard stories about them."

He arched an eyebrow.

"Consider the Greek *orgia!*" I lowered my voice unnecessarily to increase the drama. "They referred to secret religious rites, especially those in worship of Greek and Roman gods like Dionysus. These rites involve extravagant dancing, singing, and drinking to reach an ecstatic state, often in an unclothed state.

He gave me a curious look. Then he nodded his head slightly.

"Meanwhile, you have a room, go rest. It's a twelve-hour float."

Arlund licked his lips, took a bottle from the shelf. "Oh, be joyful."

I sat in an overstuffed chair and opened the latest London newspaper, weeks old. The first horse-drawn tramways were installed along Bayswater Road, Victoria Street, and

Kennington Street. The names didn't mean anything to me because I'd never been to England, but since I was to attend a reception, knowing something of the current news couldn't hurt. A hippopotamus named Obaysch arrived at London Zoo from Africa, creating a sensation. The articles were dry: "Reactionary Symptoms," coverage of Annecy, Savoy, and General Lamoriciere, articles on the fire in Red Cross Street, and the new opera "Almina," engravings of the launch of the steamship *Connaught,* and a full-page illustration of the Victoria Bridge being constructed over the Thames.

The ship's captain returned and asked me if anything I had read interested me.

I said, "Charles Dickens started publishing his novel 'Great Expectations' in installments in his magazine, *All the Year Round.* It's not a big concern to me. There are articles about a flag adopted by the Southern Confederacy and another on the signing of the Treaty of Tien-Tsin in China, which are more to my liking. Did you know that the Southern States had a flag? It's blue with a single white star in the center."

"I don't get further south than the Seventeenth Street Wharf, Mr. Hudson. My people are Maine fishermen who see little more than the contents of a net and a rolling gray sea. I went to sea to experience the world, not to make the run between New York City and Washington City. I shipped out with the Mediterranean Squadron as a boy and saw the Barbary States in Africa and the Pyramids of Egypt. It led to discontentment. When the US Steamboat Act authorized the issuance of licenses for engineers and pilots of steamboats carrying passengers, I thought that being a master would lead to travel farther than from my knee to my foot."

I told him that I'd share his name but wouldn't promise anything.

. . .

ARLUND WAS SOBER enough when we docked at Washington City.

I had visited Redmayne Tailoring with my father many years ago, and after asking around, I found the shop located in a brick building with a sign painted in the window. We learned that the founding owner had passed, and his brother, who had worked with him as a junior tailor, was now the owner. I brought a bank draft to cover our initial costs, and Bruce Redmayne, the proprietor, recognized the family name. He didn't like the idea of Sergeant Major Bisbee leaving the premises with a rack suit, altered on the fly, but when I explained the facts of life, he put on his best smile and said, "Certainly, sir."

Redmayne explained, "Fine wool is used for high-quality, tailored suits worn by upper-class men, and the price is dear. The uniform the sergeant wore is of a lower quality, which we refer to as shoddy, and the dye will run."

"Yes, we know. And my cadet uniform is of a better quality than his. What we need him to walk away with is a formal black wool frock coat, a silk waistcoat, and good dove-gray trousers. The shirt should be made of silk, if possible, or cotton if not."

He fiddled in his back room while we waited, and I wrote out a list. Arlund would need the increasingly popular sack or lounge coat for informal daywear, as well as the cutaway or morning coat for business attire.

Redmayne didn't sell beaver hats or proper shoes. That would be another stop.

By the time we reached the Willard Hotel, the Sun had set, and we had several boxes and bags for Arlund Bisbee's transformation. Whenever he complained, I reminded him that he had a duty to watch over me and, as an enlisted soldier, he wouldn't make it past the kitchens in a great house.

I looked at him, all made up like a gentleman, and gave him a secondhand gold watch on a chain with a Masonic fob that I had purchased from a pawnshop. It had been well-worn, but a gentleman about town would carry such a watch in his waistcoat. He was to be a cotton buyer or a coal magnate, not a king or prince. He tucked a revolver into the waistband of his trousers.

I put my hand out, "Show it to me, please." He put the checkered India gum rubber grips into my hand.

I held a blued-steel Belgian 7mm Pinfire Pocket Revolver with a 3-inch folding dagger mounted on a spring-loaded mechanism with a push-button release. It also had a folding trigger, a deeply rifled bore, and Belgian proofs on the cylinder, which are common for a weapon of that class.

I handed it back to him, grips first. "Close range. Don't shoot yourself while you're preening before a mirror. I will return later." I handed him a purse of silver. "For victuals and such."

He nodded his thanks.

"I'm off to pay court to a young lady at her home. I'm sure there will be a chaperone to ensure her virtue remains intact." What Arlund didn't know wouldn't hurt him.

I rented a one-horse shay at the stable across the street from the Willard Hotel, and I drove it to Lord Lyons' residence at 1710 H Street between Vermont Avenue and 16th Street, a matter of only a few minutes' travel around the White House, the residence of President James Buchanan Jr.

Stopping before the house, I wasn't sure precisely how to proceed. Victoria said that she lived next to the Ambassador. The word next was an imprecise direction, so I knocked on the Minister's door, wearing the dress uniform of a cadet corporal, complete with sword and shako.

An old liveried servant answered the door. I announced

myself, "Cadet Henry Hudson to see Major Sir Iain McKay, of the Coldstream Guards Regiment."

He appraised me with rheumy eyes. "The Major is not in the residence at this time, young man."

"Would you direct me to his residence?"

"I'm sure that's impossible without the presentation of official credentials."

I looked around. "It's a matter of urgent business."

"You may leave a dispatch with me. I will see that he receives it in due time."

"I am not a goddamned messenger, sir." I may have raised my voice because Sir Iain's wife, Maude, with whom I shared a kiss a few months before in Port Royal, appeared behind the servant with another woman of roughly equal age to Victoria, who was richly dressed and stunningly beautiful.

"Jeeves, why are you conversing with our dear Henry Hudson on the stoop?" Maude asked, and the liveried servant, whose name was apparently Jeeves, turned and looked at her and the younger lady.

"He arrived without portfolio, madam, inquiring after your husband, Sir Iain."

"Come in, my dear. Henry, may I present Lady Anne Pickering, um, *niece* to Minister Richard Bickerton Pemell Lyons, Baron Lyons."

Lady Anne offered a gloved hand.

I took it, bowed, and kissed it gently. "Your servant, Lady Anne."

"Will you have tea with us in the parlor, Captain Hudson?" Lady Anne had a soft, sultry voice.

"*Cadet Corporal*, M'Lady, and yes, I would be honored."

"Jeeves, please arrange for tea for this gallant officer and us."

We were seated when Victoria arrived as Lady Anne, and Maude and I were laughing at a joke I made. I stood immediately, and her gaze shifted between Lady Anne and me. She looked at me hard, and I said, "I came looking for you, as I was invited previously, but I didn't know precisely where to find you, Victoria."

Her mouth went from a hard line to the hint of a smile.

"The Secretary of War, His Excellency, John B. Floyd, sent orders detaching me from service at the Academy and directing me to attend a reception here at Minister Lyon's invitation."

Victoria smiled. "Yes, we were expecting you, but you did not send a cable."

"The orders were to proceed forthwith."

Maude intervened, "You'll stay for dinner, of course. Sir Iain and Minister Lyons are at Congress today. Are you hungry?"

"Yes, thank you, that would be wonderful. I have been traveling all day by paddle steamer from New York."

Maude suggested, "Perhaps Victoria could walk with you in the garden while I instruct the staff to add a sitting and oversee final arrangements. Will you need a chaperone, Victoria?"

"I think not, Henry is a gentleman."

"I am, Maude," I assured her.

Maude winked at me. She gave Victoria, who had maneuvered to my side, a wry smile. "Stay away from the misslietoe, Victoria. Dinner is at eight."

Lady Anne Pickering pouted slightly when I left the room with Victoria.

THE PARTICULARS at dinner are not necessary to relate, except to say that I met the British Queen's ambassador, Minister Richard Lyons, at dinner, which was a far more informal affair than I expected it would be. It was like sitting with family, with Victoria at my side, holding my hand discreetly under the table when she could.

Sir Iain had said of Victoria that she was the most intelligent woman he had ever met, strange in one so young. "She will end up married to the Viceroy of India, running the place in his name while the fop with the title has his fun buggering boys, or she'll commit suicide into a river during a storm, *bound hand and foot*, and will wash up on a beach four days later." He meant it as a cautionary note to me, but I didn't think about what he said at the time. I couldn't when I looked into her green eyes.

Maude, Sir Iain, and the others of our class did not view a possible match as improper or out of the question. I, on the other hand, was confused by the events until I sat with Sir Iain privately afterward, when he explained the situation we were all facing. I'll share that with you because it's crucial to your understanding of my journey.

Sitting in the study with glasses of claret that had not yet been emptied, he said, "You have been tested to the best of the ability of people who have some influence in this world and your country. You are of the right class, the proper breeding and upbringing to be a man of influence in this world. The world constantly changes, and significant shifts are occurring across social, political, and mechanical spheres. Machines are doing what people have not been able to do throughout human history.

"Your grandfather, Leslie Forsythe, is building a steam-driven, ship propelled by a screw drive that is defended with one single cannon. It's being built in England, and Leslie, being a friend of the realm, has shared his vision, which the admirals dismiss as foolish impracticality."

"Not, Rear Admiral Owain Rowley-Conway?" I guessed.

"No, not him. He sees the vision clearly, and that vision indicates how things are changing almost before our eyes in unpredictable ways. Imagine a metal ship equipped with a rotating cannon that can fire in nearly every direction, loaded from either the breach or muzzle, and hurling a projectile stabilized and accurized with rifling in the barrel. It may take time to load, being a heavy projectile, but one or two well-placed shots could sink a capital ship if struck at the waterline. Because she is not driven by wind, such a ship could maneuver away from a broadside with some ease while out-ranging the finest and best crewed ships of the line.

"Your grandfather intends to use this new ship of his for commercial purposes, but visionary men see that this mechanical ship has the makings of a device that would be transformative to navies around the world. During the Crimean War, battery ships, powered by steam and moving slowly, were used to support the war on land. Their capacity for swift maneuvering was limited, and they still fired from broadside; however, they, too, portended change — inevitable change.

"My realm fears yours. Not openly, not as a direct rival, though we have fought two wars with you in recent memory. They were nasty wars between brothers. Rome fought those wars, England fought those wars of the Roses, and otherwise, and they are vicious affairs. We believe that one is brewing within America. Do you agree?"

"It would seem to be the case, Sir Iain, but perhaps it can be avoided by compromise?"

He laughed, "We do not observe much effort toward compromise, but we will see, won't we? England would not be distraught with a divided and weakened United States. The crown might be persuaded to recognize a Southern government, but wise men in our midst raise cautionary voices about the precedent for secession in our own empire. Your revolution set that precedent once to our detriment. It could happen in this generation as well. Heavy is the head that wears the crown.

"There are always factions. Perhaps now is the time to explain things as they presently stand. One faction is supported by Prince Albert of Saxe-Coburg and Gotha, Queen Victoria's husband and consort. He holds a powerless official role, but he is a trusted advisor and confidante to the Queen, overseeing her household, estates, and office. He was instrumental in organizing the 1851 Great Exhibition, the world's first display of goods and design, which aimed to solidify Britain's industrial leadership. It is the Prince himself, a friend of your grandfather, Leslie Forsythe, who is behind what I will propose to you this evening.

"When they were first wed, the Queen's household was run by her former governess, Baroness Lehzen. Albert referred to her as the *House Dragon* and manoeuvred to dislodge the Baroness from her position over time. He's an interesting man and passionately anti-slavery. Still, at the same time, he feels a kinship to the Southern Aristocracy in America, which has pledged to stop the international slave trade while phasing out the institution of human slavery in their states over time. Perhaps within a generation."

"He's a man of contradictions."

Sir Iain said, "As are most of us." He took a sip from his glass of claret. "He and our beloved Queen have nine children together. He is persuasive at court. You take my meaning, Henry?"

"I do."

"There is a problem. Last August, Albert fell seriously ill with stomach cramps. His medical condition remains tenuous, and though he and I are both forty years old, he is frail, whereas I am not. His death would mean a weakening of *our* political influence over the Queen."

"I'm only a military cadet, and though I am a friend to

your ward, Victoria, and friend to you, I am hardly in a position to do much of anything. While I do understand what you are saying, I am an American subject, not a British peer."

"Precisely." He drained his claret and refilled his glass. Mine remained untouched. "Our faction is looking for somebody precisely like you to communicate with and thus, informally." He chuckled, "You can't imagine how difficult it is to find somebody who can keep his mouth shut, and at the same time has a head on his shoulders. We don't want you as a cat's paw. You only have value if you remain true to yourself, your own man, as it were. Colonel Hardee and your own Secretary of War have given you orders, haven't they?"

"Yes, they have."

"Why do you think they did that?"

"It's unclear to me."

"They wish to further your education, but it can only happen if you are willing. You need not travel from Washington City. Remain here for the summer *with Victoria* and learn."

I countered, "Cadets aren't allowed to marry."

"We can always defer the pronouncements of clergy to a later date, and she can warm your bed now."

I felt a trap closing around me. He found my weakness.

CHAPTER 8

Washington, D. C. and Maryland
Summer 1860

The expatriate Londoner told me that his name was John Summerhaze. He stood at six feet, was slightly stooped, bookish, with thinning blonde hair, and as thin as a rail. His reddish beard grew along the jawline, covering his chin, but with a clean-shaven upper lip. The style was variously referred to as a chin curtain, a whaler, or a Shenendoah. His choice of clothing emphasized sobriety and formality while also incorporating the specific traditions of conservative academic dress.

Victoria arrived and seemed somehow different in a way that I could not readily define. She had preferred me clean-shaven and said so at dinner at Lord Lyons' residence, not two weeks before, and suddenly she encouraged me to grow a cavalry mustache. I shaved carefully to properly groom the growth.

Women are unpredictable. I know this, but she asked about the duel on Christmas morning in Port Royal as if she had not been there and had not witnessed it firsthand. Stranger still, our lovemaking changed subtly. Where she liked this, now she preferred that. I asked Sergeant Major Bisbee, a man of considerably more experience than I had, and he said, "You never can tell, Hud. It may be the Moon."

Victoria and I took an apartment in the same block as John Summerhaze on a floor lower. He had a cat named Felix, with a calico pattern, of indeterminate age. Vadoma, his wife, told us that she was a Romani Gypsie, and Victoria debated with her over the point of who had a keener second sight.

"She cites her power as originating in Egypt, Hud. Mine can be traced to the druids—Celts like Merlin, the famous magician who advised King Arthur and his knights of the Round Table."

"Really." It wasn't a question. "It sounds like a claim of witchcraft made by you both. Sir Iain told me that Summerhaze was a man of science, not a charlatan, reading the placement of tea leaves in a mug."

"D'ye think me a witch, Hud?"

"I don't know, the jury is out on that one. You do know that they still hang witches in this country, don't you? The Christian Scientists claim to use "mesmeric" powers to harm others. I asked my father about that. He said that the court has no jurisdiction over mental powers."

"Ye're a man of little faith, Henry Hudson."

Victoria had a point. I distrusted smoke and mirrors, claims of buried treasure, Spanish cities of gold, mystic Egyptian curses, and necromancy. I had seen barkers who stood on wagons or on a pine box in the corner of a pub and sold elixir said to cure all ailments. People would line up and pay their dollar to cure the ague or to find love. None of it impressed me. Ministers of religion, who were often former medicine show drummers, spoke of the miraculous they could conjure in exchange for a generous donation. And we're back to smoke and mirrors. It didn't rain, evidence of God's displeasure, or it would rain too much, again, unmistakable evidence of God's displeasure. Locusts stripped a farmer's crops to the limb, providing proof of the displeasure of their nailed Lord. A horse came up lame during a race, changing the perceived outcome, and the Providence of the Universe was cited.

Of course, I read the Bible and drew from its wisdom. Everyone that I knew did that. My father continually referred to our laws as having been based on the texts and to the formation of the nation as anchored in divine providence. I distinguished between those medicine show preachers and evidence of something greater. I didn't want to argue with Victoria, so I didn't draw her into that discussion. Laudanum relieved pain much more quickly than invocations did, and for less money. When Autie Custer found the Venus curse in the upstairs room of a public house after interacting with a woman of the town, I took him to a doctor, not a chanter.

Vadoma's clothing choices included headscarves embellished with golden coins. In response to my question about her unique clothing, John explained Romani traditions regarding purity and pollution, which heavily influenced clothing practices. He said, "The lower half of a woman's body is considered ritually unclean, which leads to the practice of wearing long skirts to cover the legs. Additionally, the clothes she wears on her upper and lower body are washed separately."

The heat of summer and oppressive humidity made life in the apartment unbearable. I suggested that we relocate to a property owned by an uncle on the barrier island in Ocean City, Maryland, that was unused. It didn't take much convincing, and the family, Summerhaze (John, Vadona, and the cat), and Victoria didn't object when I rented a two-horse open spring carriage and loaded our goods for the two-day trip. I rigged a canvas awning to shield us from the sun as we traveled. I put a halter on Glory, and he trailed us.

As we rode, Victoria sat in the rear spring seat with the Gypsey and the cat. John told me, "We can begin our discussion of games and theory on our ride."

It was fine with me. He had boxes and objects, and began with a series of observation games as we made our way slowly through clouds of mosquitoes toward the relief promised by the seashore.

The memory and observation game that Mr. Summerhaze introduced me to was one in which players memorized a set of items and then recalled them after the items were covered or removed. It was a play that I found boringly simple. Summerhaze was frustrated. "The distraction of the road makes this too easy for you."

"I'm driving the carriage, driving around obstacles, holes, ruts, and playing your memory game."

"Quite, you don't have an appreciation of how difficult it should be."

"Mr. Summerhaze, you said that your craft, the one at which you are adept — the dark arts of statecraft require cunning, shrewdness, acuteness, and astuteness. Maybe I acquired them unaware?"

I've always had a good memory and an eye for detail. For the past two years, I have been taken to military fortifications, instructed to observe them closely, and then, sometimes days later, directed to draw pictures of what I saw. Our work was adjudicated based on accuracy in scale, detail, and overall composition. The position of the Sun at the time of observation and the orientation to the points of the compass were also included. Sometimes we had a compass, and sometimes we had to infer north from shadows and the season."

THE CONFEDERATE CIPHER

His thin lips compressed to a fine line. "We can move on to flaps and seals once we arrive. Then secret writing."

"Victoria sent me a letter penned with lemon juice and a hint in the text. I heated the letter, and the writing appeared."

Summerhaze looked over his shoulder at Victoria, who smiled, shrugged, and nodded, saying, "Maude showed me how to do it."

"That is only one element of secret writing. I will instruct you in many methods. There is the scytale, an ancient Greek device used to create a transposition cipher by wrapping a strip of paper or leather around a cylinder of a specific diameter. The sender writes a message along the length of the cylinder, and when the strip is unwrapped, the letters are scrambled. The recipient, who must possess a scytale of the same diameter, wraps the strip around their rod to read the original message. Have you heard of that?"

"No, sir, I have not."

"There is also the use of the written cipher. The Vigenère cipher, a polyalphabetic substitution cipher, is widely used by the Foreign Office. The version I will instruct incorporates nomenclators, which combine symbols and code words for common phrases or names to enhance security in written communication. It will take *some time* for you to become adept at its use."

I nodded. My summer was for vacation, not for memorization, but as an adult, the apparent demands of duty were forcing a different, not particularly interesting lifestyle. Additionally, Victoria entered her Moon cycle and became irritable, prone to complaining like a petulant child.

I could have been at the Academy's encampment, and then gone hunting and fishing on furlough with my friends. In place of that, I had a complaining Scottish brat, a stuffy London prig, and his gypsey wife on a wagon where I had become responsible for their pleasure and contentment with swarms of blood sucking insects in our wake.

The two-day journey felt like two weeks, and on the afternoon of the second day, we arrived in Ocean City and found my uncle's house, where we were to stay.

Vadona dismissed the cook I retained and prepared a gypsey meal for us all to share. Instead of cooking inside the cottage, she built a bonfire. She suspended a well-seasoned pot from a greasy, blackened iron tripod, setting about to cook goulash—a stew of meat and vegetables flavored with paprika. Something smelled off about it as I studied and practiced Vigenère ciphers in the library with John. During a break, I noticed a possum skin and asked about it. Rather than spend a dime on beef, swine, or chicken, Vadona located a dead possum, skinned it, and that was the meat in the stew. I knew that Nate's family in South Carolina refused to eat possum, but many residents of Port Royal did. Technically, there shouldn't be anything wrong with it, but the smell didn't sit well with me.

Sergeant Bisbee arrived on horseback in the late afternoon. I asked him his opinion, and he said, "Son, that possum has turned." Under something barely short of military interrogation of a prisoner of war, Vadona confessed that she had found it dead. Using second sight, she said she divined that it had passed, but only one day earlier, of natural causes.

Despite her advocacy, there was no telling when it died or the proximate cause of death.

For some unknown reason — possibly due to female bonding — Victoria stood with Vadona and John in asserting that they should eat it, regardless of the meat's quality, because Vadona had put so much effort into preparing her signature stew.

Arlund, usually a man of few words, said, "A starving, broke dick dog wouldn't lap at that plate."

THE CONFEDERATE CIPHER

It was enough for me, and I rode Glory while Arlund rode his mount to the Atlantic Inn, not a hundred yards distant, where we dined on freshly caught blue crabs, oysters, and a savory potato soup that incorporated sea bass. Arlund took a room at the inn, and I took one as well to get a quiet night's sleep. In the morning, we enjoyed fresh bread, poached eggs, pickled oysters, and smoked fish, accompanied by strong coffee sweetened by sugar and fresh skimmed cream.

I left him to read the newspaper and smoke a cigar, and rode back to the cottage. As soon as I entered, I could smell the illness. I found Victoria in bed, moaning from stomach pain, which could have been a combination of woman time and possum goulash. She said they all vomited and suffered explosive diarrhea throughout the night.

Discretion being the better part of valor, I left Victoria in the care of the sick gypsey woman and her puking mate and rode back to the inn. Her crystals and incantations didn't seem to have much impact on the flux.

I joined Arlund with a cigar and read a dated publication of the *National Republican* newspaper.

I knew Abraham Lincoln received the nomination, but I reread the drama because I didn't have anything better to do.

With the Democrats in disarray and a sweep of the Northern states possible, the Republicans felt confident.

Seward's speeches on slavery predicted inevitable conflict, which spooked moderate delegates. He was also firmly opposed to nativism, which further weakened his position. He had also been abandoned by his longtime friend and political ally, Horace Greeley, publisher of the influential *New-York Tribune*.

Chase, a former Democrat, had alienated many of the former Whigs by his coalition with the Democrats in the late 1840s. He had also opposed tariffs demanded by Pennsylvania and faced opposition from his home delegation in

Ohio. Chase's firm anti-slavery stance made him popular with the radical Republicans. But what he offered in policy, he lacked in charisma.

The conservative Bates found support from Horace Greeley, who sought any chance to defeat Seward, with whom he now had a bitter feud. Bates outlined his positions on the extension of slavery into the territories and equal constitutional rights for all citizens. These positions alienated his supporters in the border states and among Southern conservatives.

Into this mix came Abraham Lincoln. The party platform promised not to interfere with slavery in the states, but opposed slavery in the territories. It promised tariffs to protect industry and workers, a Homestead Act granting settlers free land in the West, and funding for a transcontinental railroad. There was no mention of Mormonism, which had been condemned in the Party's 1856 platform. Seward's forces were disappointed at the nomination of a little-known western upstart. Still dissatisfied, they rallied behind Lincoln, while abolitionists were angry at the selection of a moderate.

The *National Republican* carried no news of the Democratic Party's specific nominations or newly eloquent arguments.

I put the paper down and asked Arlund, "What do you think of Lincoln?"

He sighed, "The Southern States want to form a new country. They won't accept Lincoln and Hamblin." He changed the subject. "Did you read that there is now a Pony Express, carrying the mail from St. Joseph to Sacramento in ten days?"

"It was not in the *National Republican*." He tossed me his now-folded copy of the *Tribune*. "The Northern Democrats just selected Stephen A. Douglas, the Southern Democrats picked Vice President Breckenridge, and the Constitutional Unionists nominated John Bell. It will be a four-way race with Sam Houston in Texas being a fifth horse with little support from anyone outside his own Texas Party."

I said, "Houston hates Lincoln."

Arlund said, "Hardly anyone likes Lincoln in the South, and they barely tolerate him in the North."

"What will you do if there is a national division?"

"I am of the South, Henry. I have made my mark on the Army's rolls, but how could I turn against my own family?"

Not wanting to go down that road, I proposed, "Why don't we buy two of those bamboo fishing rods, line, corks, and hooks, and fish in that creek that feeds under the bridge into the ocean?"

Arlund smiled, "Now there's an idea."

We didn't catch any fish, but we had a lovely day sitting in the shade and sharing military academy gossip.

I went back to check on Victoria after we had dinner, and she was feeling better, drinking some tea, still as white as a ghost. "You were right, she said in a broad Scots brogue. My second sight failed me."

"My nose didn't fail me. That possum was purely wrong."

She turned green, "Don't ever mention that, or I'll lose it."

"Fair enough. This whole education thing isn't working the way anyone hoped it would. And I'm not sure that it's working for you and me in the way that I'd hoped it might."

"I can try harder," she said, eyes tearing.

"You shouldn't have to try. Maude and Iain shouldn't have pushed you toward me. I'll be staying at the Atlantic Inn while you, John, and the gypsy get better. Let him know. We can meet once you're all back on solid food. I'll come by in the morning and take care of your needs. There's a baker down the street. I can bring fresh bread and butter, milk, or whatever would settle your stomachs. For now, stick with tea."

"Thank you, Hud."

"My pleasure."

That went better than I thought it might, and it answered questions that bothered me while Arlund and I fished. It's a strange thing about fishing and thinking, and sometimes not thinking, that can sort out tangled problems.

The next day, Victoria found me sitting on a dune overlooking the ocean, throwing rocks into the surf, and developing a sunburn. She sat next to me without saying a word as gulls rode the wind above us, calling to each other. Then she asked me, "Have you ever looked at sand through a magnifying glass? Sand is many different things—quartz, seashells, miniature worm tubes, and little bits of creatures that once lived."

"I'll take your word for it." I took sand into my hand and let it run through my fingers. "If I were one of those gulls flying on the wind, it would just look like dirt. Perspective matters?"

"It does, and that's what I wanted to speak with you about."

"I don't seem to have much better to talk about. If I go back to Washington in the heat and with mosquitoes, it will be worse than staying here, eating soft-shell crabs and oysters."

"There are also kippers at the Inn." She tried to pour oil on the water between us.

A kipper is a whole herring or similar oily fish that has been split open, gutted, salted or brined, and then cold-smoked over wood chips, giving it a characteristic reddish-gold color and distinct smoky flavor. The curing process, known as kippering, is a method of preservation that also imparts a delicious taste, making kippers a popular food, especially when served with butter and lemon. There was almost no food that couldn't be improved by adding butter or bacon to it.

"Yes, the kippers are quite good. They make an otherwise unpleasant fish into a delicacy."

"You should finish your studies."

"I don't think I'll finish them with John Summerhaze and the gypsey. In a few weeks, I will be able to return to West Point, as classes will resume. I don't know how many cadets will resign if war breaks out between the States. Most are from the South, and they will take up arms on behalf of the oaths they swore to their states. Your country wishes to meddle in this affair, but I don't think that you will, despite what your uncle and his friends will advise the crown."

"When my parents died, their money went to my nearest living relative, Sir Iain. Therefore, I am dependent on his good graces and Maude's. Had I been born a boy, they would have been required by law to turn those funds over to me upon my reaching my majority. As a woman, there is a general, though unwritten, rule that I would contribute to my dowry when I am married. However, I know that the money is spent because they explicitly explained that. My value to them is presently established by my capacity to influence you."

I replied, "That is outrageous."

"Notwithstanding, that is the case. It is why they offered me to you unwed to do as you will with me, using me as a whore to keep you quiescent while you receive instruction from Summerhaze, who is believed to be a genius in some circles."

She looked over her shoulder. I followed her gaze to Arlund Bisbee, who sat in the shade, smoking a cigar, looking back at us. I waved, and Arlun returned the gesture.

"He is there to protect you, yes?"

"From what?"

"Why then is he there?"

I shrugged.

"Your Commandant is a Southern man with strong ties to their cause, isn't he?"

I replied, "He makes no secret of that."

"He wouldn't need to. Everyone, including the British Crown, understands that many of your leaders, including President Buchanan and the American Secretary of War, favor the cause espoused by Virginia and the Carolinas. Sir Iain explained it to me when he was in his cups. The Cadet Commandant, Hardee, is in a position to persuade the more promising among future officers toward his political cause. The same is true for many who are selected to instruct. You are a prize because you do not oppose slavery, and your family's wealth is substantial. With great wealth comes great influence."

"It is not illegal."

"But the issue is bipolar. You either oppose it or you favor it. Let me finish, and then you can decide what you want to do. Your family, and their extended business partners, represent the wealthiest and most influential people in America. You represent the ownership of railroads, shipping, newspapers, and steel, and your father presides over an influential federal circuit court. He could be considered for appointment as a justice of the Supreme Court if an opening were to occur. Tell me I'm wrong."

"You're not wrong, Victoria."

"You are potentially valuable to the Crown and to the Southern Cause. If you disregard this instruction, I will suffer the consequences. I don't know what those consequences will be. Maybe I will be married to a fat old man back in England, and he will rut with me to his heart's content. Perhaps I will be offered a position as a senior officer in the Coldstream Guards or an officer in a lesser regiment. Sir Iain will make his best cash deal. For my sake alone, I ask you to finish with Summerhaze and write a lover's letter to me when you return to your academic studies, so I can show that there is still potential to influence you. Buy me time to sort things out. In exchange, use my body as you will."

I lay back on the sand and looked up at the sky, the clouds blurring with my tears.

CHAPTER 9

US Military Academy, West Point
Autumn 1860

I returned to Washington City after the summer furlough, and John Summerhaze trumpeted my scholastic acumen to Minister Lyons, Major Sir Iain McKay, and pronounced me a master of the craft. I suspect that part of his motivation lay in being paid for his services, but he complimented me to no end.

There in Ocean City, Vadoma, the gypsie, proved to be skillful at instructing in the finer arts of disguise, false identities, and extracting information through clever interrogation schemes.

John Summerhaze devoted much of his efforts to teaching me ciphers and coded letters to ensure the confidentiality of communications, often using codebooks or systems where numbers represented words or names. He offered insight into how one might go about discovering the system of encryption an opponent would use so that I could read their letters.

THE CONFEDERATE CIPHER

Secret writing involved using a mixture of ferrous sulfate and water to write messages between the lines of innocent letters, revealed only by heat or a chemical reagent. Mask letters required a special template to reveal the hidden message within the text.

Hidden messages that he and Vadona demonstrated were concealed in everyday objects such as hollowed-out quills, buttons, or baked goods.

Hidden locations, such as hollowed-out trees, were used to store messages for pick-up by couriers or other agents. They referred to these as dead drops because you dropped the information for your agent and did not return to it. If they dropped it for you, it could be a trap.

I did it for Victoria's sake at first, but in the end, I learned because I wanted to.

As my furlough concluded, I attended a formal reception hosted by Her Majesty's Government, wherein all of the political grandees and ambassadorial class in Washington City attended. There had to be at least two hundred people who arrived by invitation, and there were nearly that many servants circulating. Without the open doors to the garden, we would have all suffocated.

The etiquette and protocol emphasized formality in dress, dining, and social interactions. The purpose was not just social but also diplomatic, as it created opportunities for conversation, relationship-building, and the representation of the interests of the respective nations.

Some of the grandees were peacocks. Others pretended to be fops while circulating with more defined political motives. Some were genuine fops. Differentiating one from the other was the function of the genuine political gamers who gathered.

Victoria's hair was parted in the middle and waved over her ears, gathered into a roll at the back of her neck. She wore a light summer hoop dress of lilac-colored silk, as the evening was still hot. It was the same general style as the other women wore, but she outshone them all.

Victoria stayed on my arm, hinting that we were engaged to be engaged once I completed my studies at the Military Academy and would be free to commit myself. I didn't disabuse anyone of the notion, and we were closely chaperoned by a servant assigned to the task at the reception to ensure that probity was satisfied.

Sir Iain publicly reiterated his dismay that I had declined his offer to purchase a lieutenancy in the Coldstream Guards for me, which impressed the small cadre of senior US Army officers and aides who were also present at the suaree with their wives.

Baron Edmond Roche, Lord Major of the Royal Horse Guards Regiment, had returned to America and was present, publicly squabbling with Sir Iain over whether I was more suited to the infantry or to the Royal Horse Guards, to which he belonged. "He's a cavalryman, Sir Iain, not a foot soldier, by God and St. George!"

The duel I fought and won was discreetly discussed, with my accuracy with a pistol highlighted. "I was there, by jove, and he shot the gray-coated scoundrel through the throat at twenty paces without the use of a sight." My reputation with a blade was also discussed. "Out of three dozen duels with a blade, he has but one mark, and that delivered by a Bavarian prince."

Their deliberate fuss and drama worked, and a US Army Captain of Engineers asked me to meet Lieutenant General Winfield Scott, who had arrived and was seated in a stout chair from which he held court in a corner of the room. The captain introduced me, and I saluted the Commanding General of the Army, one of the largest men I had ever met.

"Cadet Corporal Henry Hudson, the son of Judge Charles Hudson?"

"Yes, General."

"Then you are a Michigan man?"

"Yes, General, returning to the Academy to begin my third year."

"And how did you come to the acquaintance of these John Bull Officers who squabble for your commission in Queen Victoria's Army?"

"I met them socially last Christmas, sir."

"They speak well of you, young cadet, which is a rare thing indeed. What is your class standing going into your third year?"

I didn't want to say, but his aide, the captain, prodded me, "Answer the Commanding General."

"Third, General Scott."

"By God, we must keep a close eye on you, remember his name, Captain Jones, and send our congratulations to both the Superintendent and Commandant of Cadets by telegraph."

Minister Lyons came up behind me and put his arm around my shoulders. "What think you of my friend, Henry Hudson, General?"

"We have just met, but he is very well-referenced for a cadet corporal."

"He has been a guest in my home and is a welcome friend," the Queen's Ambassador gushed. "I think of him almost as I would a son, if I had married."

It was a relief to excuse myself, take Victoria by the arm to the punchbowl, and have two glasses dipped by a liveried servant. We escaped to the veranda and the cool night air, trailed by the chaperone.

I whispered to Victoria, "Your uncle and the rest of them are putting a lot of jam on the bread, aren't they?"

"Are they? I would think it's just the right amount."

A herald struck the marbled floor with his staff three times and announced, "His Excellency, the fourteenth Vice President of the United States of America, John Breckenridge of Kentucky, and his wife, the Second Lady of the United States, Mary Cyrene Breckinridge. Victoria and I clapped from where we stood, looking in through open doors at the couple arriving. The vice president, not yet forty, looked dapper and distinguished. His wife's features were somewhat more masculine and less flattering.

They were followed by a single strike to the floor with the staff. "Accompanying the Vice President is Colonel Robert Lee, Commanding the Second Regiment of United States Cavalry, and his wife, the Lady Mary Anna Custis Lee. The Lees made a dashing couple and, in their way, were more famous than Vice President Breckenridge.

Baron Edmond Roche came up from behind and took me by the left arm, as my right was entwined with Victoria's. "Hud, are you enjoying yourself?"

"Ed, or is it Lord or Major?"

"It's always Ed."

"I'm red-faced from your blandishments."

"Ha! I have a question for you, and it has to do with Breckenridge, Lee, and Lieutenant General Winfield Scott."

"I don't move in those circles, Ed."

"But you hear the gossip. All three men are Southerners. Scott and Lee from Virginia, and Breckenridge from Kentucky. Where do they stand?"

"Breckenridge is running for the presidency in November, so as president, he will do what he does. I don't expect him to change his position from that of President Buchanan. Should he lose, he is a son of Kentucky in the same way as Colonel Lee is a Virginian. The Old Soldier,

General Scott, would never turn his back on the Federal government in Washington."

"That is my reckoning as well. I must mingle, and I will leave you two partridges to your young love."

Ed Roche clanked off in his Royal Cavalry uniform, spurs clinking, and sword dragging.

The herald struck his staff again, "The Honorable Judge Charles James Hudson and his wife, Lady Margaret Louise Forsyth Hudson."

"Oh no."

Victoria looked up at me, "Your parents."

I nodded. "Shall we swallow the bitter pill?"

My father separated me from Victoria, and my mother took her arm and began interrogating my guest at the reception. I heard her as we drifted away from them. Lord Lyons arrived as if by magic to claim Victoria as his own, and I sighed with relief. The Queen's minister was nothing if not glib and aware.

My father said, "I was told that I might find you here. You've been gone for the summer, and I had hoped you would return home. Then Colonel Hardee explained that you were under orders from the Secretary of War on a confidential matter, most unusual for a cadet at the Military Academy."

"Unusual would explain it completely."

"We heard a rumor of a duel fought in South Carolina where you killed a captain in the militia on a matter of honor, and that your standing with Colonel Hardee and his staff was very high. I hope that you're not mixed up in the politics of the time."

I looked at my father squarely, "How could I not be? All that is discussed is politics, the coming election, the possible secession of Southern States, and the development of their militias. It was you who forced me into this."

He nodded, sighed, and confessed, "I need a stiff whiskey, son."

* * *

Upper-class cadets returned from furlough on August 28, 1860, to begin the next six months of the session at West Point. The lower two class years convened earlier, in July. After everything, it was a relief to return to the discipline, structured routine, and familiarity of the Military Academy.

As usual, we began our day with reveille at 5:30 AM, followed by a brief breakfast, then rigorous academic classes until noon. Afternoons involved more classes, military drills, and potentially some recreational activities. Evenings were dedicated to study, and lights out at 11:00 PM.

Nate Beaufort lost weight, improved in the areas where he had been weak, and turned into a first-rate cadet with a strict focus on his duties. We still shared quarters, but he didn't require tutoring. In turn, he was an exemplary mentor to lowerclassmen who struggled.

Autie Custer continually tested boundaries and rules, amassing a staggering number of demerits. Even the chaplain openly denounced him in a sermon to the Corps of Cadets for instigating devilish plots both during the services and in Sunday school. In response, Autie appeared contrite and respectful, but he doubled down with disruptive schemes designed to torment Reverand Davis.

His academic performance was always subpar, despite my efforts to help him prepare for exams. He did not allow low marks in engineering and artillery science to trouble him.

Two weeks after I returned to the Academy, I was summoned to the Superintendent's office. Colonel Richard Delafield stood when I entered, looking unwell. I saluted, and he returned the salute as I stood at attention.

"At ease, Cadet Corporal Hudson. I am informed that you recently met our Commanding General, Winfield Scott."

"Yes, sir."

"And yet you failed to report that meeting to me."

Colonel Hardee was aware of the meeting through Sergeant Major Bisbee, who reported everything, but I didn't want to bring it to the Superintendent's attention.

"I was at a reception at the home of Lord Lyons, Queen Victoria's minister to the United States, while on furlough and under orders, and the Commanding General, who was present, asked to meet me."

"And you were introduced to Winfield Scott, the Old Soldier."

"Yes, sir."

He turned the pages of a file, "And you are the grandson of former Ambassador Leslie Forsythe, the current business partner of Cornelius Vandrbilt in the railroad industry?" Your other grandfather, Hudson, owns the Michigan Central Railroad and the Farmers' and Merchants' Bank?

"I am, sir. And yes, he does."

"The son of Judge Charles James Hudson, of the Michigan Circuit Court, who is on the short list for nomination to the Supreme Court of the United States, should a vacancy occur."

"He is my father, and I was not aware of a potential appointment."

He turned a page. "A duel at Port Royal, where you killed a captain in the local militia after he shot first?"

"Yes, sir."

"Witnessed by several peers of the British realm who certified that you behaved honorably and nobly. One of them, a Baron Fermoy, acted as your second."

Nate had been my second, Ed was the master of the duel, but I didn't want to gainsay the great man.

"You are the best swordsman at the Military Academy, according to my records. Why did you not choose swords?"

"It was his choice, Superintendent Delafield. He chose pistols at eight paces."

"And he missed, and you did not."

"Yes, sir."

"At eight paces aggregated. Very well, in the future, should there be an occasion for you to hobnob with the Commanding General of the Army, I would expect to be notified immediately in advance of that meeting."

"Yes, sir."

"Your file indicates aptitudes and high marks in both Engineering and as an Artillerist, do you have a preference?"

The Superintendent was an eminent engineer. "I have always aspired to be accepted into the Corps of Engineers, but I would need to prove myself worthy of that honor."

"Yes, Cadet Corporal Hudson, it would be a great honor for you. However, you may also be a good fit for the Corps of Engineers, given your background. You are dismissed with that one caution. Please let me be the first to know, not the very last."

I saluted and reported my meeting with the Superintendent to my superior officer, Acting Cadet Sergeant George Armstrong Custer.

"You know why I'm an acting sergeant, Hud?"

"You're an upperclassman, and you deserve the rank, sir."

"No," he laughed, "they want me to fail gloriously, and it's easier to show failure as a sergeant than as a lowly cadet as justification for my unfitness for command."

"You'll be a great officer, Autie. I've told you before, you're bold, and you will lead your light brigade against the Turk without once considering that you'd fail."

"That may be true, the cavalry is my calling. What did

Dicky the Punster want with you?" Autie referred to the Superintendent by his nickname.

"He wanted me to work diligently toward being an engineer."

"Oh, Sweet Lord."

"And I met General Winfield Scott while on furlough and didn't tell him about it."

"Are you pulling my leg? You met *Old Fuss and Feathers?*"

"My father was at the same reception, and it happened."

"I may need to have you intervene with your new friend on my behalf. I just received another demerit from Alonzo Cushing, our very own First Sergeant. He aspires to be a major general."

On November 6, the day of the presidential election, Abraham Lincoln was elected president and Hannibal Hamlin was elected vice president, garnering 39% of the vote in the four-man race. Though it was in no way a convincing plebiscite, the percentage was a win.

Francis Wilkinson Pickens was sworn in as governor of South Carolina on December 14, replacing Governor Gist, whom I knew. Nate said that Governor Pickens was even more dedicated to separation than Gist had been. While he strongly advocated secession by the Southern states, he did not sign the South Carolina Ordinance of Secession.

On December 18, the Crittenden Compromise was introduced to avert civil war. The compromise proposed six constitutional amendments and four congressional resolutions. It guaranteed the permanent existence of slavery in the slave states and addressed Southern demands regarding fugitive slaves and slavery in the District of Columbia. It proposed re-instating the Missouri Compromise, which had been functionally repealed in 1854 by the Kansas–Nebraska Act and struck down entirely in 1857 by the Dred Scott decision. The proposal extended the compromise line to the west, with slavery prohibited north of the 36° 30′ parallel and guaranteed south of it. It was doomed to fail.

Two days later, on December 20, South Carolina seceded from the Union, and President Buchanan fired his cabinet.

There would be no Christmas furlough for the Military Academy.

Following South Carolina's declaration of secession, its authorities demanded that the U.S. Army abandon its facilities in Charleston Harbor. On December 26, while the citizens of Charleston recovered from their Christmas feasts, Major Robert Anderson, well known to me, who left his instruction post at West Point to take command there, surreptitiously moved his small command from the vulnerable Fort Moultrie on Sullivan's Island to Fort Sumter. Sumter, a substantial, well-engineered fortress built on an island controlling the entrance of Charleston Harbor, would be a much harder nut to crack than Fort Moultrie for the rebellious South Carolinians.

We followed the papers closely, ignoring everything but mandatory formations and perfunctory drills. The administration of the Military Academy fell into disarray.

While the Christmas season of 1860 was marked by heightened tension and political divisions, we West Point cadets remained at the Academy, observing our daily routines and witnessing the growing national unrest from within the military institution.

I returned to quarters after breakfast to find Nate packing his belongings. "I have resigned from the Academy, Hud. My father telegraphed permission for me to leave the service. I will return home to take up an artillery commission with the regiment at Port Royal."

"I know we have all been discussing this for months," I said, "but I am sorry that it has come to this."

"You can join me, Hud. My father will arrange a commission for you in South Carolina if you wish it. I'm sure that Governor Pickens will shoehorn you into any regiment you choose. He is a friend of Gist, and Gist will speak on your behalf. I'd be proud if you thought of the Panthers as home."

"I am sworn to Michigan, Nate. I can no more break my oath than you can."

Nate said, "I believe the Union is virtually dissolved, Henry. South Carolina cannot retract. Her honor demands that she secede, else she would be a byword. She will seize Fort Moultrie by force of arms now that it has been abandoned and will move on to Sumter, and hence, a collision with the General Government must follow. Everyone in South Carolina is for disunion, at least none dare avow themselves for the Union, from the accounts in the New York daily papers. I will know more when I return home."

I saw him off at the train station the next day and gave him one of my sabers as a keepsake to remember me by.

President Buchanan sent the unarmed merchant ship, *Star of the West*, to reinforce and resupply Major Anderson at Fort Sumter. The resupply attempt failed when shore batteries fired upon it on January 9, 1861. The ship was hit three times, causing no significant damage but preventing the supplies from reaching Major Anderson's command.

Mississippi adopted the Articles of Secession on the same day and removed itself from the jurisdiction of the United States of America.

Cadets were being offered militia commissions in their home states as they left the Union. Florida on January 10, and Alabama on January 11. Parental permission was required to leave the Academy, and it was given on a one-by-one basis.

On January 28th, Colonel P.G.T. Beauregard, a small dapper man with noticeably olive complexion and French features, who favored the Southern Cause and had been appointed superintendent the previous November and had just reported for duty five days earlier, was compelled by Special Order 19 to return command to his predecessor, Colonel Richard Delafield. Louisiana left the Union on January 26th, and although he had not formally announced his intention to resign his commission, Colonel Beauregard, a Southerner, was bound by honor to follow his State, which he called "my country."

SPECIAL ORDER NO. 19

U.S. Military Academy
West Point, N.Y. January 28, 1861
In compliance with War Department Special Orders No. 19 of January 25th, 1861, revoking Special Orders No. 238- Adjutant Generals' Office of November 8, 1860, appointing me Superintendent of the Military Academy. I transfer back this day the said Superintendency and the command of this Post to Col Rd. Delafield Corps of Engineers, in compliance with the above Special Order No. 19
G.T. Beauregard
Colonel of Engineers
As Superintendent Mil. Acady

ORDER NO. 9

Head Quarters, Military Academy
West Point, N.Y. January 28, 1861
Order No. 9
In conformity with the orders of the Secretary of War

received from the Chief Engineer under date of the 24th and from the Adjutant General of the 25th January inst. Requiring the attention of Colonel <u>Beauregard</u> to his former trusts and responsibilities in Louisiana, and that Colonel <u>Delafield</u> should resume his former duties at this Post; the undersigned hereby resumes the command of the Post of West Point and Superintendence of the Military Academy:– All orders issued by Colonel <u>Beauregard</u> during his Superintendence command will be strictly carried into effect.

(Official,). (Signed) Rich Delafield

1st Lt. Infy. Adjt. MA

On January 30th, Sergeant Major Arlund Bisbee sought me out after taps played, and we were dismissed from formation. He shook my hand. "I wanted to thank you, Cadet Corporal Hudson, for everything. Serving with you has been both an honor and a pleasure. I hope we can stay in touch in the future. I hope that this separation of nations won't separate us from our mutual respect."

"You're breaking your enlistment?"

"I am honor-bound to do so. I have been offered a commission as a first lieutenant in the Louisiana Guard. It is an infantry militia organization, but when they get field guns, I may be able to ply my trade as an artillerist."

I asked, "Is this Colonel Beauregard's doing?"

Sergeant Major Bisbee shuffled his feet briefly, looking down, then up at me again, "Yes, he made the offer. He—"

"The damned Little Creole."

"I could never raise my hand against Louisiana, Hud."

"Of course, he reminded you of that duty, Arlund."

"And Colonel Hardee, our Commandant of Cadets?"

"I don't speak for him, but Georgia left the Union on the 19th. I saw him packing, but it's not official yet."

I hugged Arlund like a brother. "I won't ever forget you,

Arlund. You'll let me see you to the train station. It is the *Hudson* River Railroad."

"I'd be disappointed if you didn't."

I went to the train station with Colonel Hardee and Sergeant Major Bisbee the following day. It was just another sad day among many. Some of the cadets chided me for being too close to traitors, but they were careful not to call me out over a matter of honor. I started carrying the Düsack Sword even though it violated uniform regulations. The eyes of cadets both south and north were drawn to it, and it reemphasized a point that I didn't want to discuss. Honor was honor.

I made it plain that I was from Michigan and would serve the United States as honor and my oath demanded. I also hinted that I wasn't beyond dueling with anyone who accused me of treachery for treating kindly with my classmates and those of our academy who had been friends. I feared that soon enough, those with whom we shared camaraderie would be shooting at us.

Cadet Emory Upton attended Oberlin College in Ohio before his appointment to West Point. It was the first desegregated college in America, adopting a policy to admit Black students in 1835. In 1841, Oberlin became the first college to offer a coeducational program, granting baccalaureate degrees to women. Emory did not shy away from sharing his views against slavery. The fact that he had attended Oberlin made him a target of ridicule and taunting by cadets from Southern states. He was very loud in his accusations of treachery, and as I returned from the train station, he accosted me.

"You didn't board the train south with your slavers, Hudson."

"This is not the time to run your mouth, Upton." My hand went to my sword hilt. "I see that you are armed."

"Those lice don't deserve to—" That's as far as he got before I threw a right cross, discovering his glass jaw. He went down like a stone, and I stepped over him. I didn't run him through even though I had been tempted.

Colonel John F. Reynolds, who succeeded Colonel Hardee as Commandant of Cadets, gave me one demerit, a light sentence, for *unauthorized contact* with Cadet Emory Upton. Fighting was strictly prohibited, but the fact that we were both outside the academy grounds near the train station and out of uniform provided him with a loophole.

Though I didn't have the same sort of experience with Colonel Reynolds that I did with Colonel Hardee, he was the sort of man I always hoped I would grow to be. He reminded me very much of my father and my grandfathers in that he was larger than life. His honor and integrity were inextricably linked to who he was. There was no affectation or false humility to his being. He fought with steadfast courage in Mexico at the battles of Buena Vista and Monterey. He led his troops against the hostiles in the Rogue River War in Oregon.

In many ways, both he and Colonel Hardee, who fought as a Texas Ranger and in Mexico, shared a similar warrior ethos. With such men on either side of the contest now unfolding, the affair was likely going to be extremely difficult to resolve.

Colonel Alexander Hamilton Bowman, USMA 1825, served as our new Superintendent. Like his predecessors, he was a very skilled engineer.

The resupply of Fort Sumter became the first crisis of Abraham Lincoln's administration, inaugurated on March 4, 1861. On the same day, Brigadier General P. G. T. Beauregard, the first general officer of the newly formed Confederate States Army, was placed in command of Confederate forces in Charleston. General Beauregard, an engineer, strengthened

South Carolina's batteries around Charleston harbor aimed at Fort Sumter. Both Beauregard and Anderson were familiar with their business, and Beauregard played to his advantage as conditions in the fort deteriorated due to a food shortage.

The Confederate government issued an ultimatum to Major Anderson for the immediate evacuation of Fort Sumter. Major Anderson refused.

Beginning at 4:30 a.m. on April 12, the Confederates bombarded the fort from artillery batteries surrounding the harbor. Although the Union garrison returned fire, it was significantly outgunned, and after 34 hours, Major Anderson agreed to evacuate. There were no deaths on either side as a direct result of this engagement. However, an accidental gun breach explosion during the surrender ceremonies on April 14 caused the death of two U.S. Army soldiers.

A week later, on April 19th, a violent clash between Copperhead Democrats and the recently raised Sixth Massachusetts Infantry marching to reinforce Washington, D.C., took place as they passed through the center of Baltimore, Maryland. Soldiers and civilians were killed as widespread support was voiced from both North and South for further military action. President Lincoln called for 75,000 volunteers for 90 days to augment the small regular standing army and suppress the rebellion.

This effort led to the secession of four additional Southern states, which subsequently joined the Confederacy.

The effect on the cadets was electric. Twenty-one cadets from the graduating class remained loyal, and sixty-five resigned in favor of commissions in the Confederate Army. The Federal Army changed the oath we would swear.

> I, _____ , do solemnly swear (or affirm) that I have never borne arms against the United States since I have been

THE CONFEDERATE CIPHER

a citizen thereof; that I have voluntarily given no aid, countenance, counsel, or encouragement to persons engaged in armed hostility thereto; that I have neither sought nor accepted nor attempted to exercise the functions of any office whatsoever under any authority or pretended authority in hostility to the United States; that I have not yielded voluntary support to any pretended government, authority, power, or constitution within the United States, hostile or inimical thereto. And I do further swear (or affirm) that, to the best of my knowledge and ability, I will support and defend the Constitution of the United States against all enemies, foreign and domestic; that I will bear true faith and allegiance to the same; that I take this obligation freely, without any mental reservation or purpose of evasion; and that I will well and faithfully discharge the duties of the office on which I am about to enter, so help me God.

The West Point class of 1862, though initially intended to graduate in 1862, graduated in June 1861 due to the rebellion. This accelerated graduation occurred in response to the urgent need for officers in the Federal Army. The class of 1862 was unique, as it was the first class since 1824 in which no *graduates* served with the Confederacy. Many cadets left *before graduation* to join the conflict.

I wrote my father, wishing to graduate two years early. Against his better judgment, he wrote to Lieutenant General Winfield Scott, who is said to have remarked on our meeting at the party at the home of Minister Lyons the summer before. "We will need every man, and he is a fine figure, trusted by all. I will sign the waiver on his behalf."

Thus, I graduated from the US Military Academy two years early with the classes of 1861 and 1862. Commandant

Reynolds ordered me to his office. I entered at his bidding, and he had my academic file open.

"I see from these notations from the Commandant and Superintendent that you are personally acquainted with General Scott." He lifted a telegram. "And he telegrammed. You must have made quite an impression last summer. You move in the circles of the elite British Guards."

"Socially only, Colonel Reynolds."

"Sometimes that is more important. For these reasons, General Scott has chosen to put you into service as a second lieutenant. Since there is nobody else in your class graduating with you, the choice of branch will be for the needs of the army." He flipped a page, then another. "You are a good horseman, and we need cannon fodder to go up against hundreds of thousands of Confederate volunteers, so I'll endorse this for the cavalry. You and George Custer are both from Michigan, both friends?"

"Yes, sir."

"God save the Union. Get out of my office, pack, await official orders, go where you are sent, and take that misfit Custer with you. Sweet Lord Jesus, Custer is to serve as a cavalry officer even though he has 726 demerits." Colonel Reynolds had a paper at hand. "I do not know this cadet, but he is renowned for misconduct, including poor housekeeping, being late, and almost every possible breach of academy rules. He had piles of rubbish outside his tent during encampment and kept his room messy. Found to be late for formations and parades. Demerits for keeping cooking utensils in his chimney and bombarding classmates with snowballs. And on and on."

CHAPTER 10

US War Department Building
17th Street and Pennsylvania Avenue NW
Washington, D.C.
May 1861

I received orders to report to the Headquarters, Department of the East at Camp Troy, New York. They were not expecting me and redirected me under orders to Headquarters, War Department, Washington, D.C., in response to a general request for junior regular officers to serve staff duty in support of the rapidly growing Volunteer Army's requirements.

It was in this way that I served as a generally anonymous second lieutenant (Cavalry) who stood ready to carry messages from General-in-Chief Winfield Scott's staff to the points of the compass as required.

General Scott proposed that an army of 80,000 men be organized to sail down the Mississippi River and capture

New Orleans, strangling the Confederacy in the west. The U.S. Navy would blockade Southern ports along the eastern and Gulf coasts. He wanted to fight a war of attrition, focusing on controlling their capacity to acquire weapons of war from European monarchies intent on supplying them for profit and national advantage.

Since General Scott was seventy-five years old and physically unable to lead this force against the Confederates, President Lincoln searched for a more suitable field commander.

The Regular Army was not expected to provide a trained cadre from which officers and trained non-commissioned officers were drawn to command units of US Volunteers. It was to remain as unchanged as possible, supplemented by a much larger temporary force, which would be engaged for specified periods of temporary service.

This temporary force was designated the US Volunteers. General Scott envisioned that the permanent Regular Army would maintain a modest size and structure, and retain most of its officers and enlisted personnel. Some would operate on the frontier against the hostiles or in garrisons supporting fixed fortifications.

Units of the US Volunteers were to be recruited on a state-by-state basis, with each State fulfilling a stipulated quota of men to serve under officers appointed by the State. Each State raising units for the US Volunteers was expected to identify and nominate commanders for its units. Suitable candidates with the ability to learn and lead were sought from all walks of civilian, professional, and political life; however, those with military training or experience were in high demand.

By necessity, men with little or no military credentials whatsoever took command as Colonels of many US volunteer regiments, trusting that their civilian leadership qualities would suffice to supplement eager hands-on learning in the field. Volunteer Company officers rarely had military expertise, and the majority would be expected to learn on the job. Wherever possible, field grade officers of the regular Army (Colonel, Lieutenant-Colonel, and Major) were allocated to command brigades, divisions, and higher formations. Junior officers (Captains and Lieutenants) were highly valued for their training and for commanding volunteer regiments.

Officers and General Officers could be appointed to a grade in either the United States Army (USA) or the United States Volunteers (USV), or both concurrently. A grade in the US Army was a permanent promotion in the Regular Army that would remain in effect after the end of hostilities.

I was the most junior second lieutenant in the Regular Army, and seniority, determined by date of rank, mattered for purposes of assignment and precedence. According to the Senate's confirmation resolution, the date could be earlier or later than the confirmation date. Otherwise, rank would be determined by the order of names on the lists of officers confirmed in the exact resolution made on the same date, to rank from the same date. When seniority was in question, rank in the US Army was deemed higher than the equivalent rank in the US Volunteers. For example, a Brigadier General in the US Regular Army outranked a Brigadier General in the US Volunteers. However, a Major-General in the US Volunteers outranked a Brigadier-General in the US Army, although the circumstances where such a command was asserted were uncommon.

The US Army was usually punctilious in ensuring that US Volunteers promoted to senior commands also received promotions, both in the USV and the USA, appropriate to their status and necessary authority. The use of Brevet ranks was a helpful expedient on occasion. Before the rebellion, the Army itself had no professional personnel system. Traditionally, most officers entered the service from the US Military Academy at the lowest rank and received promotions based on seniority. Volunteer officers were commissioned without formal training; they learned on the job.

As a result of the seniority rules, the General Officers, chief staff officers, and full colonels of the small pre-rebellion Regular Army were almost all of advanced age. The General-in-Chief, Major-General USA Winfield Scott, was appointed on 25 June 1841 and was first commissioned in 1808. Brigadier-General USA John Ellis Wool was commissioned on 25 June 1841 and was first commissioned in 1812. Brigadier-General USA David Emanuel Twiggs was commissioned on 30 June 1846 and was first commissioned in 1812. Brigadier-General USA William Selby Harney was the "youngster", ranking from 14 June 1858, although first commissioned in 1818. Brigadier-General USA and Quartermaster-General Joseph Eggleston Johnston was promoted to the staff on 28 June 1860, but was first commissioned in 1829.

Among the top field officers, 11 of the 19 colonels of the line had fought in the War of 1812 as commissioned officers. Thirteen of these individuals stayed with the Union. The ineffectiveness of an army based on seniority advancement was quickly exposed during the war, and a formal retirement system was deemed essential. In 1861, Congress established a provision for compulsory retirement due to incapacity.

The US Volunteer force expanded rapidly, creating opportunities for men who had commanded no more than a company or a militia unit, perhaps even in the somewhat distant past, to be appointed as colonels of regiments. There was stiff competition to secure the most promising talent from among current and retired officers to command new Volunteer units. Anyone with military training or experience was prized. Many Regular Army officers were induced to retire to take a higher command and receive more rapid promotion in the US Volunteers. State origin often influenced the appointment of officers – and also directed the choices of the officers themselves – but it was not essential to hail from a particular State to receive a commission in the US Volunteers.

A dilemma arose for all Regular Army officers. Should they retain their secure, permanent regular commission or resign to seek a temporary, but more lucrative and senior commission in the US Volunteers at a much higher rank?

As the most junior second lieutenant in the US Regular Army, attending to my senior officer's needs, there was no pressure for me to depart immediately to command a volunteer company. In the same way, I was more than content to learn. Although my orders were for detached service, I was officially assigned to the First U.S. Dragoons Regiment, headquartered at the Presidio in San Francisco, California, even though I was designated as a cavalry officer. The plan to redesignate all dragoons as cavalry began, and I was caught in the paperwork in between.

When South Carolina signed the Articles of Secession, 198 Regular Army companies were formed into 10 Regiments of Infantry, 4 Regiments of Artillery, 2 Regiments of Dragoons, 1 Regiment of Mounted Rifles, and 2 Regiments of Cavalry.

The US Regular Army had been organised primarily for operations on the western frontier. The majority of field forces were deployed along the western frontier and in the newly acquired territories, including my regiment. To compound the confusion, my new commanding officer, Colonel Fauntleroy, resigned on May 13, 1861, to join the Confederate Army, and was succeeded by Colonel Benjamin Lloyd Beall, a 60-year-old who was reportedly in too poor health to travel east with the regiment.

The Department of Utah, which had a mandate to keep an eye on the Mormon Church first and the hostile tribes second, had three companies of dragoons, three companies of artillery, and four companies of infantry. There was a heated discussion within the War Department as to how many of those soldiers were needed to keep the Mormons under heel.

At the beginning of the secession, Lorenzo Thomas became the Adjutant General, succeeding Samuel Cooper, who joined the Confederacy. The Adjutant General's Corps was a key administrative body within the U.S. Army. It managed crucial tasks, such as organizing recruits into companies and regiments, maintaining records, and overseeing personnel during mobilization.

Colonel Thomas did not get along well with Secretary of War Edwin M. Stanton, and this assignment, which took him out of the inner circle in Washington, D.C., was considered a form of banishment.

At the time, Colonel Thomas stayed at the Willard Hotel in a room adjacent to mine. He asked me how a second lieutenant of cavalry managed to secure a room next to his. I sheepishly explained that it had been reserved permanently by the Peninsular and Oriental Steam Navigation Company, which had recently received contracts to construct armed steam-powered first and second-class sloops for the US Navy.

"What are you to that company?"

I said with as much humility as I could muster, "I stand to inherit it when my uncle passes to walk the streets of glory."

"Oh, you're the chum of General Scott. I heard about your meeting at that suaree with the Limeys last summer. I had a case of the ague and couldn't attend. I was his Chief of Staff before my upcoming assignment as Adjutant General."

I stood there at attention.

"Do you have any way of keeping them Limies and their big fleet out of this war while we attend to our business?"

"I'm a second lieutenant, and I fetch and carry for the staff. I don't know what I could do."

He grunted and unlocked the door to his room, muttering to himself, "Damned child belongs in the Navy."

The knock on my door was indistinct, more like a scratch followed by a second. I opened it to find Victoria's face staring out from under a riding cloak.

"Isn't it warm for that?"

"I'm trying not to be recognized, but the longer I'm in this hallway, the less likely that I'll be successful, Hud."

I invited her in.

"Today is Monday, July 15th."

"Yes, Victoria, take that warm cloak off and sit for a while. I can put tea on the fire for you." The rooms came with a coal oil warmer that could be used for tea or coffee.

She seemed different, somehow, more focused, more closely attuned to business, more like her old self. Like the girl I made love with at Port Royal.

She came to the point immediately, "The Confederate Army will attempt to capture Washington City a week from today, on Monday, July 22. General Beauregard will approach from the south, and General Joseph Johnston will slip past the Federal pickets and come east from Harper's Ferry to pin the Federal Army and defeat it, ending the war."

I looked closely at her. "Maybe something to fortify the tea. I have whiskey and gin."

"Give me a pour of gin, a short pour. I don't have long. I will be missed."

She reached into her dress and withdrew three pages. "I copied this for you. It is General Beauregard's battle plan."

I looked over what she wrote.

The Army of the Potomac will be divided into brigades with the following assignments. Their objective is to hold the fords over Bull Run Creek through which the army shall wish to pass.

    1st Brigade (Bonham) shall cover Mitchell's Ford

    3rd Brigade (Jones) shall position itself at McLean's Ford

    4th Brigade (Longstreet) shall cover Blackburn's Ford.

    5th Brigade (Cocke) shall cover Island, Ball's, and Lewis Fords

    6th Brigade (Early) shall support Jones' 3rd Brigade and exploit the situation as may present.

    7th Brigade (Evans) will extend the line to the stone bridge.

The Army of the Shenandoah will reinforce the Army of the Potomac, push through, and gain the advantage to reach Washington.

    1st Brigade (Jackson)

    2nd Brigade (Bartow)

    3rd Brigade (Bee)

    Col. Hampton's Legion will screen as necessary, supported by the 30th Virginia Cavalry (Whitehead, Alexander, and Terry)

    The Washington Artillery will suppress Federal movements and will position itself as is most advantageous.

    1st Louisiana - Wheat's Tigers - Irish - to act as a reserve

"How do you know this, Victoria?" I handed her a glass of gin, which she drank in one gulp.

"I overheard, and I'll say no more on the matter. Generals Beauregard and Johnston believe that it can be won in a single bold stroke. Colonel Hampton has been reporting on the Volunteer Army's readiness as it is forming. He probes, and he reports."

"Hampton?"

Victoria said, "Patterson took Harper's Ferry, Butler showed spunk on the Peninsula, but McDowell appears to be timid, and they sense an opportunity to possibly end the war by pushing him. They appeal to President Davis for all available support, characterizing McDowell as preparing to march to Richmond. Davis will send them what he has by hollowing out the Southern host that guards the Rappahannock Line."

"Why didn't you write this in code?"

"Nobody suspects me, and your commanders are poorly organized. I have no love for your President or his Army, but I was concerned for you. *We* know of your early commission and of your presence on the staff of your General-in-Chief."

"My small role is hardly notorious. I run dispatches."

"There is one more thing. Prince Albert, who favors the Southern Cause, has a wasting disease. Nobody believes that he will last out the year. His death will weaken what the Crown is attempting to do."

She held out her glass for another pour, which I obliged. Then she put on her cloak and left.

When I arrived at the War Department the next morning, I took what I had to General McDowell, commanding the Army of Northeast Virginia, and charged with the defense of the nation's capital.

"How did you come by this information, Lieutenant Hudson?"

"We all know people on both sides of this military contest." It was a bold assertion from the newest second lieutenant in the Army, but I didn't know my place at the time.

General McDowell asked, "Do you judge it to be reliable?"

"If I didn't, I wouldn't have brought it forward to you, Sir."

"Hudson, you're the son of Presiding Judge Charles Hudson, aren't you?"

"I am, sir."

"Then I will take it seriously. Maybe we shall strike them a day early, before they are ready, and take the starch out of that Little Frenchy. I am under pressure from the politicians to strike south. I have spent my time as a supply officer, not as a battlefield commander. I understand logistics, but there are among us those more qualified to command the Volunteer Army. My men are not ready for this scrap, but if I do not take advantage of Beauregard, he will take advantage of me." General McDowell seemed out of his depth.

"Yes, Lieutenant Hudson, maybe we can disrupt them and rout them. Please convey this message to General Scott that I intend to move on July 21st to seize the railhead at Manassas." He scribbled a note. "I shall require his approval and support. Please ask for orders, and when they are written, return them to me. Also, please take a note apprising the Treasury Secretary, Salmon Chase, of the situation."

He then began to speak to himself, "I must convene my division commanders immediately. It's not too soon to start ordering our movement." He had a nervous tic that became pronounced when he spoke to himself. "General Runyon's militia remains disorganized, but we will need every man to confront the Little Frenchman's party. He's moving to Washington. How audacious is his treachery? It knows no limits." He wiped his face with a handkerchief, "It's hotter than dog's balls in here."

I saluted, but he was too preoccupied to return it. I left the office, walked down the stairs quickly, and passed and saluted as I left the War Department. Audie Custer, also on detached service and working as a dispatch runner, sat with two other second lieutenants, drinking coffee near the front door.

THE CONFEDERATE CIPHER

"Audie," I called to him, beckoning him. He set his coffee down.

"What mischief?"

"Sign us out to the General Commanding and the Secretary of the Treasury." I held up my dispatch case, "From Major General McDowell - urgent."

Standing orders required newly commissioned second lieutenants to travel in pairs when transmitting urgent messages from general officers. I suspect they were concerned we'd get lost.

He signed us out and ran to catch up with me. Our mounts were tied near water and provender in front of the War Department and guarded by a corporal.

The corporal saluted, and we returned the honor.

As we walked our mounts, I told him. The Confederates are to attack next week. The Army of Northeast Virginia will strike before they can take the Capitol."

"I swan to mercy, Hud, do they intend to capture Washington?"

"General McDowell has intelligence in detail of the Confederate plan."

UPON OUR RETURN after delivering the dispatches as ordered, General McDowell had one for each of his division commanders, who were called to a council of war. I delivered mine to Colonel William Sherman, commanding General Tyler's third brigade, since the General was indisposed, then to Colonel Samuel P. Heintzelman, commanding the third division, which included the Michigan regiments.

Major Alonzo F. Bidwell, commanding the First Michigan, saw me and called to me, "Lieutenant Hudson, can you share a moment?"

I raised my dispatch case and marked it as "Urgent business."

"Hold, lieutenant," He called. He wasn't supposed to interfere with an officer carrying dispatches.

I stopped my horse, and he asked, "Hud, what newsmongering?"

I bent low and whispered, "The Army will move to Manassas to stop Beauregard and Johnston, who plan to take the Capital."

"Johnston is in the Shenandoah."

"Not for long."

Major Bidwell asked, "Is this idle prattle?"

"I ride with urgent orders from General McDowell. Please don't give me up to Colonel Heintzelman. He's been called to an urgent council of war."

"I won't, but the First Michigan will quietly assemble and will be ready when called. Thank you for extending confidence, Hud."

I saluted, he returned it, and I rode to Colonel Dixon Stansbury Miles, who commanded the New Yorkers.

Dismounting and handing my reins to a private, I saluted a captain who was seated by the door of Colonel Miles' command tent, smoking a cigar.

"Second Lieutenant Hudson, with urgent dispatch for Colonel Miles."

"He is indisposed, Lieutenant."

"My orders require that he receive this dispatch personally. I must place it in his hand."

The captain said, "He is pursuing a Brannagan and is thoroughly stupefied there in his tent. I will take you to Colonel Davies, commanding the Second Brigade. His tent is yonder."

I presented the orders to Colonel Davis, M. A. Class of '25, who took them and read them. "Do you know why

THE CONFEDERATE CIPHER

General McDowell has called an immediate council of war, Lieutenant?"

"I can not speak for the Major General, sir, except to say that he asked that this dispatch be delivered with haste."

"Did he expect a written response?"

"No, I am to return immediately and report to him directly."

Colonel Davis said, "I will follow you within the quarter hour and will bring Ludwig Blenker with me from the First New York Brigade. My superior is ill after eating bad oysters. He is indisposed."

I returned to General McDowell and reported that the dispatches had been delivered.

"You have done the Army and me a great service, Lieutenant Hudson. I would hesitate to order the Army's movement on the word of a lesser man than the son of Judge Charles Hudson, but upon such things wars are won and lost."

Autie Custer looked through the open door and, seeing me with General McDowell, knocked on the door.

General McDowell beckoned him in and told me, 'When this affair is better organized, I will want more details of how you came by the information that is causing us to move to Fairfax.' You are staying at the Willard at your shipping company's suite on the second floor?"

He seemed remarkably well-informed. "Yes, sir."

"We shall speak tonight informally. Generals usually do not take counsel from second lieutenants, but I must know your source. For now, we must prepare to move. Armies are ponderous human organisms. Time is of the essence."

He turned to Autie. "How many demerits, Lieutenant Custer?"

"Seven hundred and twenty-six, sir."

"That is amazing - and yet you graduated and were

commissioned to the cavalry with Lieutenant Hudson. Graduated early, or you'd have even more demerits. Well, report, Lieutenant, are my division commanders coming?"

The Prelude and the July 21st Sunday Picnic
South of Washington, D.C.
July 1861

VICTORIA MET me at my suite in the Willard Hotel on the late afternoon of Wednesday, July 17th, and we frolicked a bit. She was back to her former self. I untied my uniform sash that held her wrists, and she sighed, "If it isn't rough, it isn't fun."

Later, we joined her uncle, Major Sir Iain McKay; her mother, Maude; Senator Kingsley Bingham, a Michigan Republican and friend of my father's; and Rose O'Neal Greenhow, a Washington socialite and friend of Maude McKay, for dinner at the Willard in a private room. The private rooms were difficult to book and featured French menus and elaborate etiquette.

Senator Bingham thanked me for securing the room and acting as our host for the evening. Maude introduced Rose Grenhow, an attractive forty-year-old widow who dropped names and wore expensive clothing.

Before dinner, Victoria told me something of Rose Greenhow since she would be the only one joining us whom I had not met.

"She has lived a sad life, Hud. Rose's father was murdered by his negro valet when she was a teenage girl. Her mother, Eliza, raised four daughters on the income provided by a cash-poor farm. Lacking the means to introduce her daughters into society properly, Eliza arranged for Rose and her sister, Ellen, to live with Mrs. Maria Ann Hill, her aunt, who ran a stylish boarding house at the Old Capital Building.

"She married Doctor Robert Greenhow, a prominent doctor, lawyer, and linguist from the Tidewater. Her sister, Ellen, married Dolley Madison's nephew, James Madison Cutts. In 1856, their daughter, Adele Cutts, married the famous Stephen A. Douglas, a widower and senator from Illinois who lost the recent election to Abraham Lincoln.

"Her husband, Robert, died in an accident in San Francisco in 1854, and she returned to Washington City, where she met Maude, and they became friends."

Rose Greenhow and Senator Bingham sparred over the blame for the Southern Rebellion. Bingham, a free-soil Republican, squarely opposed Greenhow's pro-secession stance. Sir Iain intervened, apologizing to me for bringing bitter politics to what had been intended to serve as a meeting of friends.

Greenhow turned to me, "Yes, I apologize, but I was under the impression that you did not directly oppose slavery in the South, Lieutenant Hudson."

"As the most junior officer in the Federal Army, I'm afraid that my opinion doesn't count for much. I have always shared my father's views. The law did not condemn the institution of slavery, and the foundation of the nation was rooted in an acceptance of it." I went back to carve off a piece of steak and place it in my mouth. "Ma'am."

"Yet, you serve an unjust repression of the Free South."

"I follow my oath." I looked plaintively at Victoria, who sat next to me.

Victoria said, "Hud is also a friend of Lord Lyons and the British Crown, as is his grandfather Forsythe."

Rose smiled and turned her attention to her plate as well.

Senator Bingham asked me, "Do you move south with the Army of Northeast Virginia to oppose the rebels, Hud?"

"Nothing so glorious. I deliver dispatches from the War Department, spending my days on horseback or at the coffeepot next to the telegraph office, waiting for orders to deliver. I'm an errand boy."

After the dessert, I settled the bill by signing on behalf of the Peninsular and Oriental Steam Navigation Company. Sir Iain and Maude escorted Rose Greenhow. Senator Bingham departed for his townhome in Georgetown.

I offered Victoria my arm and asked if she'd accompany me on a walk to allow dinner to settle. She kissed my cheek, and we set off, only to meet Major General McDowell, who appeared to have aged ten years in the past ten days.

"Lieutenant Hudson."

I saluted, and he returned my salute.

"Your young lady?"

"May I present Victoria McKay, ward of Major Sir Iain McKay, military aide to Minister Lyons of Her Majesty Queen Victoria's government."

"I commend you on your taste, Lieutenant. This lady is ravishing." General McDowell took her gloved hand and kissed it gently, clicking his heels.

"We have something to discuss, Lieutenant, but it will keep. I offer you a good night."

General McDowell continued through the Willard Hotel, accompanied by an artillery captain and Lieutenant Autie Custer, who made a funny face at us when out of the General's gaze.

"You know the lieutenant."

"Yes, my friend, Autie. He graduated when I did. We both graduated early; he a year ahead of me. We're both from Michigan."

"And you know General McDowell."

"He received the list you gave me. I think that's what he wants to speak to me about. He wants to know how I came by the information."

She looked concerned.

"I'll explain how it was passed to me by the Peninsular and Oriental Steam Navigation Company without attribution. It won't be a lie, I'm only a conduit."

"Let's not go for a walk, take me to your suite and amorous congress."

Who was I to deny a lady?

Around 10:00 pm, previously ordered fresh oysters with mignonette sauce arrived by room service. The sauce, a favorite of both Victoria and me, was made with vinegar, shallots, and black pepper. Two chilled bottles of Perrier-Jouët Champagne also arrived in an ice bucket.

Victoria and I set to work on the oysters. "Hud, I have a confession."

"Whatever it is, I forgive you." The champagne on the heels of a minor athletic event in bed had gone to my head.

"You aren't the only person that Summerhaze trained."

"What do you mean?"

"Just that, he trained an American Army officer a year or a year and a half before he trained you."

"How close were you and this officer?"

"I never met him, but I hear things. He's much older than you, Class of 1840, a captain in your regular army with service in the Second Seminole War, and the battles of Palo Alto and Resaca de la Palma in Mexico. He was disgruntled with his lack of promotion and went over to the Confederacy. They made him their Adjutant General in Richmond. He's now a brigadier general.

"What is his name?"

"Thomas Jordan."

I wrote the name on a pad of paper with a pen dipped from the inkwell.

"He set up a network of spies in the capital to report on matters of interest to Richmond. He left one of his protégés behind to run his team."

"Let me venture a guess before you tell me. It's the lady I met at dinner, Rose Greenhow."

Victoria gave me a coy smile, took a ladylike sip of champagne, and said, "She uses the same twenty-six-symbol cipher that Summerhaze gave you. Naturally, Queen Victoria would be distressed to know that her people were aiding the Confederates directly in that way. It could lead to unpleasantness."

"It will balance because I know the key, and if we intercept anything, I can read it.

"She has been passing information to General Beauregard on Federal troop strengths so that he can plan his invasion and capture Washington City by using the couriers that Captain Jordan recruited for the effort."

I asked, "How do you know so much?"

"Oh, I think you know Hud. I believe that it's clear to you what's going on here. My country is working to divide yours along any available point of fracture. We're doing it secretly, and your Northerners are too thick to understand what is going on. You remain a plum to be plucked, but you won't go along with it in the end because I know you."

I nodded. Then I drizzled mignonette sauce on an oyster and slurped it down, washing it down with champagne and recharging my glass.

I knew what to do. Alan Pinkerton had been posing as a spy catcher and detective. He'd been a railroad bull for the Illinois Central Railroad, which was a rival business to my family's. He was well read, but that notwithstanding, he had a crude thickness about him that made him unpleasant to be around.

"Who are her runners?"

Victoria thought for a moment. "She has several that Captain Jordan used as his whores when he was here in Washington City and spying directly. Lily Mackall uses her charms and her wit. She hates men, which makes her ideally suited to use them."

"What do you think of your countryman, Alan Pinkerton?"

Victoria said, "He's a Glaswegian tinker with airs of self-importance. He can be flattered to do anything, and he's always broke, so between money and flattery, he can be directed, Hud. But you know that, don't you?"

"Yes, I do. I can set him against these women. He will take all of the credit, giving none to those who put him on the scent, absolving your people of any involvement. In character, he's much like George McClelland, who has held his leash more than once. Both are driven mercilessly by self-importance. Pinkerton will stomp his big feet over any detail that could embarrass you."

Victoria asked, "And you can drop the hint?"

"I'm a dispatch rider, I can go anywhere and be admitted anywhere. I'll drag Autie Custer along with me to embellish anything that needs exaggeration."

* * *

ON JULY 18TH, General McDowell arrived at the War Department early. I had been there for over half an hour at the telegraph office and the coffee pot.

"Ah, Lieutenant Hudson, let us retire to my office for a moment before this day takes us in different directions again." He removed his ornate major general's kepi and put it on a hook once we reached his office."

"This information about an impending attack that you gave me. I do not doubt your word, but I need more."

"Yes, General, my family has shares in the New York Central Railroad and an outright ownership in the Michigan Central. We employ detectives to deal with company interests, and they come on information through their skullduggery that they pass on from time to time." It was not precisely a lie, so I'll call it a calculated truth.

General McDowell nodded as he lit his first cigar of the day.

"May I fetch the general a mug of coffee?"

"That would be splendid, Lieutenant."

I returned with a coffee mug on a small wooden platter with sugar cubes. He dropped all of them into the coffee and stirred it with the end of his pen. Yes, it would make his hand sticky when he went to write, but he was a general, and I was not.

"You were saying, railroad detectives?"

"The Farmers' and Merchants Bank uses the same slinkers, General. They gave me the information. Perhaps I should have gone to Mr. Pinkerton with it rather than to you. Isn't he the Army's man?

"He belongs to Little Napoleon, now jumped up to be a general, I would never have seen it. No, Hudson, you did the right thing by bringing it to me. Look at this map. I'm sure it's familiar to you. We are moving, concentrating on Centreville to cross Bull Run Creek on Sunday morning, taking and holding the fords as we move on Manassas Junction. If we control the junction, we control the Confederate capacity to reinforce from Front Royal along the Manassas Gap Railroad —Johnston's Army of the Shenandoah. It splits the Confederate force. Beauregard will reinforce from the Orange and

Alexandria Railroad, but he has fewer men available without Johnston. We need to take that crossroads early in the day.

"Word has leaked of our intentions, and many of the nation's most august and influential wish to accompany our grand army and watch it crush the vile little Frenchman and his cohorts."

I asked, "Would you like me to contact Mr. Pinkerton on your behalf and determine what he has learned?"

"He is McClelland's man."

"He's a railroad detective, and my family owns railroads outright and stock in many of the rest. It also owns a bank that lends to the railroads we don't own."

A wave of relief washed over General McDowell's face. "Would you do that favor for me, lieutenant?"

"It would be an honor. Pinkerton is known to take an egg and biscuit at the Capital Boarding House in the morning. He is a late riser."

General McDowell took his sticky pen, dipped it in an inkwell, and wrote a dispatch commending Mr. Pinkerton for his excellent work and asking for his assistance in providing the information the army needed. Then he handed it to me, "Only if you need it, Lieutenant. I leave the matter in your hands."

"May I take Lieutenant Custer with me?"

"By all means."

We found Alan Pinkerton, wearing a soiled white shirt and a food-stained tweed waistcoat lapping over his ample belly, eating from a platter of ham, eggs, and biscuits slathered with heavy jam. He sat by himself in the dining room of the Capital Boarding House with the daily paper, scribbling notes. He was known to pass news off as secret intelligence. That was his intent when Autie Custer and I walked up wearing our aiguillettes. General McDowell had issued them to all of his dispatch rider-officers who represented him on important business. They set us apart from other officers. The aiguillettes are decorative cords or braids with metal tips worn on our shoulders and across the breasts of our military uniform. Because Autie Custer and I were cavalry, the braid was yellow. If we had been infantry officers, they would have been light blue. If we had been artillery officers, they would have been red. They originated from the practical use of securing plate armor, evolving into a badge of office for officers serving as aides-de-camp or adjutants to ranking officers. In this case, only General McDowell's staff wore them.

"Mr. Pinkerton, a word if you will, sir?"

He looked up at me, squinting, trying to place my face. "My name is Lieutenant Henry Hudson, and this is Lieutenant George Custer."

"Do ye want me to buy ye breakfast because I won't."

"We've eaten, Sir, thank you. I come from General McDowell on a matter of some sensitivity."

"Hudson? Do I know you? You look like a young version of that old rascal Elijah Hudson."

"He's my grandfather, sir."

"Well then, sit down, Mister Hudson - Custer, is your family important?"

Autie Custer blushed.

"I guess not, you can stand. So, Lieutenant, what have you for me?"

I passed a note to Pinkerton, who palmed it immediately. "Lily Mackall?" he asked.

"She is an information runner for a spy den - slavers here in Washington. She reports the Army of Northeastern Virginia's progress to General Beauregard. She does it for this person." I passed another slip of paper. "Rose Greenhow directs the operation from her home. She is a former confidant of the Confederate Adjutant General, Jordan, who formerly served in our army here. She is an ardent secessionist, and one could gain favor by collecting the information they have and demonstrating their guilt. I would use our detectives if it were the business of my family's bank or railroad. With the situation we find ourselves in, I thought it best to come to you. General McDowell agrees." I showed him the dispatch and took it back.

Pinkerton pushed his chair back from the table, crumbs and crumpled wet egg yoke dripping onto his trousers, "Leave this matter to me and my detectives, Mister Hudson. You have done me a great favor, and I remember my friends."

I could only smile. Pinkerton had no friends. Only customers.

"And Lieutenant Custer - don't forget that he, too, is your friend."

CHAPTER 11

The Battle of Manassas Junction
July 1861

We joined Fifty regiments of infantry, ten batteries of field artillery, and one battalion of cavalry on the hot, dusty roads that led to the Fairfax Courthouse.

There were hiccups. General McDowell ordered that the 30,000 men would have cooked rations in their haversacks. That hadn't happened. It took the better part of two days to put that right, and there was some confusion as we threw reconnaissance forward.

Hostilities began early in the day, twenty-seven miles from the nation's capital, as large bodies of poorly trained volunteers, led by officers steeped in Napoleonic traditions, attempted to recreate the Battle of Waterloo as their officers had been trained to do at the US Military Academy.

Autie Custer and I spent the Sunday battle within the fog

of war, running dispatches to the divisions, which did not respond well to direction.

Bull Run flowed from the northwest to the southeast, and had steep banks, making it difficult to cross except at the fords located both above and below a stone bridge that spanned the river where the turnpike intersected it. Rebel infantry held the fords below the bridge. As I attempted to cross early in the engagement, delivering a dispatch, I almost lost my life. I do not know which battalion of Confederates fired on me, but only the hand of the loving Almighty God spared me. I returned to headquarters, and they redirected my path to Sudley Springs, above the bridge where we held the crossing.

McDowell and Beauregard had the same idea. Each attempted to turn the other's right flank by striking with their left. General McDowell, a supply officer by trade, while active on the battlefield, became involved in the minutiae of directing any unit close to him rather than coordinating the army as a whole, leaving division commanders to make choices on their own rather than in concert.

General Robert Patterson, at age 69, was well past his military prime. His Pennsylvanians failed to hold General Johnston's Army of the Shenandoah in the Valley. Johnston, who outgeneraled Patterson, used his limited supply of railcars to bring his army up piecemeal, thereby being present and fully supporting General Beauregard at the point of contact.

The Federal Army, accompanied by picnickers and gawkers, behaved more as if they were on a lark than an army intent on destroying the enemy.

During the fog of war, the Federal Army became panicked and unmanageable, out of control of its officers. Once the Zouaves broke and we lost batteries in the center of the action, the men, hungry, thirsty, tired, and demoralized, believed they had been mismanaged. One old soldier I saw as I rode with a dispatch to General McDowell began to cry, "Betrayal!" It was about that time that I heard a shrill yell, turned in my saddle, and saw a long gray line of infantry crossing the field toward us at the run, their bayonets gleaming in the hot summer Sun.

The officers on horseback slapped the infantry with the flats of their sabers to get them back into line, but the fear gripped them, and they ran. Some threw down their rifles so that they could run faster.

I delivered the dispatch to a captain near McDowell, and he said, "Remain here, Lieutenant Hudson, to form a bodyguard." I wondered if it was that bad, and then I looked more closely at my surroundings.

We remained close to General McDowell, who was a beaten man, fearful that P.G.T. Beauregard would follow up on his victory and chase us to the gates of Washington.

Though we didn't know it, Generals Beauregard and Johnston had their problems and the dead to mourn. They won a victory, but it was not exploitable because their volunteers were as challenging to manage on the battlefield as ours were. Colonel Jackson lost fifty percent of his Virginians, killed, wounded, and missing on the battlefield. They stood like a stone wall, fighting alone for almost four hours, but did not break. General Bee was mortally wounded, and his brigade was routed on the battlefield.

General McDowell ordered the balloon, *Enterprise*, sent aloft to determine how closely we were being pursued, but the professor of aeromancy didn't see the enemy close on our heels.

The general and his staff, Autie and me among them, relaxed as we walked our tired horses back to Centreville. I was sent forward to the divisions with orders. We were to regroup as much as possible to form a blocking force around Centreville.

General Irvin McDowell knew he would be relieved of command after our defeat. He told us somewhat openly that he expected to be relieved by Little Mac, the American Napoleon who lobbied heavily for the top job.

Some men paused at Centreville, but they mostly rushed on to the Potomac in a panic.

WHEN I RETURNED to my suite at the Willard, still attached to the War Department as a dispatch rider, I read in the newspapers that Pinkerton and his detectives descended on the home of Rose Greenhow. The papers called it Fort Greenhow, a Confederate bastion in our midst. They found voluminous information implicating her. The courts put Greenhow and her accomplice, Lily Mackall, under house arrest. There was no mention of me, Victoria, or the British Mission. The newspapers trumpeted Pinkerton's brilliance as a detective. The Union needed some good news in the face of dire and forlorn headlines.

George Custer managed to detach himself from courier duties. He received orders to serve with the Second US Cavalry Regiment in the nation's capital. They were tasked with screening the Army and probing for possible Confederate movements toward the Capital.

Victoria joined me for breakfast at the Willard Hotel a week or so after things calmed down and everyone licked their wounds. I rose and held her chair to seat her at my table. I pointed to my newspaper, "Did you read this? *A brick house turned prison* - an ordinary brick house on 16th street where Greenhow and other secessionist women are imprisoned highlights the seeming contradiction between the house's prison character and the casual appearance of the sentinel guarding it, while also mentioning the limited access granted to the women within."

Victoria's eyes were filled with mirth. "They don't know how to handle ladies, and the fact that these ladies have carnal knowledge of half of Washington's married elite provides a situation that would not be available to women of the town."

My father, Judge Charles Hudson, joined us a few minutes later. "It's a pleasure to see you, Henry, and you're lovely as usual, Victoria."

"Are we to talk politics at breakfast?" I asked my father, who tried to avoid political discussions over meals, but given the swirl of intrigue around the city, it was impossible.

My father looked at her questioningly, "You don't care for such discussions, my dear?"

"The Confederacy pins its hopes on European dependence on Southern cotton for its textile industries. They believe that such will lead to diplomatic recognition and intervention, in the form of mediation. That mediation will, they hope, lead to a recognition of a free and independent Southern Confederacy." Victoria smiled girlishly.

"Well put, Victoria," my father said. "Jeff Davis expects events to accomplish diplomatic objectives and recognition. The blockade of Southern ports has begun. I'm not sure how effective it will be. The men Davis selected as secretary of state and emissaries to Europe have been chosen for both political and personal reasons, rather than their diplomatic potential. They won't depart anytime soon. He wants the cotton scarcity to impel the Europeans to demand meetings."

We ordered breakfast and took a brief break from serious discussion to focus on the summer heat.

"How long have you two known each other?"

I answered, "We met socially while I was in the Military

Academy. Victoria's aunt and uncle are friends of a former classmate of mine who now serves in the military with a commission from the Confederacy."

"I was present for the famous Christmas duel," Victoria said casually. "We had met at a reception the evening before, where satisfaction had been demanded."

My father looked hard at a man wearing red livery, who was accompanied by a woman in a semi-formal dress, standing in attendance about twenty feet away.

I identified them. "Victoria's footman and our chaperone."

Father scrutinized me. "You've changed, Henry. And it's not just the fancy uniform and the cavalry mustache."

Victoria said, "I've asked him to shave it off."

He paused, drinking from his coffee mug. "What do you think of the battle you were in?"

"I carried messages, Father, but the Confederate officers who led their effort were my schoolmasters at the Academy and my classmates. Many fought in Mexico and on the frontier. Their artillery was well handled, and they carried away much of ours to add to their batteries. All that said, they were unable to march down the streets of the Capital."

"It was too close." Turning to Victoria, he asked, "How do you find our fair country?"

"It is a lovely place, Judge Hudson. Your son was kind enough to escort me, as he has had time to visit. Had it not been for Henry, I would have been closeted away."

Breakfast passed, Victoria excused herself and left with her chaperone.

My father became all business. "President Lincoln sent letters to me, my brother Samuel, and Leslie Forsythe asking us to meet with the new Navy Secretary, Gideon Welles." He handed me his copy, and I read while he paraphrased. "We're requested to meet jointly with Secretary Welles on an urgent matter of great interest and concern to the Federal Government. We sent telegrams to each other and then to Secretary Welles to arrange our schedules. We will meet at the Navy Department's office in the Winder Building on Pennsylvania Avenue between twenty-first and twenty-second streets tomorrow at 9:00 a.m. to hear what Secretary Welles has to say. I would like you also to be present."

"Me?" I asked. "What business do I have with the Secretary of the Navy?"

"Family business. You are Samuel's heir, as he has no *sons*, and he has taken a liking to you. Under the legal doctrine of coverture, a married woman's legal identity is subsumed by that of her husband. Samuel is not well disposed toward Madeline's or Abby's choices. Their husbands are financial leeches and are not that bright. He doesn't want them to control the shipping company or his finances. You can give them an allowance after he has passed. He doesn't want the husbands to manage their inherited real estate and personal property, or sell it without their consent. Frankly, I thought that your older brother, Robert, being a lawyer, would have been a more suitable heir and manager, but he wants you to be treasurer and sole decision maker."

"And his — our company has a contract to build mechanical steam warships for the navy."

"Yes, I didn't know if you could be free of your duties to attend the meeting?"

"I will ask Captain Prentis today. He directs the commanding general's aids at the War Department, but it should not be problematic."

My father looked disappointed.

"Since we lost the battle, the Army is encamped for the defense, and the need for close coordination is not as acute as it was."

"Is there anything I should be concerned about in your relationship with Miss McKay?"

THE CONFEDERATE CIPHER

"No, father. She is the niece and ward of Major Sir Iain McKay. As you saw today, she is escorted and chaperoned when she leaves her home. Her uncle, who crosses the Atlantic frequently now, will travel less when a reliable transatlantic telegraph cable can be put into service."

"Yes," my father said, "the first one was short-lived."

"His wife, Maude, looks after Victoria in his absence and supervises her social calendar."

My father departed for meetings, and I rode Glory to the War Department. Captain Prentis was opposed to giving me time the following day, but when I explained that I had a personal meeting with my family and the Secretary of the Navy, his tone changed.

Captain Prentis said, "The Peninsular and Oriental Steam Navigation Company? I've heard of it."

"Yes, sir, the meeting has to do with the construction of warships of intermediate size. I am involved because of my Uncle Samuel. I am his heir, and he has not been well. I doubt the condition is serious; it may be due to the night air. He gambles aggressively through the night."

GIDEON WELLES GREETED US, and I found him cordial and serious. His beard was not well-groomed, but he was fastidious in his dress and organization.

"Yes, Samuel," he addressed my uncle when we were seated and pleasantries had been passed, "this blockade business, sealing the Confederate coastline to prevent the exchange of cotton for war supplies, is essential to the success of the war, but it could just as easily backfire. I will need a tenfold increase in fighting ships and crews to carry it off."

"Then what is the problem, Gideon?" My uncle asked.

"It would be more effective as a de facto, undeclared

measure. The pettyfoggers say that formally declaring a blockade will grant the Rebellion belligerent status, allowing them to seek aid from other nations. You don't blockade your ports. You blockade the ports of hostile nations. By issuing the formal blockade, we lend legitimacy to their claim that they are a sovereign nation. We skate on very thin ice from a legal perspective.

"When I arrived to take over the Naval Department, it was in disarray with Southern sympathizers - the best of the officers - resigning en masse. Our Navy started the war with forty-two commissioned ships of all classes. With the warships you are building and the others on order, I expect to have nearly 264 ships by Christmas. Congress has been generous with funds, and the lost battle at the Capitol's gates has them scrambling to allocate still more to the Navy.

"We will move against Hatteras Inlet within weeks, showing North Carolina what the Navy can do, but what officers remain are, upon the whole, men of less ability. During the twenty years preceding this Rebellion, the naval affairs of the United States were influenced by Southern men. In Congress, probably no one man so much determined naval legislation as Stephen R. Mallory, of Florida, who has been anointed as the Secretary of the Navy for the Southern Confederacy. He was chairman of the Senate Committee on Naval Affairs before switching sides and openly settling the question of treason.

"Lieutenant Hudson," he said, pinning me with his gaze. "Your uncle's business interests are primarily with two of the five bureaus that I oversee: the Bureau of Navy-Yards and Docks and the Bureau of Construction, Equipment, and Repairs.

"The Bureau of Navy-Yards and Docks is vested with the construction and maintenance of the docks, wharves, and buildings within the navy-yards. It has general control of the administration of the yards. Their several commandants reported to the bureau's chief. The Bureau of Construction, Equipment and Repairs is charged with the designing, building, fitting, and repairing of wood and iron hulls; and with the equipping of vessels with sails, anchors, cables, fuel, galleys, blocks, and yeomen's stores."

Uncle Samuel nodded.

"And it's all askew. The first indications in the Navy Department of the approach of the Rebellion were the tendering of resignations by Southern officers. From November 12, 1860, immediately after the election of President Lincoln, until January 24, 1861, forty-seven naval officers from South Carolina, Florida, Georgia, Alabama, and Mississippi resigned. My predecessor, Toucey, accepted each resignation as soon as it had been tendered. In some instances, this was of doubtful propriety. Those officers implicated in the surrender of the Pensacola Navy Yard should have been first court-martialed, and only the innocent should have been permitted to resign. Toucey might at least have hesitated to accept the resignation of an officer who declared that he wished to be released from his obligations to the United States so that he might be free to act against the Union, retaining personal honor if you can call it that." He sighed, "But now that's all water under the hull, and we shall move forward to strangle this Rebellion like an anaconda.

"Judge Hudson, I asked you to be present because I have concerns about the intentions of your father-in-law, Leslie Forsythe. I'll come right out with it. Is he a damned rebel too?"

I choked when I heard those words, and after I finished my coughing fit, my father responded, "He is a Michigan man and above the petty squabbles of Southern interests."

Uncle Samuel backed him up. "Charles is correct, I've known the man for thirty years, and he is no traitor."

Welles said, "Yet I have intelligence that he is fitting out the first of a series of speedy, metal-clad screw pickets that would seem to be of a design in keeping with running a blockade." Welles pushed paperwork across the desk. "These are copies of bills of lading acquired by our agents in Liverpool."

I spoke, "Mister Secretary, he began these designs years ago. I know this for a fact because he talked to me about it. There was never a discussion of rebellion or a blockade, only fast commercial business. The ship is small, the coal bunker is small, but when the wind fails or there is a need to cross a bar, the steam power is available."

My Father, being as judicial as is humanly possible, said, "Leslie Forsythe is beyond reproach in this matter. Let me recount his mindset for everyone present. In 1854, Congress appropriated $3,000,000 for the construction of six first-class steam frigates, to be equipped with screw propellers, namely the *Merrimac, Wabash, Minnesota, Roanoke, Colorado,* and *Niagara*. They were objects of admiration and envy to the naval architects of Europe, who modeled some of their ships after them. My father-in-law, being an innovative man, thought that he could do better with a smaller ship, still armed, but able to engage in commerce while protecting herself. That was the origin of the sloop-built, screw packet *SS Seraphim*, now close to completion in Liverpool. Ships are his hobby. He and Vanderbilt are in the railroad business."

Uncle Samuel said, "The Navy could have had better ships than they ordered from me if the Bureau of Construction had listened. They wanted yesterday's ship, not tomorrow's."

"And what is tomorrow's ship, Mister Hudson?"

"Look to my friend, and visionary, John Ericsson, who designed the United States Navy's first screw-propelled steam frigate, *USS Princeton*, in partnership with Commodore Stockton, who unjustly blamed him for the Peacemaker tragedy."

I was unaware of the tragedy they discussed, and my expression may have shown my ignorance. Secretary Welles said, "Lieutenant, when the then *Captain* Stockton pulled the firing lanyard on a long gun called the Peacemaker, the gun burst. Its left side failed, spraying hot metal across the deck and fragmentation into the crowd. John Ericsson had nothing to do with the flaw in the gun's design. Given that the Secretaries of the Navy and State were killed among four others and a dozen or two more were injured, and all were blaming Stockton, *he* felt it prudent to blame the young foreign genius, Ericsson." Welles then changed his focus to my Uncle Samuel as if to agree with him. "Ericsson is working to build a design by Robert Fulton at the moment. It will be shot-and-shell proof and propelled only by steam. The Navy Board does not want the war steamer completed."

I recalled my grandfather's discussion of his gun system. "Ericsson's design for a single muzzle-loading gun on a revolving pedestal using a hoop construction to pre-tension the breech with an improved recoil system was incorporated by my grandfather on the *Seraphim*. Steam power in combat removes the mandate for a broadside to be effective."

Welles' bushy eyebrows shot up. "You are more than a mere second lieutenant and apple polisher, young man, if you understand such things. Yet you are in the cavalry, not the artillery or engineers."

"I graduated two years early because of the war. The cavalry branch was the option offered to me."

Secretary Welles said, "I need an officer to undertake a secret mission to determine what the damned confederates are up to in Liverpool, Bristol, and Plymouth. Given that the brains went south, I am left with only bad options, but Leslie

Forsythe's grandson, commissioned by Congress, admittedly, an Army commission. Who is your commanding officer?"

"Wait a minute, Gideon," Uncle Samuel said.

"Captain Prentis, on General McDowell's staff," I said quickly.

My father gave me that look, but didn't say anything.

"And I am acquainted with Minister Lyons of Her Majesty's Government," I added.

"More than one would think, Lieutenant. You might not be in danger from the British crown, but the Confederate agents would pose a significant threat. Let me think on this and confer. I can send it to General McDowell for your release. We will have to go through the Secretary of War and, likely, President Lincoln, but yes, we will consider this plan. Samuel, you will give young Henry leave to represent your steamship company in England for a time, won't you?"

I could see the gears turn in Samuel's mind.

"The Navy will need hundreds more ships if it is to deflect Confederate commerce—hundreds of lucrative contracts. There is no law specifically against war profiteering, although it is frowned upon. A law, the Confiscation Act, will authorize the government to confiscate property, including slaves, used to support the Confederacy. That is how we will pay for these ships."

Samuel nodded and smiled. My father elbowed his brother in the ribs.

CHAPTER 12

SS Spirit of Ohio
Mid-Atlantic
Late Summer, 1861

The *Spirit of Ohio*, owned by the Peninsular and Oriental Steam Navigation Company, was a modern commerce vessel, constructed of seasoned live oak and propelled chiefly by sails, but also having auxiliary steam power. As with all steamships, the engines were to be used principally in calms, in leaving port, and as aids in storms. Few naval experts foresaw that steam was destined to supplant entirely sails on board naval vessels because coal took up so much space.

I learned a great deal about ships and nautical matters during my brief period between secret orders from the Secretaries of War and the Navy, countersigned by President Lincoln. Copies of those orders rested in the War Department's safe and with my father.

Victoria McKay, her Aunt Maude, and two servants also booked passage on the *Spirit of Ohio*. In addition to twenty-one first-class passengers with cabins aft, the ship carried sacks of dried corn and crates filled with manufactured goods for trade.

As I learned upon boarding the ship, first-class passengers had the means to consume liquor freely in their private cabins or the ship's saloon. A variety of alcoholic beverages, such as fine wines, champagne, brandy, sherry, and port, rounded out spirits, including whiskey, gin, and bourbon. The captain and officers preferred that the passengers remain besotted for the voyage as they caused fewer problems. I had the owner's cabin, reserved for my Uncle or luminary guests making the crossing. The wine and spirits cabinet took up half the cabin.

When Victoria first saw the cabin, she began undressing and demanded that I pour her the best vintage available. I reminded her, "We have not left port."

"And as I have been told, we will not sail for some time. You must occupy me for hours; we will still make the departure to wave at lesser mortals ashore and stroll the deck."

The crew managed to cut the lines that connected us to the shore and activate the steam engine, which propelled us, belching huge clouds of black smoke. Victoria and I, having made our presence known, returned to my cabin for another round.

First-class passengers and the officers who dined with us enjoyed fine meals, prepared by a chef and his staff, to our gastronomic delight. I asked the First Engineer what the crew ate.

"The crew eats salt junk and hard tack at sea, which means salted meat and sea biscuit. On Sunday, they eat lobscouse and duff, which is plum pudding with a generous spirit ration rather than the daily rum."

Victoria crinkled her beautiful nose. The Engineer set her straight. "Princes do not sit down at their tables, groaning beneath a thousand delicacies, with greater contentment, or enjoy their luxurious viands with a higher relish than those which the tempest-tost, weather-beaten sailor squats by the side of his greasy tarpaulin, and devours his humble dish of lobscouse on Sunday."

Neither Victoria nor I was taken with sea illness, nor was Maude, but their servants were ill for most of the trip, which was convenient in the event proper chaperoning had been required. None of the ship's crew commented that Victoria shared days and evenings in the Owner's Stateroom. The servants stayed in her cabin and retched.

Some of the dinner conversation with full-bearded Captain Israel Matlock, sitting at the Owner's Table, revolved around naval controversy since we had a rule against talking about the politics of slavery or secession.

He left the US Navy to work for my Uncle Samuel amid heated debates over assimilated ranks, which caused much bitterness and jealousy on both sides. He explained that the "line" was defined as those officers whose essential duty is to fight the enemy, and who were eligible to hold naval command. The line grades were those of captain, commander, lieutenant, master, and midshipman. The "staff" comprised those officers whose duties were auxiliary to the line and who could not hold naval command. The staff officers were the surgeons, pursers, engineers, chaplains, victuallers, and gunners.

He said, "The civilian may have some difficulty in understanding the character and importance of assimilated rank. To the naval man, the nature of this incorporeal hereditament is real. In naval and official life, and especially in the society aboard ship, rank confers precedence, social rights and privileges, and the esteem of your fellows. It determines the apartment in which an officer sleeps, the position of his chair at the table when eating, his relative position on entering or leaving the ship, his place of promenade on deck, and the fashion and decorations of his clothes. The official worth of a man on board his fellow officers is read from the buttons and gold bullion on his coat, and he is esteemed accordingly. To be without rank is to be penniless of the current coin of the naval realm. An officer with rank may demand privileges as his right; while without rank, he may accept them, if offered, *as a courtesy*."

I understood his point, having just spent three years at West Point. Maude and Victoria lived the life of privilege and precedence every day as they maneuvered through the nearly Byzantine world of peerage and honors. Major Sir Iain McKay GCB of the Coldstream Guards, recently awarded the Victoria Cross for his service in the Crimean War, had been honored for valor in combat and for his loyalty to the realm. As a Knight of the Grand Cross, he received considerable deference even though he was not a royal peer. In America, class distinctions revolved more closely around the amount of money one had. Thus, the merchant class was looked down upon, but at the same time, it could not be disregarded.

Captain Matlock continued, "The surgeons were foremost in presenting their case and urging their claims to status. The pursers were scarcely less insistent, and soon the engineers had increased in numbers and began to make demands. The line naturally resisted the assignment of rank to the staff. An institution that has developed traditions and a corporate life, and that enjoys a monopoly of rights and privileges, is wont to resist strenuously its being cheapened or made common either by undue additions to its membership or by extension of its privileges to others. The line argued with reason that rank, owing to its very essence, belonged peculiarly to the military corps of the navy, and that it was incongruous to clothe the staff in the garb of the line. It urged that the granting of rank to the staff would injuriously affect the discipline, harmony, and general good of the service; that the wearing of epaulets by both classes of officers would lead to confusion; and that to admit staff officers to seats on courts-martial was not *military*."

It explained why Captain Matlock changed his employment rather than be made common by an act of Congress.

The upper ranks of the navy were overstocked with old and incapacitated men, who impeded the flow of promotions. The younger officers urged that the quarter-deck was not the proper place for the lean and slippered pantaloon of old age. Accepting a privately owned ship imparted a socially acceptable alternative and the opportunity to receive a financial share of the cargo delivered. Often, the amount of compensation was influenced by the time it took to transit. Whereas a sailing ship could take more than forty days to make the crossing, Captain Matlock felt we would drop anchor in less than ten days with steam power to augment the wind. With luck, as few as eight days.

My instructions before departure included the latest information available regarding the Confederate Navy, which was still undergoing formation. They acquired ships through a combination of purchasing vessels from abroad, converting merchant ships into warships, and capturing existing Union vessels. They intended to employ commerce raiders built or bought in Europe and made technically legal under letters of marque to disrupt Union shipping.

One unexpected bit of serendipity on the journey came from the most unlikely of all possible people.

He dressed for dinner that first night at sea in what Maude observed before he spoke, wearing a uniform pattern that British lancer regiments had adopted. He introduced himself in the dining saloon as Lieutenant Colonel Jonnathan Martin Smythe-Armbruster of the Calcutta Light Horse, in transit to England by way of the vast emptiness of the Atlantic.

He wore a version of the Polish Uhlan uniform, including the czapka-style headdress. His dark blue and double-breasted tunic was slightly too small for his bulk. The uniform he wore had scarlet facings on the collar, lapels, cuffs, turnbacks, and the piping around the pockets. He wore a white sash and white breeches with twin stripes in the facing color.

"He's quite a dandy, Hud," Victoria whispered to me.

"One of your countrymen."

She and Maude nodded knowingly.

After a dinner of beef stew served with Yorkshire puddings, followed by a trifle, the men retired to the small wardroom, which was made up like a library with leather couches. Port was served, and cigars were passed as the ship rocked through the swell.

I walked up to Lieutenant Colonel Smythe-Armbruster and offered to light his cigar.

"Thank you, old chap." He puffed it to life.

"You're a long way from India."

"Oh, I am indeed a very long way, but my business is in Indian cotton, and so with this rebellion situation underway, I expect that the demand and the price will increase as the supply diminishes from the American South."

Smythe's impeccable manners showed good breeding. He held his position in the Calcutta Light Horse for many years. Although still technically a military unit, the regiment had evolved over the decades into a de facto social club, where an evening at the clubhouse bar could be recorded in the regimental ledger as attendance at a parade. For two weeks a year, the unit took the train from Calcutta through

Bengal, camped out in tents on a manicured lawn, and played polo on the newly established grounds at Silchar, Assam.

The Light Horse became a home to many young British gentlemen on their first assignment to Calcutta. They made contacts, enjoyed horse-related sports, including betting on race outcomes, and climbed socially.

"Most of our members are overweight, out of shape, and the weapons we have are as dated as the combat tactics, but it's still a jolly good show, and the mess dues are affordable. For those single men who feel the need, there is female company nearby, with a come-hither welcome. The proprietors ensure that the girls are clean and smile, accommodating the needs of young gentlemen far from home."

I nodded with understanding and sipped my port as the deck moved under us.

"You are quartered in the owner's stateroom?"

"I am," I said. "I have an ownership interest in the Peninsular and Oriental Steam Navigation Company. The *Spirit of Ohio* is one of the flotilla."

"When I was in Atlanta recently, I made the acquaintance of a gentleman by the name of James Dunwoody Bulloch. I have his card somewhere. He made preparations to travel to Liverpool to buy ships for the Confederate States that would run the American Naval Blockade. He was to act as a sales agent for Confederate cotton, and with those sales, he would dispatch armaments and war supplies to their armies. He offered me an investment opportunity. I explained that we were rivals in the cotton trade. It didn't seem to matter to him. An investment in ships could pay for the blockade runner in two or three successful journeys; thereafter, it was all profit."

"If the Federal Navy didn't capture or sink them."

Lieutenant Colonel Smythe-Armbruster tapped the side

of his head. "I considered that, and did not invest. Not yet anyway."

I asked, "Would you be willing to make an introduction personally for me in Liverpool if you can find his card? I do have some guineas to invest and possibly ships to sell, including this one, if the price is favorable."

Smythe smiled and said, "I'd be delighted."

Thereafter, he sat at the owner's table when we dined. He entertained Maude, who made it plain that she was married.

I asked him whether the Confederate agent, Bulloch, figured out how to avoid British neutrality laws. Smythe said, "The ships are built in British shipyards but are not armed there. The ships are met at sea by other vessels carrying weapons, Confederate naval officers, and crews. Alternatively, they are victualled and armed in France. The French are neutral, but what happens in the dark of night need not be reported."

He invited me into his cabin, "Let me show you how he proposed that we communicate from a distance." He poured water from a pitcher into a basin. Then he plunged a handkerchief with a red border into the basin. A chemical from the cloth was released into the clear water, visibly. Then he immersed a green-trimmed handkerchief in the same basin of water, and a chemical reaction produced a complete message that was easily read on the green-trimmed cloth. "Once they dry, the message becomes invisible again. It requires a specific ink. I have a bottle."

"Is there a message you plan to send soon?"

"He wishes that I use this method to contact him, but I haven't known about when it might be yet."

"Is there a secret method to disguise the text of the message? Did he share a cipher?"

It was an improvement over using lemon juice or urine to create a hidden message. I didn't know how it was accomplished chemically, but it worked. I wasn't aware of anything like that being used by the Federal Army, and if Summerhaze knew how to do it, he never told me or showed me.

'It's very secret, Henry," he told me. "But I don't have a method of code to use."

"I won't tell a soul."

"No, of course not, and gentlemen shouldn't read other gentlemen's mail. But it happens. What is the world coming to?"

I wagered that James Dunwoody Bulloch would use the Confederate 26-symbol cipher for encoding messages, just as the turncoat Captain Jordan and his agent Rose Greenhow did. They would employ the Confederate Cipher, as taught by John Summerhaze. He may use the handkerchief trick to hide the message.

The problem with secret codes and ciphers comes when your opponent can read what you write.

I traded his bottle of secret ink and both kerchiefs for a bottle of the best Scotch whiskey on board.

Birkenhead, England
Late Summer, 1861

THE BIRKENHEAD DISTRICT near Liverpool was home to shipbuilding. The Great Float in Wallasey Pool formed an immense dock system set apart from the rest of Liverpool. The docks were used for manufacturing, and they received cotton shipments from the American South. King Cotton ruled in Liverpool and supplied the textile mills in Manchester and Birmingham.

Liverpool expanded steadily, becoming England's

second-largest city, only behind London. As I took a carriage from the docks where the *SS Spirit of Ohio* was unloading its cargo to the luxurious Adelphi Hotel, I was struck by the poverty. My driver drew my attention to the overcrowding. He lived in the courts, or courtyard housing.

"The City is home to St. George's Hall and Lime Street Station, sir." The hack said. "And of course the Adelphi, for my betters such as yourself. The greatest people have stayed at the Adelphi."

Maude, Victoria, and their servants shared my coach. They would spend the night in Liverpool and continue to London the following morning. The London and North Western Railway ran the West Coast Main Line. Depending on stops, they would arrive in the afternoon.

When we arrived at the concierge's desk, he summoned Mr. Radley, the hotel manager. Radley, a snob, touted the turtle soup served at the hotel. He explained that a unique system of heated tanks in the basement kept live turtles for the soup, which he claimed was consumed by British peers, world leaders, and industrialists. He presented us with tickets to attend a performance by Dr. Charles Bertram van der Mark, known for "Dr. Mark and his Little Men," a popular traveling band of young male musicians. We were to be his guests for dinner, featuring turtle soup, followed by the show.

Maude and Victoria were shown to their rooms, and I had the bellman deliver my steamer trunks. I excused myself and took a shay to John Laird Sons & Co's Birkenhead Iron Works, where The Forsythe Atlantic Steam Ship Company had commissioned the *Seraphim* to be constructed.

The driver cautioned me, "It's acceptable for a gentleman such as yourself to walk through the docks during the hours of daylight, but as the sun sets, it becomes the domain of the cut-purse, footpad, flash, and the dips. I can introduce you to honest men who can serve as guards to your person if you plan to remain."

"I don't have an appointment with John Laird, having just arrived this morning from Washington City. I'm hoping that he will have the time to speak with me."

William Laird was on the premises when I arrived, and I presented my card, identifying myself as Henry Hudson, Co-Owner of the Forsythe Atlantic Steam Ship Company. "You must be Leslie's grandson; he speaks so highly of you, as does Cornelius Vanderbilt. It's an honor to have you here. We have been engaged to build three more ships in the same class as the *Seraphim*, and believe they will be capable of fifteen knots in situations where they follow the Gulf Stream."

We shook hands. "I'm looking forward to seeing the open revolving gun turret and the nine-inch Dalghran Gun with its compensated recoil system."

"Certainly. The Dahlgren cannon can rotate, allowing the ship to target enemies from any direction without requiring the entire vessel to maneuver, Mister Hudson. It will give a smaller packet ship the capacity to defend itself against much larger vessels. Ericsson's design employs a built-up system of wrought-iron bands to reinforce the gun barrel, enabling it to withstand the high pressures generated."

"When does the *Seraphim* launch?"

"Christening is scheduled for two weeks from today, after which there is some finishing work dockside, but the ship is mainly complete. It has not been victualed or prepared for sea. Your grandfather specified that the water tanks used to supply both the boiler and drinking water be made with the galvanized patent process. The water on a ship might taste pleasant for the first time in history. The steel tank is coated with zinc, and it will not rust."

"May I see it?"

"It would be my pleasure, Mr. Hudson."

As we walked toward the *Seraphim's* dry dock, William Laird explained the legal situation. Queen Victoria issued a Proclamation of Neutrality in May. The proclamation recognized both the Union and the Confederacy as belligerents, allowing Britain to trade with both while officially remaining neutral. The Foreign Office and the law officers of the Crown interpreted *Seraphim's* trading intentions to avoid including her design as being subject to the proclamation.

I'm not sure I could find the ship among so many construction projects without a knowledgeable guide. And as we crossed the makeshift bridge from the edge of the construction dock to the boat, I was surprised. A large man stood on the deck, one foot on the rotating platform supporting the big gun, sketching and taking notes. There was something familiar about him.

William Laird called, "Who are you?"

Arlund Bisbee dropped his sketchbook, turned to face us, and I noticed that he held the Belgian pimp pistol with the hinged blade on the barrel.

"Hud, what are you doing here?"

"It's my company's ship. Forsythe Atlantic Steamship Company is owned by Leslie Forsyth, Cornelius Vanderbilt, *and* Henry Hudson. I admit that I'm the junior partner, but it comes with being an heir."

"No, I mean, why aren't you in school? You have two years to go."

"The war that your people started, Arlund, remember. The class of 1862 graduated early. Remember Autie Custer? He graduated with over seven hundred demerits, but they needed officers."

He nodded, "Meat for the grinder."

"I quit." I lied. "It was allowed, and I thought that pursuing business interests made more sense than wearing a blue jacket."

"You could have worn gray."

"I'm from Michigan, Arlund - is it Lieutenant or Captain Bisbee? And I repeat myself, what are you doing on my ship?"

William Laid said, "Technically, it's still the property of the Birkenhead Iron Works. And while Mr. Hudson seems to know you, I do not."

Arlund hinged the blade back and pocketed the pistol. "I work with James Dunwoody Bulloch, who has commissioned ships to be built here at your yard, Mr. Laird. I believe there is a discussion of the construction of *Laird Rams* that could break the Federal blockade."

William Laird turned to me. "Our architects are sketching two ironclad ships, the *El Tousson* and *El Monassir*, that would fall outside of the Queen's neutrality guidelines because they are only armed with a pointed iron ramming bar. We are building *Enrica*, an armed screw sloop-of-war, which we will have to redesign due to the Queen's proclamation."

I turned back to Arlund, who I noticed was ushaven. "What is your part in this?" I looked at the sketch pad on the deck.

"I am an artillerist, Hud. Called to serve my country."

William Laird said, "Perhaps we should all return to my office and have a dram of Ardbeg."

"That suits me," Arlund Bisbee said.

I nodded, and we walked back. "Would you have shot us, Arlund?"

"These are challenging times, Hud. There are about 100 cotton agents between Liverpool and Birmingham, and possibly a thousand people when you include their employees and family members. The Confederate states produced over 2 billion pounds of cotton annually last year, with about two-thirds of that being sold here in England. That's even real money to the Hudsons, Forsythes, and Cornelius Vanderbilt. To win the war, the Northern States must choke off our commerce. You understand commerce, Hud."

I nodded.

"Whatever happened to that Scots lass, Victoria?"

"She and Maude crossed with me on the *Spirit of Ohio*. We arrived today. They'll take the train to London tomorrow morning."

"You should marry her, Hud."

I looked over at William Laird, "See, we know each other well enough for Arlund to guide me in nuptials."

He nodded, "Aye."

Arlund asked, "Are you still friends with Admiral Lord Owain Rowley-Conway?"

I turned toward William Laird, "Baron Langford."

Arlund continued, "And Lord Major Roche?"

I said, "Baron Fermoy, who is a major in the Royal Horse Guards." Nodding, I added, "And Maude's husband, Major Sir Iain McKay of the Coldstream Guards—also, Minister Lyons. Yes, you know that I am acquainted with all of them."

"It's just that James Bulloch is looking for new friends who have sway in the House of Lords and might be able to soften the terms of neutrality."

"Why would I want to do that, Arlund?"

"Two billion pounds of cotton. Fifty-five million guineas. It's a king's ransom—a nation's ransom."

We arrived at William Laird's office, sat, and he poured generous quantities of Scotch into crystal tumblers. Raising his glass, he offered a toast, "To commerce."

We all drank to that.

Arlund said, "Fifty million guineas will buy a lot of armed

ships and war supplies," as William Laird recharged our glasses.

"Aye," Laird said, his blue eyes twinkling.

Adelphi Hotel
Liverpool England
Two days later

I HAD dinner with the ladies and sent them off at the train station. The next day, I had breakfast with Lieutenant Colonel Smythe-Armbruster of the Calcutta Light Horse, after which I saw him to the station with an additional bottle of the best whiskey to sweeten our deal. He boarded the first-class coach that would take him north to Glasgow via Carlisle and Gretna.

He trumpeted, "My business with Brown Brothers Harriman concluded successfully and most satisfactorily."

"Who are they?" We enjoyed a traditional, sumptuous English breakfast while chatting.

"Oh, I forgot that you are not in the trade. They provide financing for cotton exports and imports between America and England. They have agents in various Southern cities to solicit cotton consignments and facilitate trade. They understand that there may be an interruption in business and are willing to pay me top dollar in Calcutta, and then to enable export separately. We contracted at a favorable rate, and I can return to India with confidence."

"What business do you have in Glasgow?"

My new friend Jonnathan said, "There are Scottish companies importing jute. It is in high demand for the manufacturing of sacks, ropes, and other textiles in Scottish mills. The Sepoy Mutiny led to the British Raj's decision to take direct control of India, and the John Company's monopoly ended."

I wasn't aware of the potential impact on trade. There was so much to learn. "So even tea? You could import tea without interference?"

"Yes indeed, tea, pepper, cinnamon, and cardamom. I also have a meeting to discuss the importation of indigo."

I asked, "Then home, or do you have further business with the American South and the gentleman we discussed? What was his name? Bulloch?"

"Yes, quite. Bulloch, the Confederate man. I didn't anticipate the enthusiasm of Brown Brothers Harriman. They changed everything."

I signed for the meal and telegraphed my grandfather in London from Lime Street Station.

By midday, I received a reply to my cable.

> Henry Hudson, Adelphi Hotel, Liverpool
> Remain Liverpool- STOP - we launch *Serephim* within fortnight - STOP - Cornered Indian opium harvest - STOP- Will join you there - STOP

Two weeks in Liverpool with very little, if anything, to do had a small appeal. There were a few people from my class and a vast number of people living in grinding poverty in the city. I was told that Manchester and Birmingham were worse.

Yes, I could have gone to Scotland with Smythe-Armbruster, but I found him difficult to take in large doses. Liverpool in August was not the sort of place where royalty gathered. The putrid stench of the city, the forges belching coal smoke, the odor of the fish catch drying in the sun, the guts sloshing in the tides, rotting. Inland, the slaughterhouses pour gore and blood into the Mersey, which meets the Irish Sea in a brackish melange. Then there was unseasonable heat.

My hotel suite was very elaborate, with flowers masking the humors leaking in from outside, but the only possible escapes were to sea or ashore somewhere. I spoke to the concierge, who recommended Wales with a more sulubrious climate, which could be reached by coach or rail.

"I can telegraph the St. George Hotel at Llandudno and advise them of your arrival. It is well-appointed, with indoor plumbing and a water-operated lift. The hotel sits astride the promenade. A horse-drawn bus service runs from the Conway railway station to the hotel."

"Very good. Leave a note to forward telegrams to me there on my account, and should Leslie Forsythe arrive and inquire, tell him where to summon me. What is the train schedule?"

He consulted a ledger, "It leaves in five minutes promptly, you won't make it, sir."

"Hire a private coach for me. How long by coach?"

"Four hours."

"Do it. And have the bellman bring my luggage down. I'll be in the saloon."

I walked into the dark saloon and ordered a gin. The Adelphi had its own ice house, and the ice in the crystal glass was remarkably clean.

As I finished my first and motioned to the bartender for another, a man, shorter and older than I was, with facial hair and a dapper look that reminded me of Colonel Ambrose Burnside, wearing a full gray, wool, business suit with a red silk waistcoat that must have been hot to wear, walked up to my table.

"My name is James Bulloch. No need to rise."

"I don't intend to. What is your business, Mr. Bulloch?"

"May I join you?"

"I don't usually drink with strangers, and I will soon be on my way."

"I bribed the concierge, who said you were here awaiting a coach to Wales — more specifically to Llandudno."

"It's good to know that information is so readily available, Mr.?" I knew who he was and what his business was, but I wanted him to work for it.

"Bulloch, Mr. Hudson."

He seated himself, motioning to the bartender for a drink, and withdrawing a business card from his waistcoat. He slid it across the table. I read it aloud. "James Dunwoody Bulloch, President, Port Royal Planters' Association, Port Royal, South Carolina."

I thought for a moment. "I know Port Royal."

"And Port Royal knows you, Mr. Hudson. You're a famous pistolero, and from what I have heard, you are clever with a blade. Colonel Beaufort sends his best regards to a friend of the Beauforts and the South."

"Did Arlund Bisbee tell you where to find me?"

"Not precisely. He said you'd be staying at the best hotel in Liverpool. The sea turtle soup is legendary."

"Have a bowl with my regards after I'm gone. Put the bill on my room tab."

"I thought we could discuss commerce. I am informed that you left the Military Academy two years early."

"Everyone else was leaving, and my family marooned me there to separate me from a married lady with whom I had formed an attachment."

Bulloch said, "You are not opposed to Southern rights? You are not an abolitionist?"

"I'm the son of a jurist. By upbringing, I tend to follow the law, which seems remarkably fluid these days. It seems foolhardy to shed blood over negroes."

"We did not leave the Union over the darkies precisely."

"No, I understand the issues. States' rights are closely intertwined with the slavery issue, though. The federal government's failure to uphold its constitutional obligations to protect slavery and the rights of slaveholding states and their agrarian economies has brought about a crisis that entwines us all."

"Precisely, *their obligation*, sir."

The bartender brought two iced gins.

"The topic has caused so much grief in my life that I am not inclined to chew the bone with you or anyone else, Mr. Bulloch."

"I know from Laird that your grandfather, Leslie Forsythe, plans to ship chests of opium in his fast ship, the *Seraphim*, possibly the fastest ship on the Atlantic. The fastest armed ship."

"It is not a warship; the cannon is for the ship's defense."

"Of course, Mr. Hudson." He winked.

"The Confederate States would like to buy your cargo for delivery at Port Royal. An army doesn't run only on bullets and food. All people in the South need medicine, and we will pay top dollar for the cargo on delivery."

"On delivery? His name is *Forsythe*. I expect he will want the payment delivered to his bank before setting sail, along with commissions and transportation costs. The Union will likely consider that cargo to be contraband of war. The ship and all of my grandfather's holdings would be forfeited. That's a high price for a cargo of opium."

Bulloch softened his request, "Then I will take the opium and find shipping."

"It's not mine to sell."

He finished his drink, agitated. "Would you ask him for me?"

"I'm informed that he bought the balance of the harvest being shipped to England. The focus of the opium trade is export from British India to China. There is another English Opium War underway in Cathay to ensure continued access to the Chinese market for opium."

"Thus the scarcity," Bulloch said. "He bought one hundred thousand pounds of opium - the civilized world's medicinal supply."

"And you would deprive your countrymen in the Northern States of opium to relieve pain?"

"At a considerable profit to Mr. Forsythe and his financial empire. I would also pay you a significant commission in gold guineas. As a young man new in the world, there is much you could buy with that sum for entertainment or investment, depending on your tastes."

The concierge appeared at the door of the saloon and motioned to me.

"My coach has arrived, Mr. Bulloch. Thank you for introducing yourself. Give Arlund my best, and of course, Nate, senior and junior, when you return to Port Royal. They are dear friends." I stood.

"I have gold to buy friends and influence in England, Mr. Hudson. The peerage thinks well of you. We would pay in gold to achieve an end to British neutrality."

"I'm willing to entertain your suggestion. We can discuss the matter further on my return." I needed to stretch this out and to draw him out, and I wasn't prepared to discuss this matter of concern to him so soon into our conversations.

I walked to the front of the hotel and checked the security of my trunks on the carriage. It wasn't a new coach by any means. The upholstery was on the verge of threadbare, and the wood's lacquer was worn and dull. The driver had a long, thin face with a high forehead. He wore a soft felt, broad-brimmed hat often worn by working-class men. His clothes were likewise nondescript. The horses that pulled the carriage were a matched pair and looked to have some life left in them.

I looked up at the driver as I boarded the coach, "Let's be off."

CHAPTER 13

On the Highway from Liverpool, England
to Llandudno, Wales
August 1981

*A*s I have described, the day was hot, the coach springs rocked, not being new and being prone to sway as old leaf springs do. The horses pulling the traces were trotters, and the driver alternated between the trot and the walk depending on the gentle grade. I began to doze in the heat after taking a stiff drink from a flask.

Voices outside of the carriage and an absence of motion woke me, and I was instantly alert.

"Stand and deliver your passenger, I say again and won't say once more." It wasn't an English-accented voice, and it was muffled. I looked out the carriage window and saw a slight man wearing a flour sack over his head, with holes cut for eyes. The mask gathered around his neck. He held three horses. As I stepped from the carriage, I could see two men, one holding the reins of one of the trace horses and the other holding a revolver. They were larger men, and they too wore flour sacks with eyeholes cut into them.

I drew and cocked the Le Mat Grape Shot Revolver chambered in .42 caliber that my father gave me and that I always carried with me. Holding it near my leg so as not to be seen, I stepped from the carriage.

"Are you looking for me?"

The man held a Colt Model 1851 Navy revolver chambered in .36 caliber in one hand and a scrap of paper in the other. Holding it up while looking at me, he turned to the man who held the reins and said, "It's him. It's Hudson," in a guttural tongue.

I walked forward, closing the distance to the armed man, who had his pistol trained on the driver.

"You stay right there." My movement surprised him.

"Can I help you, gentlemen?"

"John, tell him to stop," The man holding the carriage horses said.

I fired my pistol into the heart of the pistolero twice, rapidly, and as the other man dropped the carriage lines and grabbed for a handgun in his breeches, I shot him in the chest twice, too. He clutched his chest and gasped loudly, saying, "I am a dead man."

Cocking the pistol once more, I trained it on the smaller of the three, holding their horses, and said, "Pull off your mask and put up your arms or suffer the same fate."

When the mask came off, I could see it was a woman dressed in men's garb. She held her hands high and wet her trousers.

"You killed them," She said breathlessly in a typical English accent.

"And I am within my rights to kill you as well, so make no sudden movement or join them in hell."

As this drama unfolded, another carriage approached us, heading north in the direction of Liverpool. I called up to my driver, "How far are we from Liverpool?"

"Not five miles." He spoke to the other carriage driver, "Summon the constabulary from the Bridewell at Brick and Duncan Street. Tell them that two highwaymen have been killed in the commission of a kidnapping and a third is held at gunpoint!"

I holstered my pistol and set the woman inside my carriage. She shook like a leaf. "I'll hang for sure." I didn't disabuse her of the notion.

"If you attempt to escape, I'll shoot you like I shot your friends."

"They're not my friends. They paid me two shillings to hold these horses."

About an hour later, two mounted constables arrived and took my statement. Fifteen minutes later, a more senior man arrived on horseback and retook my statement, along with those of the driver and the accompanying woman.

The senior man admired my LeMat pattern handgun. "I haven't seen one like that, Mister Hudson."

"It was developed in New Orleans in 1856 by Jean Alexandre Le Mat. John Krider of Philadelphia made the revolver under license."

"Nine shots and a grape charge. You could have kept shooting."

"Yes, but I didn't need to."

"No, they're dead."

"What about the woman?"

"She, a sixpence whore from Market Street, who is known to us. Her name is Bernice Hobbs, but she goes by Bettina in the scarlet trade. She says the highwaymen, who are not well known to her, hired her to hold their horses after sampling her favors in a bawdy house."

THE CONFEDERATE CIPHER

"Do you believe her?"

"Yes, I believe her. She's terrified, and of course, she'll hang for this. The men have no identification on their persons, and I don't think they're English or Irish. Perhaps they are Welsh. They carried American pistols, and you're an American, so there is that connection. They had a sketch. They said it was of you, but when I look at it, the sketch could be any man with a mustache."

I recounted, "From what they said, they wanted to take me. Kidnap me, not just empty my wallet. They had my name."

"We haven't seen a highwayman in these parts for a long time. Maybe twenty years, long before my time. There are stories, but they're from a different age. This lot didn't expect you to be armed. You just walked up to them and shot them?"

"What else should I have done?"

He laughed, "Americans. The magistrate will want to hear your story. We can put the bodies in the coach with Bettina. Please come back with us. You can sit atop with the driver."

A runner summoned the magistrate of the Assize to the Bridewell, which was their term for the police station. He pronounced me free to go and took my statement regarding Bernice Hobbs' involvement.

"If we need to contact you within the next week, where will you be?"

"My address for the next few weeks is the Adelphi Hotel, but I have plans to take in the sights at Llandudno. The concierge at the Adelphi telegraphed the St. George hotel in Wales and made arrangements, but I can stay closer if it's a matter of law."

"No, Mr. Hudson, you're free to travel. Check in with Constable White at the South Bridewell if your situation changes. I apologize for my country. I thought we had rooted out his behavior, but you have found an exception to the rule."

I was suspicious of the concierge, whom I knew to be susceptible to bribery, and the unscrupulous Confederate agent, Bulloch. Still, there would be no time to arrange such an abduction. As the constable pointed out, the sketch they had could have matched any male with a mustache. The constable didn't hear them call me by name, though.

I returned to the Adelphi Hotel, unpacked again, and spent the evening.

Bulloch sat in the restaurant reading the daily paper when I came down in the morning. "I see you have been busy, Mr. Hudson."

"I made the paper?"

"Above the fold in the *Liverpool Mercury* and the *Daily Post*. Both publications pay the police to feed them stories. There have not been highwaymen in this part of the country within recent memory, and you brought down two in rapid succession with shots through their hearts. The news is salacious and superseded the latest information from the Confederacy."

"Ah, so we know for a fact that they had hearts?"

Bulloch laughed. "At two and four paces."

"I didn't want to miss."

"You didn't command them to throw down?"

"Does the law require it?"

"No, but it is polite."

"I didn't want to give them time to turn their revolvers on me."

"And they met the same fate as Captain Ezra Pervis at Christmas."

"I backshot Pervis."

"I'm too polite to bring that detail up, Mister Hudson. May I call you Hud? You can call me James or Jim."

"Shall we order breakfast? What is the news from *your* war back home?"

"On August 10, our army, including the Missouri state militia, routed a Union army led by General Nathaniel Lyon southwest of Springfield, Missouri. The papers are calling it the Battle of Oak Hills. The Federal Navy captured Forts Hatteras and Clark on the North Carolina coast. They will undoubtedly continue to attempt to blockade Southern ports along the Atlantic coast.

"The Federal Congress passed the Confiscation Act, allowing for the seizure of property used in rebellion, including negroes, but you know about that."

I raised my hands in mock surrender. "They have no choice."

"And you should pick the winning side."

"Why, Mr. Bullock?"

"Why indeed, when you can play both ends against the middle - smart business, Hud."

I didn't want to brush him off because he was a trusted agent of the Confederacy, and I was under orders to gather information on their intentions in the British Isles. I could play the dandy, and he wanted to pull me into his circle. If I allowed it too quickly, I thought it would raise red flags. The presence of Arlund Bisbee, now a Confederate officer, bothered me more than I think I let on.

Arlund and I were, by definition, enemies, and even though I didn't want it to be like that because I liked and trusted him, we were on opposite sides of a war, had taken oaths, and there wasn't any way around it.

Nate Beaufort, Arlund Bisbee, Colonel Hardee, and others left West Point before I petitioned for promotion and received it. I didn't show up for my class, and although I briefly served on General McDowell's staff, few people knew what happened to me. Washington, D.C., was a jumble, particularly after the Battle at Manassas Junction. The paper said that General McDowell had been relieved of command, replaced by George McClelland, the Little Napoleon. New divisions and brigades were being formed with the newly minted volunteer army, and freshly commissioned volunteer officers were being promoted. Regular officers were being promoted to higher ranks and reassigned.

The situation in the Federal Navy was more dire since they lost the cream off the milk and kept the blue john. Headlines quoted by Bulloch of a Federal Navy victory at Hatteras were only achieved by sending everything that could float, along with the entire Corps of Marines. Somewhere over two thousand marines remained with the Union, but some of their handful of officers went South. I thought it unlikely that the Navy would create a massive volunteer force as the Army did.

Prime Minister Lord Palmerston and Foreign Secretary Lord John Russell enforced British neutrality. Even though I knew that they privately sympathized with the Confederacy, they publicly upheld the policy of neutrality to avoid entanglement in the conflict. This policy had been influenced by public opinion, which opposed slavery and supported the Union.

That the peasant farmers and the poor who worked in factories in America and England were little more than slaves themselves never rose to the public consciousness. Marx's Communist Manifesto, published in February 1848 in London, was written in German under the title *Manifest der Kommunistischen Partei* and was frequently quoted by union organizers in circulated pamphlets. The Amalgamated Society of Engineers, formed in 1851, served as a model for other craft unions, such as the carpenters and joiners. My family was directly opposed to trade unionism.

There would be worker discontent if the Federal Navy choked off the cotton trade, as they intended. Although some Indian cotton would arrive from five times the distance in Liverpool, it would not be enough to keep the industries running, and unemployed workers would become a problem.

This was the leverage on which the Confederates rested their hopes.

LESLIE FORSYTHE, read about me shooting the highwaymen and sent a telegram congratulating me on my victory, but cautioned me about my impetuous nature. Victoria said in a brief telegram that she showed the paper to our friends. Still, they'd all read the sensationalized account of the brave American, Henry Hudson, of English ancestry, who took his time, took careful aim under fire, and blew their hearts out their backs with a big-bore revolver.

I never allowed them to return fire, but the part about blowing their hearts out their backs was technically close to accurate. The portion of the incident in which a soiled dove was hired to hold the horses was included and sensationalized. The papers predicted that she'd swing for her crime.

Nobody asked about the Colt 36s, which bothered me. The men had been identified as Manx thugs from Peel who left the Isle of Man one step ahead of the law and landed in Liverpool, up to no good. Based on my inquiries, the pistols were less common, although many of them had crossed the ocean with Southerners engaged in the cotton trade. They were also in demand by army officers who wished to buy a private weapon. The Colt Navy had a modest recoil, making it more popular in England than the Royal Army's Adams and the improved Beaumont-Adams revolvers, which were available in different calibers.

One of the thugs had a newspaper article mentioning my arrival in Liverpool, which included an artist's impression of my face. One of the thugs attempted to copy the picture from the newspaper, and that's what I found in his hand when I shot him.

As I walked through the hotel from the salon to the dining room, the concierge, whom I suspected of setting up the robbery, pointed me out to a tall, thin gentleman, well-dressed, wearing a top hat and a handlebar mustache.

"I say, Mister Hudson!"

I stopped, looking at the concierge who pocketed a coin.

"Yes?"

"My name is Faversham, Charles Faversham. He handed me a card with his name on it. Will you walk with me?"

I said, "I am headed to tea."

"That suits me. I need a moment of your time. I represent the Birmingham Small Arms Trade and the London Armoury Company."

"Both of them? I've read in the papers that they are rivals."

"At times, they are, and in other circumstances, they work in concert where notable clients are involved," Faversham assured me.

"What business do you and they have with me?"

"They are both interested in selling Pattern 1853 Enfield rifles, and because you are in the shipping business, and are known to Mr. Bulloch, I thought that you might like to transport them for us to New Orleans, which remains an open port."

"For now."

"Yes, for the moment. The *SS Spirit of Ohio*, here in Liverpool, is searching for a cargo to fill its hold for the return journey."

"Shipping violates the Queen's neutrality proclamation and the United States' Constitution. Article III, Section 3 defines treason as levying War against them [the United States], or in adhering to their Enemies, giving them Aid and Comfort. I am not a traitor."

"There are ways around the law."

"And I am not inclined to ship your rifled muskets."

"The fee would be generous."

"Not for any fee, Mr. Faversham."

AND SO IT WENT. The newspapers wanted to interview me. Some of the reporters wanted to heft the heavy LeMat pistol, which I had to carry in a sling holster, supported by my shoulder and strapped to my chest. I didn't grant interviews, and it drove them to a frenzy. The lack of highwaymen waylaying travelers made this a story of stories at the end of the Summer of 1861, when people had already grown tired of the Family Feud in the Americas.

Bettina, the prostitute, gave her story and named customers, none of whom were known to me. I suspect that she selected men from the elect of Liverpool society somewhat at random, and it led to her alleged suicide by hanging in her cell one night. A note was not left, but since Bettina couldn't write, the papers composed notes on her behalf in absentia, blaggarding society, and the need to support aging parents, by selling her body, and so forth—anything to sell a penny paper.

It began to interfere with my life and the reason I was in Liverpool in the first place. I decided to hire a detective, also known as a private inquiry agent in Old Blighty—the British version of a Pinkerton—to compile a list of shipbuilders who had contracts with the Confederate States to build its Navy.

Charles Frederick Field, a former London police officer

who operated in the model of the former Home Secretary, Robert Peel, retired and opened offices in London and Birmingham. His agency aimed to provide investigative services to individuals and organizations who sought answers to complex cases and mysteries. I didn't know much about the business, but after probing the situation, I learned that Parliament had passed a Private Detectives Act two years earlier. Some of the more questionable inquiry agents had been driven from the trade.

To get to Birmingham, I boarded the line, initially operated by the Grand Junction Railway, which connected the Liverpool and Manchester Railway to Birmingham via Warrington, Crewe, Stafford, and Wolverhampton. They had been absorbed by the London and North Western Railway when I took the trip, but the first-class car still bore a brass plaque showing construction took place under the suzernity of the GJR. I departed from Lime Street Station and, hours later, arrived at Curzon Street Station in Birmingham, where it shared facilities with the London and Birmingham Railway, providing a seamless connection between the two cities.

The Charles Field Agency had an office on Curzon Street, so the walk a few blocks wasn't unpleasant, even though it rained on me. I telegraphed my intentions, and the burly gent, who wore a cheap suit and a bowler hat, met me as expected.

"My name is Albert Grace, your lordship, and I'm excited to be engaged by yourself and the Peninsular and Oriental Steam Navigation Company."

We shook hands, and he asked, "Are you the same American Henry Hudson who dispatched the highwaymen on the road to Wales?"

"Yes, I'm sorry to say."

"That was a cool bit of work if I do say so myself. Blew

their hearts out their backs with your American nine-shooter."

"That's not why I'm here."

"Of course not, let me get my pad and dip my quill, and you can tell me what inquiries we can make on your behalf."

"The Peninsular and Oriental Steam Navigation Company is interested in which firms are potential rivals in the shipping trade between the American South and Liverpool. William Miller and Sons has a contract to build a warship called the *Oreto*. I have heard that Harland & Wolff in Belfast may be drawing up a construction design. There are the Short Brothers of Sunderland, and I have visited with John Laird & Sons, who own Birkenhead Iron Works. They are building the *Seraphim* for the Forsythe Atlantic Company, of which I'm also co-owner."

Albert Grace scribbled furiously in a strong hand, dabbing the ink with a sponge when he dripped.

"Though it is not an immediate concern to me personally or to my company, Mexico is borrowing more than it can repay from European creditors. If the Federal Government is successful in blockading Southern ports, it may be possible for the Confederacy to get around the blockade by sending cotton to Mexico by rail. I want your firm to research a particular opinion. Matamoros could become a crucial channel for exporting Southern cotton to European markets. The Mexicans would claim that cotton was grown in Mexico, and it would be exempt from the Union embargo and British neutrality. If opened, this trade route would enable Mexico to repay its debts to France, Spain, and England. There are rumors that England, and particularly France, plan to invade Mexico to repay the debt. Such an invasion would interfere with Southern exports. British and French interests are to seize assets in Mexico. They don't want the Mexicans to use the Confederacy's commerce to make payments."

He finished writing and looked up at me, "This is more than we are accustomed to doing."

"Will you do it?"

"We will—try."

"Get on it and send me your bill." I handed Mr. Grace my solicitor's card. "Payments will be facilitated through our lawyer in London."

Was I stretching my remit? I admit that I did, but being in England, there were so many undercurrents and the level of intrigue internationally, from the opium wars in China to an impending engineered coup in Mexico, staggered me. When Maximilian was first mentioned as a possible emperor of Mexico, the idea seemed far-fetched, but circumstances were changing with the onset of the War Between the States.

Apologies here to you, dear reader. I neglected to mention the visit I had with Edmond Roche, the first Baron Fermoy, who visited me at the St. George Hotel in Wales. As with everyone else on the Island, he'd read about my encounter with the highwaymen, so he knew I was in town. It didn't take him long to track me down and quiz me on the possible export of cotton from Mexico. I knew nothing about it, and the thought hadn't occurred to me. The potential seemed obvious with the declaration of a blockade that would exclude a Mexican port.

"You see, old chap, we don't want to see that happen," he said to me over whiskey, sitting and watching the waves roll in at Llandudno. "We don't want Mexico to be able to repay the debt. We want to put a—."

"Puppet."

"Yes, quite, I didn't want to sound gauche by using the word, Henry, but yes, a puppet on the throne. Think of a Mexican Empire. Maximilian is a descendant of Charles V, Holy Roman Emperor and King of Spain, who, when the Spanish conquered the Aztecs, first brought Mexico under Spanish control. Maximilian is a perfect catspaw—the correct hereditary right to be emperor and all that. The divine right of kings. His wife, Marie Charlotte Amélie Augustine Victoire Clémentine Léopoldine of Saxe-Coburg and Gotha, is Queen Victoria's cousin. Once he is in place, England and France can export Mexican cotton to fill the need. The idea isn't original with me; it's politics. Lord Gladstone supports the Confederate claim strongly and the importation of Southern Cotton. His family has deep ties to the West Indies slave trade."

"And you'll use Indians in Mexico rather than Africans to pick *Mexican* cotton," I suggested.

"You're sharp, Henry, that's precisely what we'll do. Political expediency will be satisfied, and no transatlantic slaves will be used. So we must put our man on the throne in Mexico. He won't even be British; Maximilian, the hereditary heir, with support from our financial partners in France, will cement the trade." He gave me a sly glance, "The Manchester Textile Guild will renounce processing Confederate cotton produced by slaves later this year."

"But they will find cotton picked by indians to be acceptable."

"Precisely."

"When will all this happen?"

"Later this year, when the weather is more clement. Why would one invade that intemperate place in the summer? Half the army would die of fever before they met the enemy."

That made some sense to me. "What can I do to help you?"

"Where once we would have opposed the blockade, we now support it tacitly and would like you to do what you can with your family connections to make the right people aware."

I asked, "Can you stop the construction of a Confederate Navy here in England?"

Lord Fermoy said with a wink, "We can slow it and obstruct it under the law without being obvious."

I asked, "And all that intrigue with the Beauforts and the South? You know that they're counting on British intervention."

"We'll sell them Enfields and gunpowder, and your grandfather will sell them opium and medicines, and they can battle it out as best they can. Maybe they'll win. It's difficult to say at this point. But the odds are against them if we don't send a navy to break the blockade and land an army in support."

So there you have it. The opium deal was closed without my involvement. The *Seraphim* would soon sail, likely with a hold full of opium chests sold at a premium price in England, with cotton profits banked before hostilities began, and the blockade could take effect.

"She's in your room," Lord Fermoy said.

"She?"

"Victoria came up on the train with me to keep you company."

THEREFORE, as soon as I returned to Liverpool, I summoned James Bulloch and Arlund Bisbee to my suite in the Adelphi and agreed to facilitate the transshipment of opium. I told them I'd have to discuss how the Enfields would be transported with my grandfather once we met.

Victoria was in the adjacent bedroom, possibly listening in when I made the deal, and we shook hands. After guessing correctly that it would be shipped on the *Seraphim*, I told them I'd personally sail to Port Royal with the cargo.

Bulloch was delighted, but Arlund Bisbee was more circumspect, accepting the news more quietly. Bulloch may or may not have known that the business was a *fait accompli*, but he played a deeper game than that. The American Federal Government and the Confederate Government seemed to play checkers, whereas Europeans, and the British in particular, played chess. I thought that Bulloch likely had a game of chess going, too. The question in my mind was whether I was a pawn and, if so, when I would be sacrificed.

When my Grandfather Forsythe arrived at the hotel, he did not seem surprised to see Victoria at my side, clinging to my arm possessively. I introduced them, and he made all the right moves, but he is my grandfather, and I had grown up with him.

We boarded the *Seraphim*, which was tied up to the dock at the ironworks, looking very shipshape and Bristol fashion with a picked crew on board.

William Laird personally gave us the tour and stayed on board as we cast off under steam, and the ship cut through the water.

"She's as fast as a homesick angel," my Grandfather announced.

Victoria spent time in the cabin that had been earmarked for my use and said, "It's lovely, Hud, and large enough for two."

The gun was demonstrated against a wreck on the shore north of Liverpool at range and was remarkably accurate.

Three rounds were fired into the same portion of the hulk, splintering wood and causing destruction. After the firing demonstration with the turret gun, the crew began cleaning it.

We returned to port under sail, which took some time to set, but once in place, it seemed very well organized; however, it was slower than steam power.

"When do we sail?"

Grandfather said, "*You* will sail at dawn in two days, will load cargo in Plymouth, and then on to Port Royal. I'm told you have good friends there."

"Yes, and so does Victoria, don't you, dear?"

Victoria nodded demurely.

He reached into his coat and brought out a formal-looking, multi-page document, written on vellum and sealed with a ribbon winding through brass grommets. He handed it to me. "It is a bill of transfer from the Ironworks that built it. Think of it as an engagement present."

"Engagement?"

"It would be inappropriate for a single woman to share a cabin with a young, eligible bachelor on a sea voyage, even with a Captain as upstanding and Christian as Robert Amadon acting as chaperone."

"You're gifting me the *Seraphim*?"

"Yes, it should stay in the family, but far enough from the family's treasury in the unlikely event the Federal Navy seized it."

He turned to Captain Amadon, a large, fair-skinned, broad-shouldered man in his late thirties with curly blonde hair and an easy smile. His curly yellow hair was bound in a queue.

"I am a witness to it! Congratulations, young Master Hudson."

I looked at the documents. My name was boldly ascribed to it, as was the name of the *Seraphim*, Liverpool, England, launched in 1861, the sole property of Henry Hudson (no longer attached to the Forsythe Atlantic), of Detroit, Michigan, United States of America. The document bore the British Customs seal featuring the Royal Arms of the United Kingdom, including a quartered shield representing England, Scotland, and Ireland; the Order of the Garter surrounding the shield; a crowned English lion and a chained Scottish unicorn as supporters; a crest with a crowned lion; and the motto "Dieu et mon droit," *God and my right,* on a scroll. The red wax customs seal included the phrase "Customs and Excise" around the edge. It was attached to documents with a cord in addition to the blue ribbon.

Details of the ship, including its construction and purpose for Commerce and trade, as well as other basic information, were contained on subsequent pages.

Victoria kissed me on the cheek. "Congratulations, Hud."

I gave her a sideways glance.

Grandfather smiled with one side of his mouth, sardonically. "I'm sure you two lovebirds will enjoy your voyage. I've given you a fast ship that will sail in harm's way if necessary and an able crew that can handle her."

"And after Port Royal?"

"She will travel south to take on a cargo of Mexican tobacco there, attested to by the alcalde of Tampico and sealed by the Customs officials there. The documents are in your cabin. The Law of Suspension of Payments, passed in Mexico last month, affected the collection and management of customs revenue; however, your documents attest to faithful payment in gold guineas."

I looked at Captain Amadon, who said, "The documents speak for themselves. It will be a legal, properly taxed foreign cargo. We will sail when you are ready from Port Royal, where you are visiting friends despite recent unpleasantness, introducing your fiancé."

Leslie Forsythe said, "For Baltimore, Henry, your destination is Baltimore, Maryland, unless they secede from the Union between now and your arrival, and then it would be Boston, perhaps." My grandfather looked at Captain Amadon.

"S.E. Thayer has tobacco wharves and warehouses in Baltimore and Boston," Captain Amadon clarified.

I asked, "Is there credible word that Maryland will leave the Union?"

My grandfather said, "The Assembly discusses it. Governor Thomas Hicks leans towards the Confederacy. The *London Morning Post* published an article yesterday documenting that the Union has moved volunteer troops from New England to the area to secure the State. The matter is unresolved as far as I know. Who knows how things will change between now and when you arrive?"

I said, "If Maryland goes to the Confederacy, Washington City and the District will be surrounded."

My grandfather shrugged. "We live in turbulent times, taking our friends where we can."

"Did we deliver a cargo to Tampico, where we picked up the tobacco?"

Captain Amadon said, "It's listed in the ledgers and bills of lading in the owner's cabin. Finished textiles, bolts of cotton and linen, and machine parts for cotton gins: hoppers, revolving cylinders with saws that separate the fiber from the seeds, ginning ribs, and metal brushes, packed in marked crates."

"That's good to know, Hud," Victoria looked up at me from where she clung to my arm possessively."

"Commerce and trade," I said.

THERE WERE a few loose ends that needed to be attended to.

Before we departed, James Bulloch sought me out. "I would like you to take a package to Nate Beaufort, Senior, for me."

He handed me a box. Arlund Bisbee had sealing wax, a seal, and a box of lucifers.

"Before I seal the box, I want you to know its contents because you will be curious." He opened it. There were fifty gold guineas wrapped in two handkerchiefs—one with a red thread embroidering the edge and the other with green embroidery. "See, nothing suspicious."

Arlund dabbed hot wax on the enclosure.

"Why are you sealing it? Don't you trust me, Arlund?"

Arlund looked at James Bulloch.

"*Pro forma*, Henry."

Albert Grace delivered a preliminary report and promised to forward the final, complete inquiry results to my home in Detroit. It was the only permanent address I had to give.

Constable White provided me with a release from the Magistrate of the Assize, acknowledging that the Crown understood I was departing for the Americas and gave permission and approval. It wasn't necessary, but if the question arose, it would provide a documented response.

CHAPTER 14

The Approaches to Port Royal, South Carolina
September 1861

Our transit was swift. We traveled under steam power south to the Canary Islands on the Canary Current to replenish our coal and fresh provisions. We anchored off Puerto del Rosario while we waited for our turn to top off our coal bunkers. *Seraphim* ate through twenty long tons a day at full power with both boilers turning her twin screws. The clean hull allowed for a speed of sixteen nautical miles per hour with the current. Three and a half days was considered a quick passage.

Our crew was divided into three departments, each led by an officer under Captain Amadon. The captain had four marines assigned to secure the ship in port and to protect the cargo. The Deck Department was responsible for navigation, steering, lookout, handling lines, maintenance of the hull, and the single gun, should it be needed, as well as non-machinery components. Should the engines break down, they would manage the sails. The Engine Department operated and maintained the steam engines, which included stoking the coal. The Chief Steward, not technically an officer, oversaw services for the crew and, in our case, the two passengers. The Steward, Francis Howland, who also served as our butler, prided himself on keeping fresh fruit available at every meal and on catering to our wishes. He had two cooks in his department who were responsible for the meals and victuals for everyone.

During the seven-day, 2700 nautical mile journey to Bermuda, we avoided the significant storms of the season. Tall, slow swells indicated that storms were brewing over the horizon somewhere, but they did little to slow our transit.

We coaled the *Seraphim* in Bermuda and allowed the crew to go ashore. The marines wore uniforms approximating those of the Royal Marine Light Infantry: Red coats with dark blue collars and cuffs, and black cocked hats. Captain Amadon, who always dressed formally, wore a dark blue jacket with gold lace trim and white facings, a white waistcoat and trousers, a white linen shirt with ruffled cuffs, and a white cravat. The coat had gold shoulder straps to denote rank. His first officer, Horace Gordon-Greeves, wore similar clothing with only one gold shoulder strap.

Our pseudo-Marines took shifts on deck armed with rifled muskets while we were in port. They managed the British ensign, referred to as the red duster, which was raised and lowered according to the situation and tradition.

British warships flew one of three ensigns, depending on which of the three squadrons of the Royal Navy it was assigned to: the Red, the White, or the Blue. Thus, considering the gun, which was covered by a tarpaulin but unmasked in port, *Seraphim* could have been confused with a warship, by design.

On the day we departed Bermuda for Port Royal, I opened the small chest containing the cipher and the guineas by breaking the wax seal. I unmasked the code by dipping the handkerchiefs in a basin of water, as Lieutenant Colonel Martin Smythe-Armbruster of the Calcutta Light Horse demonstrated to me almost two months before, when on the *SS Spirit of Ohio*.

A message was unmasked, and I applied the cipher that John Summerhaze demonstrated to me a year before.

JB TO PANTHER BUSINESS GOOD. HH ASSISTS THE CAUSE - CAN BE A USEFUL ALLY. FIRST SHIPMENT OF MEDICINE. WILL PROCURE MORE.

I presumed that HH was me, and James Bulloch's endorsement was required.

I put out the handkerchiefs to dry, then repacked them, using the same wax-melting spot that Arlund Bisbee had.

Two days out of Bermuda, lying in bed with Victoria's head on my shoulder with the ship gently swaying beneath us and the steam machinery rattling as it did, she spoke her mind. I knew what had been bothering her. I could tell when she was vexed because she unconsciously slipped into a thick Scottish brogue, whereas most of her daily chatting was in the Queen's English.

Englishmen became *Sassanacks*, do you understand, became, *dee ye ken*? Unwell was *Peely Wally*, a glance was a *shooftie*, and saving a little money became *mony a mickle maks a muckle*.

She said, *"We're handfasted tae be mairried tae quiet the clishmaclaver o' ithers."* meaning, we are to say that we are engaged to be married to satisfy the curiosity of others.

"So my grandfather instructed."

"Captain Amadon could marry us under the nautical laws of England."

"And make it official?"

She said, *"Tha mi air aontachadh a bhith do bhean,"* meaning, I have consented to be your wife.

"I could arrange it, but under British law, the captain of a merchant ship has never been permitted to perform marriages. The captain can't perform them. The Marriage Act 1753 requires that a minister conduct marriages."

She said, "Scotland has had different marriage laws for a long time, and it is possible to marry there by common law agreement without strict adherence to the requirements of the English Marriage Acts."

"This is not a registered Scottish ship."

I sighed as she fidgeted, explaining, "My mother would skin me alive if I married you without the benefit of proper clergy. She would demand a setting where she could host a formal reception and invite every notable figure in Michigan. The preparations would take months, and during a war, senior officers would be expected to leave their regiments to be present in Detroit. You have only met my mother once."

"Yer Maw seemed couthie." Your mother seemed nice.

"She is, but she is every bit a Forsythe and cunning as Lucifer when it comes to formal life in Michigan and rivalry with others in her circle. Victoria, when my grandfather announced our betrothal, I contacted a solicitor. I asked under what conditions a ship's captain might marry a couple, and he said there were no conditions under which it could happen legally."

Her green eyes filled with tears, and her broad Scots became more English as she considered what she said. "I have not been with another man—only you. I am used as chattel to satisfy the machinations of great men. I am like a papier-mache tree in a play that is moved around the stage, not quite real and available for disposal when the game is finished. If you give me your name, it will take away my shame and will make me respectable."

I said, "The Raj played the Great Game with the Russians over control of India and Central Asia. It's still going on. They're doing the same thing in the Americas now, playing both ends against the middle in a game of divide and conquer. You and I were both dragged into this, not wholly of our making, but here we are."

She dropped a card, spinning quickly back to Scots, *"Bidh thu gam lìonadh le do shìol dà no trì tursan sa latha. Uaireannan barrachd. A bheil thu a' faighneachd carson nach eil mi trom le leanabh?"* You fill me with your seed twice or thrice in a day. Sometimes more. Do you wonder why I am not pregnant?

I admitted, "The question crossed my mind, but a gentleman doesn't ask such things."

She moved back to English. I'd become used to this when she was agitated. "I drink the gypsey Vadoma's mint drought at the behest of my Aunt Maude. It ensures that my womb is barren. They want me to serve you, but they want me to be a toy for your use, not an encumbrance that you would throw overboard."

"I would never—"

"It happens, Hud. A long sea voyage, an unwanted child, and a mistress who grows large and unattractive as the child within her grows. *Thug an tonn antrin mòran leis!*" Meaning: The odd rogue wave has taken many.

I reflected on what Sir Iain told me of Victoria — *too smart for her own good, dropped in a river.*

She looked at me like a lost puppy.

"Do you trust me, Victoria?"

She nodded tentatively. "Aye, but *ah dinna ken.*"

"We are both in the middle of this war and this game. Allow me time to figure things out before we settle things between us."

She thought long before responding. "I'm getting older, passing beyond marriageable age. They will replace me with a younger and prettier version. Perhaps with the niece that graces the home of Lord Lyons? You remember Lady Anne Pickering, don't you? She's lovely, beautiful, and two years younger than I am. I remember how you looked into her eyes, Hud. I will be betrothed to an old man in need of a bride - maybe a widower whose body smells of old cheese and whose breath is that of an old army tent."

Yes, I remembered Lady Anne Pickering. Changing the subject, I said, "We are in the North Equatorial Current and will soon enter the Gulf Stream. From there it won't be long to Port Royal."

"I remember when I first saw you when you and Nate stepped off that steamer with the band playing and the flags flying. Port Royal and the Carolinas are now under a different flag."

I stepped out of bed and began to dress. "Nothing stays the same, and the future is unwritten. We won't fly any flag as soon as we enter the Gulf Stream. We will be pirates, but since we are under steam power, we will approach the Port Royal Sound during the hours of darkness without relying on the tide or the wind. We will stand off where it is safe before coming to the dock in the morning. They will burn pyres on promontories to aid in navigation. The Federals will fear deceptions that would land them in the mud at night with treacherous tidal marshes and will stand well off."

Now dressed, I stepped out of the Master's Cabin and ascended the ladder to the quarterdeck, taking in the breeze and trying to clear my head.

. . .

WITH THE WIND in the doldrums and the *Seraphim* two cables offshore at anchor as the sun, masked by fog, rose slowly. Cable length was a different measure of distance in the US and British Navies - underscoring how a common language separated us. In the US Navy, it's 720 feet. In the British Navy, it's 608 feet.

A boat rowed from shore and asked that we wait an hour or two before getting up steam and coming forward into Port Royal to unload cargo and take on coal.

Captain Amadon agreed. I stood on the quarterdeck with him, wearing a somewhat nautical garb, short of announcing myself as a ship's officer standing next to Victoria, who wore a brilliant white, large hoop skirt with many petticoats.

The rowboat set off for shore.

"What do you think of this, Captain Amadon?" Victoria asked.

He said, "I think that they're organizing a welcome party."

Two hours later, after breakfast but still in the morning, a band struck up tunes beginning with *Dixie's Land*, followed by the *Bonnie Blue Flag*. Then, as we gathered steam to oppose a brisk offshore breeze that blew up, they played *God Save the South*. A rattle of musketry from a line of militia infantry provided a salute, followed by a single saluting round from a six-pound Napoleon gun.

The *Seraphim*, coal smoke pouring from her tall stack, moved toward the dock slowly and surely, with our four uniformed marines parading on deck.

Ashore, bagpipes began to skirl. I asked Victoria if she recognized the tunes. She said, "The first one they played with fiddlers and pipes was *Farewell to Oban*, and this one is *Garryowen*."

Captain Amadon ordered his signalman to hoist the South Carolina Flag from the yardarm, and the people ashore cheered. The band played *The Palmetto State Song*.

Because I had been part of General McDowell's staff, I knew that the 1st, 2nd, 3rd, 4th, 5th, and 8th South Carolina Infantry regiments opposed the Federal divisions at Manassas and expected to remain in Northern Virginia. It would explain the thin showing of two dozen uniformed infantry in the honor guard.

The gangway dropped, and Victoria and I made our way to the quay to meet Captain Nathaniel (Nate) Green Beaufort (M.A. Class of 1863), currently serving as the officer commanding, Company B of the 6th South Carolina Infantry Battalion, CSA. His father, the colonel, stood behind him in full dress uniform, beaming.

"Welcome, Hud and Victoria, it has been too long." I shook hands with Nate and his father. Both men took their turn kissing Victoria's hand.

Captain Amadon came ashore, and I introduced him and his first officer. Although the journey took two weeks and included shore excursions, I exaggerated the danger and the time spent at sea.

Colonel Beaufort said, "We have two dozen capons roasting, mountains of sweet potatoes, fresh roasting ears, and fresh peach pies for you and your gallant crew."

The first officer obtained a signature attesting to the safe arrival of the cargo and bowed out of the party to work with the stevedores who would unload the *Seraphim*.

We walked down the dock to cheers from the citizens and three official "huzzah" cheers from the small militia unit. They presented a tasting table for us with different vintages of peach brandy to sample and judge.

I told Colonel Beaufort that I had a chest for him that I agreed to deliver into his care. He seemed anxious to receive it, and I asked the Steward to fetch it for me.

We tasted the brandy and then sat at the table of honor to have a meal and celebrate the ship's arrival.

Nate sat next to me and shared the events underway. "Our army, under the direction of General Beauregard, is in the process of constructing defensive fortifications around Port Royal Sound."

"I thought he commanded the Army at Manassas?"

"He did," Nate assured me, "But he is first and foremost an engineer, and he returned to us after his great victory. We are constructing Fort Walker on Hilton Head Island and Fort Beauregard on Bay Point to defend Charleston, Savannah, and Beaufort."

His father said, "The blockading squadron has been reinforced. I'm surprised you didn't run afoul of them."

"Captain Amadon brought us in under the cover of darkness."

"Of course." Nate Senior said, "We just learned the squadron is to be divided, and the South Atlantic Blockading Squadron will be formed under Flag Officer Samuel F. Dupont." I'd heard of him through his niece, Marie, with whom I shared sporting moments before being sent to West Point: Marie Dupont Cholmondeley, the source of so much trouble for me.

Nate Senior continued, "Dupont has been ordered to capture Port Royal Sound to establish a base for his squadron and disrupt our trade and naval operations. He sailed to accomplish this task along with Brigadier General Thomas W. Sherman and 13,000 troops, who would ravage the area once taken. Last week, as they prepared their attack, a devastating hurricane impacted the fleet as it passed Cape Hatteras. Several ships were lost or damaged, including the *Ocean Express,* which carried the army's ammunition. They had to call it off. We expected you and were concerned that you'd receive a warm reception if you sailed into the entire squadron."

"Lucky for all concerned."

"Take all the coal you can. We will set fire to it and will burn the town before we allow it to fall to the Federals. This is likely to be our last celebration at our home. We will retreat inland to our defensive positions. It won't be easy to hold Port Royal against their onslaught once it begins. I attached a six-pound gun to a caisson to bring it here to salute you. The rest are in embrasures protecting the port."

"We didn't see them as we sailed in."

"No, but we saw you."

I smiled, turning to Nate Junior. "Nate, I've missed you, and I'm sorry that we meet under these circumstances."

"Once we've eaten and your ship is unloaded, you must prepare to sail when the sun sets and get out to sea, and away from the squadron should it return."

"You will load tobacco?"

"That is our agreement, is it not?"

"Yes," I said, and I have paperwork attesting to Mexican origin, should we be searched?"

Nate assured me, "It will be loaded by dusk."

"Has Maryland seceded?"

"Not to my knowledge," Nate Senior said. "We have many friends there, but they have been occupied by Connecticut's Volunteer Army and Illinois cavalry. I don't think that they will be able to follow their inclination."

We ate, visited, drank peach brandy, and relaxed. Colonel Beaufort left with the chest in hand. A few minutes later, he returned, still smiling. "We hear great things about you, Hud." He read the ciphered message. "But I fear for your early return to Port Royal until the situation here has been resolved. Perhaps Savannah will be a better port for you to visit?"

"And what of you, Victoria?" the Colonel asked.

"Hud and I are engaged, but the war interferes with our plans to settle."

He nodded his large head, "It is a sad story playing out through our pleasant land now that the war has been joined. The only choice now is victory."

After the banquet and a brief dance held in our honor, it was time to return to the *Seraphim* and prepare the ship to sail first East into the Atlantic and then north along the Gulf Stream to our destination in Baltimore.

October 1861
Washington, D.C., Navy Yard

CAPTAIN AMADON TOOK on a cargo of locomotive parts bound for Brazil. He would travel with Brazilian molasses in the *Seraphim's* hold to England and load with more chests of opium, but I would not travel with him.

Victoria took up residence at Minister Lyon's home when we arrived in Washington City. I left her with a hundred pounds sterling from the treasury aboard the *Seraphim*. Our parting was businesslike as she reoriented herself. As Major Sir Iain McKay said, she was the most intelligent woman he'd ever encountered.

I reported to the Navy Department, was redirected to Secretary Welles at the Navy Yard on the Anacostia River, and delivered my report in person. I explained my understanding of the Confederate ships —both those in planning and those under construction —as well as the agents involved, and the British resolve to uphold the letter of the law regarding neutrality. British companies would attempt to smuggle small arms into Southern ports and would take on cotton bound for England in exchange without the crown's official knowledge."

THE CONFEDERATE CIPHER

"I read an account in the papers published here of an American named Henry Hudson, who killed two men intent on robbing him in Liverpool by shooting their hearts out past their spines. It was sensational. I assumed that was you."

"I did not seek the encounter."

"Neither did you back down. You stood your ground. You're a good man, Lieutenant Hudson. And while I'm at it, a promotion came to my office in your name. You are now a first lieutenant, time in grade, academy affiliation, all that, I suppose. I will share your observations with the Secretary of War and the President at lunch tomorrow. I hereby release you and look forward to your formal report when you are able. You are back in the uniformed service of the Army."

I told Secretary Welles that the *Seraphim* would bring a cargo hold full of opium to Washington City for sale to the Union. He noted it and said he would pass it on as well.

The following morning, I reported to the War Department in uniform, accompanied by a note from Secretary Gideon Welles.

Major General George B. McClellan commanded the Military Division of the Potomac, the primary Union force responsible for defending Washington, D.C. General Winfield Scott was still officially the General-in-Chief of the Union Army. Still, rumors were rife that he would replace Old Fuss and Feathers soon as General-in-Chief of the Union Army.

The news wasn't good. The Missouri legislature seceded from the Union. Five thousand Federal troops under Brigadier General Joseph Reynolds fought a mixed group of primarily Confederate infantry to a standstill at Greenbrier River, suffering a handful of casualties. One of my classmates at West Point was wounded in the battle. He served with a Confederate Cavalry unit from Augusta County, Kentucky, under Captain Franklin Sterrett. The casualty lists were posted at the War Department. The report of the fight indicated that neither side seemed well enough organized to accomplish much.

There was correspondence from Autie Custer, who was in Monroe, Michigan, recuperating from an illness at his sister's home. His service on General Philip Kearny's staff during the battle, now being called the Battle of Bull Run, was insufficient to distinguish him from the run-of-the-mill officers serving. He felt that his illness was somehow connected to the cure he took for the Venus plague, but he was not sure. Based on what he wrote, it was the same upper respiratory infections and episodes of diarrhea he experienced at West Point. He asked that I visit him if I took a furlough in Detroit.

Adeline Stone wrote me a newsy letter, thanking me for helping her, her brother, and her father. All were doing well. My mother invited her for tea to quiz her about my comings and goings, of which she could share little since we had little to do with each other. She hoped that my service at the War Department would be meaningful and contribute to resolving the conflict.

My sister, Louise, wrote to me about her first child, a baby boy named Charles, who was born two months ago. She asked if I could return to Detroit on a Christmas furlough and assured me that both she and Robert would be there. Robert was engaged to a railroad heiress—of course. I thought about Victoria. She was growing on me, but I didn't want to let on. Minister Lyons had invited me to tea.

General McClellan knew my family well, as Brigadier General Fitz John Porter mentioned to me. "The general is aware of your return and your service abroad to the country under difficult circumstances. He read of your running gun battle with rogues in England and thought that a cavalry regiment might suit your talents, but he wants you to have input into your assignment before orders are issued."

Porter had a storied career in the army, but I knew the type. He looked good, spoke well, and curried favor with senior officers. He would spend more time looking for a scapegoat than he would leading. He had been in the right place at the right time with the correct assignment and the right friends. If a senior officer wished to mount his wife, that officer would be presented with a warm, moist towel to clean himself afterward. Maybe not literally, but that characterized Brigadier Porter.

"Is it true," he asked, "that you were offered lieutenancies in both the Coldstream Guards and the Queen's Horse Guards after you shot a Confederate through the throat in a duel?"

"A South Carolina militia captain, there were no Confederates then. He turned to run, and I shot him through the throat from behind. Several British Royal Officers were present to ensure that honor was maintained. They were concerned that I might be mistreated upon my return from Christmas furlough to West Point, so they made offers to purchase a commission should I be dismissed or dishonored." I knew that Fitz John Porter had served as an instructor at West Point before my time there and was familiar with some of the staff members. It was a small club. He came from a family prominent in American naval service; his cousins included William D. Porter, David Dixon Porter, and David G. Farragut. There was a strong likelihood that he had been privy to at least part of my most recent assignment in England. He answered my question.

"I understand that you had personal orders from President Lincoln in your last, uh, posting."

"I'm not disposed to discuss what may or may not have been directed to do by the President."

"Of course not. Perhaps a return to your previous assignment at a regular cavalry regiment would be a fitting continuation of your service to date. The First Cavalry Regiment consists of professionally trained soldiers, not volunteers. It was renumbered this year; thus, the First Cavalry is the senior regiment, signifying its long-standing importance and service to the nation. They are moving from the Pacific Coast and the Arizona Territory. You will know that some of their number fought at Bull Run. We are concentrating the regiment here under General McClellan's command.

"Several officers commanded the 1st U.S. Dragoons due to their reorganization and movement. Initially, Colonel Robert E. Lee was appointed to command, but he resigned before taking up his post in the regiment. Additionally, Captain James E.B. Stuart of Company K resigned. They will need to be replaced. Colonel Benjamin Lloyd Beall currently commands, but he is old and is in place due to his seniority. He's a stopgap because of Bobby Lee's departure.

"As with all cavalry, their role is to scout and screen." He looked at me questioningly. "It's different from what you've done since your early commission."

CHAPTER 15

B Company, First United States Cavalry,
Washington, D.C.
November 1861

General McClellan inherited an army with three companies of regular cavalry. He brought Barker's Chicago Dragoons with him to his new command, but they were on a 3-month enlistment. The Merchant's Troop of Philadelphia arrived in Washington City with their own horses. Most of the cavalry was attached to division headquarters as scouting units. The First United States Cavalry was the exception, but there were not many of us— barely a dozen.

The creation of a volunteer army did not run smoothly. In the first few months of the war, the States had not been authorised to raise cavalry regiments. They were only permitted to organize and enlist volunteer infantry regiments.

Authority to raise volunteer cavalry regiments rested with Secretary of War Simon Cameron. Cameron believed that wealthy people would fill out cavalry regiments, bringing their personal mounts from home. The US government paid the cavalrymen an extra forty cents per month for the use of their horses. The Confederates did the same thing. The difference was that there were Confederates who agreed to serve as private cavalry soldiers in sufficient numbers to make a difference. Few men from the North who were wealthy enough to afford a horse wanted to be a private soldier.

The Federal government sent buyers to Canada to purchase cavalry mounts, and General McClellan requisitioned horses as soon as they became available.

In August, three unmounted and unarmed cavalry regiments marched into Washington, D.C.

> The Kentucky Light Cavalry, which had been organized in Pennsylvania, was folded into the Merchant's Troop as Company A, Abraham Lincoln's Bodyguard, as Company D.
>
> The Pennsylvania Reserve Cavalry (seven companies) was given government mounts as they became available.
>
> The Cameron Dragoons were an ethnic Jewish regiment that also arrived, unmounted and unarmed.

All the cavalry of the Federal army was placed in a single brigade under Brigadier General George Stoneman. General McClellan wanted to concentrate his cavalry for a climactic campaign that would march into Richmond and seize the Confederate capital.

In early September, six companies with horses but lacking saddles, weapons, and uniform equipment arrived from Indiana. By the beginning of October, another five unhorsed, unarmed regiments arrived. They were Halstead's

THE CONFEDERATE CIPHER

Horse (later 1st NJ Cav), Lincoln Cavalry (later 1st NY Cavalry), 7th US Cavalry (later the Ira Harris Cavalry and then the 2nd NY Cavalry), Van Alen's Cavalry (later 3rd NY Cavalry), Dickel's Mounted Rifles (later 4th NY Cavalry)

During October, the 8th Illinois Cavalry arrived with horses, 1st Michigan Cavalry 4th Pennsylvania Cavalry, and the 8th Pennsylvania Cavalry

The 8th Illinois had had horses purchased for them by the US government from Illinois. The others arrived without horses, and the supply of available horses was drying up. It was not possible to horse the 4th Pennsylvania Cavalry, although the 8th PA was (and was brigaded with the newly redesignated 3rd PA Cav to form a brigade under Averell).

Given the situation on November 7, General McClellan requested that no more cavalry be accepted for the Army because of the lack of horses and equipment. It was in this chaotic mess that I arrived with Bayard and Glory, my two black Andalusians.

In December, Rush's Lancers, who brought actual teak lances to the fight from Pennsylvania, arrived and were accepted.

THE HEADLINES ALARMED ME. On November 8, 1861, the *USS San Jacinto*, under the command of Captain Charles Wilkes, intercepted the British mail ship *RMS Trent* and removed two Confederate envoys, James Mason and John Slidell. This seizure of the envoys, who were traveling to Europe aboard a British vessel, sparked a diplomatic crisis between the United States and the Crown.

The Secretaries of War and the Navy, along with President Lincoln, viewed it as a means of sticking their finger in the eye of the Confederacy out of spite. In contrast, the Confederacy and, more importantly, Queen Elizabeth and her government viewed it differently - as an act of war that had to be answered. The papers lagged genuine events by weeks as tensions mounted. I read of Minister Lyons's attempts to intervene and stop the impending war.

Although somewhat disconnected from those events, I knew that the act would prompt the British to move forward with their plans to undermine the Confederacy by dispatching troops to Mexico under the pretext of debt collection. Mexico had suspended payments to European creditors while I was there.

There had been meetings, and some plans were discussed. The Royal Navy would send its Caribbean Squadron's Royal Marine Light Infantry, a force of about seven hundred, commanded by Commodore Hugh Dunlop. The Spanish would commit its Army of the Americas, a mixed-arms force of almost 7,000 infantry, cavalry, and artillery. The French would commit the troops garrisoning their holdings in the Sugar Islands, consisting of 2,500 infantry and light artillery. In effect, the European creditors would deploy forces already stationed in the area.

The development of Mexican cotton to supplant the need for importation from the Southern States couldn't happen instantly, but commercial interests were intent on developing alternatives. The seizure of Confederate States ambassadors on the high seas from a British ship became the perfect trigger.

It was a clumsy move that smacked of Alan Pinkerton's machinations. I sensed that if anyone could topple a house of cards, it would be Pinkerton.

While I read everything I could, my post didn't involve the machinations of state. I had a minimal command that awaited fleshing out with the arrival of experienced cavalry troops that had been suppressing hostilities on the frontier.

. . .

THE CONFEDERATE CIPHER

Pádraig Mac Giolla Chuda's name was also pronounced Patrick McGillicuddy. The surname was derived from the *son of the servant of St. Mochuda*. His father farmed the land near Mountville, Virginia, having immigrated from County Kerry, Ireland, with coins in his pocket. With the help of neighbors and an indentured negro named Oliver, he built a tavern in Mountville on the Snickersville Turnpike because he liked to drink with his friends and enjoyed being hospitable to travelers.

They constructed *the Kerryman*, a well-made two-story brick building in the Greek Revival style, set on a raised basement, with a one-story porch supported by Doric columns and a box-patterned railing.

Those who were apt to quench their thirst drank below, then they paid their dollar to crawl upstairs to a well-kept boarding house.

When he went South with the O'Sullivans to join Roberdeau Wheat's Louisiana Tigers because no Sassenachs from Boston were going to tell him what he could and couldn't do, the place remained empty for a few months. The location made it a point of passage and contention between Union and Confederate forces.

I arrived as the only officer in the First US Cavalry deployed with the Army of the Potomac, and I declared The Kerryman to be the First Cavalry's regimental headquarters, screening (in part) General Archibald McCall's Pennsylvanians, who made up the 2nd Division of the I Corps, Army of the Potomac.

When Colonel George D. Bayard, my temporary nominal commanding officer, commanding the First Pennsylvania Reserve Cavalry Regiment, rode up to The Kerryman and saw the somewhat idyllic appearance of the ground, I was sitting on the porch. I stood and walked out to meet him, saluting.

He took in my cavalry guidon fluttering on a flagstaff —a red-over-white swallowtail flag that designated the unit. The letters U.S. were displayed in white on the red bar, the letter B identifying the company was shown in the red bar, and the large black 1 bisected both the red and white bars.

Colonel Bayard sniffed and looked down at me. "You're under my command. First US Cavalry. Lieutenant?" He turned to his aide, who whispered in his ear.

He said, "Lieutenant Hudson."

He looked around, "Black horses, you all have matched blacks - ah, and they're calling you the *Black Horse*." He pointed to my mount, hobbled and eating grass. "I will have that horse for myself."

"His name is Bayard, sir, same as you, but you can't have the horse. He is my personal mount."

"Why, you insolent puppy, I'll have you broken."

"All respect, Colonel Bayard, you're a volunteer. You were appointed by somebody in Pennsylvania and given a rank, what, three months ago? I am a regular army officer here by order of Brigadier General Fitz John Porter, who is also a regular army officer. I suggest that you take the matter up with him before you try to reeve my horse."

His aide whispered in his ear, "A duellist are you? The Articles of War, which govern the US military's justice system, specifically outlaw dueling."

I said, "I expect that you are a Philadelphia lawyer, Colonel."

"I was before putting on blue and wearing gold eagles."

And as if a guardian angel was looking over my shoulder, Brigadier General Fitz John Porter, with an escort of ten cavalry troopers, rode up.

Colonel Bayard and I saluted. General Porter saluted and dismounted, and Colonel Bayard dismounted, sniffing, digging a pocket kerchief, and dabbing a red, bulbous nose.

"I am reviewing the disposition of my command, General."

"Yes, I placed Lieutenant Hudson and the First US Cavalry here by design."

The colonel deflated a bit.

"The colonel fancies my horse, General." I pointed to Bayard.

General Porter laughed. "Ha, both your horse and the colonel share the same name."

Nothing more needed to be said. The fact that Brigadier General Porter knew my horse's name did not bode well, and the lawyer in him was sharp enough to pick up on it.

I offered the hospitality of the tavern to both senior officers.

"Thanks, Hud, but I'm delivering an invitation from General McClellan. He would like you to be his guest at dinner tonight. He is entertaining President Lincoln and Archbishop Hughes."

Colonel Bayard had a hopeful gleam in his eye that General Porter extinguished. "I'm sorry, Colonel, there's no room at the table for one more. Hud is a social friend of General McClellan and is known to the President, who pointedly requested that he join us."

Colonel Bayard sniffed, "I must be about the Army's business, General Porter." He saluted, turned about face, walked to his mount, and rode off with his staff officer trailing.

"I think that he wanted this building and my horse, General. You came along at an opportune time."

"He's a volunteer."

"And I'm a first lieutenant, sir."

"By God and the Great Horned Spoon, you're regular army, Hud. He will never be one of us. I'll have a word with General McCall. General McClellan is sending you twenty more seasoned troopers from the Second Cavalry to beef up your post."

"Thank you, sir."

"Oh, and bring that young lady you favor to dinner—Victoria McKay, the daughter of Colonel McKay, the British officer."

"If I'm to do that, I must leave now to pick her up and arrange for a coach."

"Then I'll leave my escort behind to help secure the place, and you can escort me back to Washington." To his lieutenant, "Chambers, you and the men will remain here until Lieutenant Hudson returns sometime tomorrow. There are worse jobs than securing a well-stocked tavern."

A FEW THINGS have happened that you may have noticed. Victoria and I are still a couple; her uncle was elevated to lieutenant colonel, and I'm Brigadier General Fitz John Porter's new best friend because I am in favor with General McClellan, the Little Napoleon, the President of the United States and Alan Pinkerton, who owes me for feeding him a spy, which put him in the newspapers and expanded his role in Washington.

My orders to the First US Cavalry meant that I was the only officer from the First US Cavalry in the Eastern Theater. The remainder of the regiment was in the process of moving, along with its baggage, from Washington State, California, and New Mexico.

Victoria risked life and limb to come to *The Kerryman* from time to time, along with her chaperone, now that I had settled in.

There are a few other developments I will also make you aware of.

*　*　*

WADE HAMPTON'S Carolina Legion screened General Beauregard's 32,000 Confederates in front of me. I met Colonel Hampton when the bugler blew stand-to. I walked out on the porch of *The Kerryman*, holding my LeMat pistol to face four or five hundred well-kitted Confederate cavalry under a white flag of truce. Given that they outnumbered my command by at least twenty to one, I asked. "Is it your intention to surrender?"

Wade Hampton introduced himself as a friend of Colonel Nate Beaufort and explained that he was delivering two boxes of cigars as a favor from Colonel Beaufort.

"The least I can do is offer you and your officers a drink." I holstered the LeMat. "Since we're under a flag of truce and it would be a breach of etiquette to parley sober."

Hampton swept his hat off, "Allow me to present my horsemen. The Edgefield Hussars, Brook's Troop, Congaree Mounted Riflemen, and The Beaufort District Troop, some of whom are acquainted with you." Half a dozen hands went up, and I waved back.

Hampton left one officer mounted with his men, and the rest joined me in the tavern for a drink.

"I thought my post was a secret," I told Colonel Hampton, who was close to my father's age.

He laughed warmly. "You pose little threat, and Colonel Beaufort, Governor Gist, and others hold you in high regard, though they were distressed when they learned that you decided to wear blue."

"No threat? I don't know if I should take offense at that."

We had a drink and then another. Wade Hampton explained that although he had no military experience, his years of managing plantations and serving in state government were considered signs of leadership. Furthermore, wealthy men were commissioned based on their social standing and were expected to finance military units.

"I had the funds to organize Hampton's Legion, six companies of infantry, four companies of cavalry, and one battery of artillery."

"Your reputation strikes fear in the hearts of my countrymen."

"Posh, we have most of the good officers; we have all of the breeding stock for fine cavalry and men who ride like the wind. One day, if we don't take Washington first, you will be our match. But not this year, and I don't think the next one. You have more people and more industry. That will tell if the war extends."

I took the cigars, shared one box with his officers, and sent another box with a dozen bottles of popskull out to the officer on picket duty, asking that my friends from Beaufort all be able to drink to my continued health. My men later said that it was like delivering whiskey to Lucifer's host. They did it, but they didn't like doing it. That was the difference between commanding regular troops and recently enlisted volunteers.

When his officers mounted to leave, he shook my hand. "It is unfortunate that we had to meet under these circumstances, Hud. If it comes down to a contest, we will not hold back, and I don't expect that your men will either."

After he and his legion rode south, First Sergeant Nelson, my senior non-commissioned officer who was himself a regular army non-commissioned officer, said, "There is no real hatred between us yet."

"No, Sergeant, we can still have a drink and smoke a cigar. We all have a great deal in common. We're all Americans, some of us are friends. We're men, just trying to support our states and live our lives. Hampton's legion is encamped a mile or two yonder, and we're a pitiful screen for McCall's 2nd Division."

"There is the First Pennsylvania Volunteer Cavalry with Colonel Bayard leading them." He laughed, and I couldn't help but smile. "Twenty Bayards are not worth one Wade Hampton. When we cross swords, you'll see, and Bayard will return to his law practice, broken in the ranks if he survives." I handed First Sergeant Nelson one of the cigars from my friend Colonel Nate Beaufort.

Word of the meeting got out as far as the White House and piqued the attention of the great and near great.

By mid-November, a new division under Sumner was created and placed between McCall and Smith, and Don Carlos Buell had been sent to the Army of the Mississippi, replaced by Keyes. Keyes had no cavalry regiment, as they were not screening a sector of the front.

Rather than being used as messengers and orderlies, the Federal cavalry began to behave like cavalry. The divisions holding the Northern Virginia frontage each had a cavalry division assigned to screen their front (two in Porter's case). My small squadron from the First US Cavalry fell under Brigadier General Cooke's reserve. That reserve included Rush's Lancers and batteries C and G of the 3rd US Artillery, in the process of receiving and training with the new three-pound ordnance rifles. A wrought iron, muzzle-loading rifled gun known for its accuracy and range. It was a significant improvement over smoothbores for certain types of fire, but loading smaller with both shell and cannister shot.

Now that each regiment covered a frontage every day, a company within the regiment would be designated as the orderly company, and its captain would report to divisional headquarters, post guards from the company, assign messengers, and so on. We lacked a dedicated headquarters guard. That didn't apply to my command because we were so small.

Because I had not received a furlough and General Porter intervened on my behalf, I was granted a thirty-day leave for Christmas. I telegraphed Victoria and went to see her.

She did not speak in broad Scots, though I could tell that she wanted to.

"Would you go to Detroit with me for Christmas so that we can announce our engagement and we can give my mother time to prepare?"

She hugged me and kissed me without saying a word. "Victoria Hudson. You'll have to try the name on for size."

I looked down into those green eyes, and she said, "I have an engagement present for you."

"Oh?"

"But I fear that the disclosure will prevent us from traveling to visit your family at Christmas."

"Tell me, and we will work it out."

I went to the War Department with the information Victoria provided, presumably plans that had been shared with the British at some level.

Brigadier General Fitz John Porter was present at the War Department when I arrived.

"Lieutenant Hudson, I was under the impression that you were on furlough, intending to visit home."

I said, "I have information that I believe to be reliable upon which the Army may wish to act, General Porter."

"Should we involve General McClellan in this discussion?"

"Let me share the information, and you can decide what to do with it." I walked to a map of the Shenandoah Valley on the wall. "General Jackson successfully disrupted the Baltimore and Ohio Railroad last May with a raid that led to the successful seizure of rolling stock and the destruction of rails.

"He plans to launch an expedition north to retake the railroad and the Chesapeake and Ohio Canal. The goal is to cross the Potomac and reach Hancock Town. They wish to sweep Federal forces from the lower Shenandoah Valley and Alleghenies, disrupting our tracks, seizing locomotives, and rolling cars. If he can put a pontoon bridge across the river and cut the tracks, he can threaten Washington from behind."

I handed the general a list of units earmarked for use in the attack. General Porter spoke as he read. "The Stonewall Brigade, Rockbridge Artillery, and William Wing Loring's Division!" He said, "Loring and Jackson hate each other. Loring has Anderson and Gilham's Brigades under his command. Jackson will try to strip most of their strength from him." General Porter tapped his head, "Politics, Hud. Tom Jackson won't want to share the credit with anyone."

Reading on, "He will use Turner Ashby's Cavalry to screen his movements. That makes sense. When does Jackson propose to move on the Romney Crossroads?"

"On New Year's Day."

General Porter whistled and slapped me on the back. "Just like Tom Jackson. Exploit surprise, bad weather, and furloughs after a night of merriment. He's thinking of Washington crossing the Delaware. He's a professor of military history; we should have anticipated this, but we did not."

"My source of information must be protected, General."

"Word of your parlay with Wade Hampton and his entire cavalry regiment made some doubt your loyalty. Many feel that your survival is proof of treachery."

I must have flushed. "Calm down, Hud, we who know of your larger missions are convinced of your fidelity. I expect that your source is not Hampton."

I shook my head, "No, it's not him. He would not do that.

Hampton acts the gentleman in all respects, but he is devoted to his cause and South Carolina."

"Take your furlough and a Christmas present from General McClellan." He shuffled through an old, scuffed, leather valise. "Here it is. Signed yesterday. Your brevet promotion to Captain." He shook my hand. "He would not have promoted somebody in whom he lacked trust, Hud."

Detroit, Michigan
Christmas 1861

I presented Victoria to my father and mother before boarding the train to Monroe to visit Autie Custer. I telegraphed ahead. Autie might have loved pulling pranks, but he did not like being pranked.

I found him sitting in front of the fire at his sister's hearth, freshly shaved but looking thin and miserable.

He stood when his sister let me in and grabbed my hand. "Captain Hudson, what news is this?"

"*Brevet* Captain, commanding a company of regular cavalry screening for McCall's Division, opposite Wade Hampton's Legion."

His blue eyes grew wide. "Do you exchange fire with them?"

"Not yet. My colonel is seventy years old and anticipates imminent retirement. He is content to have us remain in quarters through the winter." I told him about my parley with Colonel Hampton, including cigars and whiskey.

"That doesn't sound much like war to me, Hud, but you have been at war, haven't you? I read about your duel in England. It reached the newspaper here in Monroe because you're a Michigan man, I expect."

"They tried to rob me, and I killed them. There wasn't much more to it."

"That is not how the papers told the story. They described a shoot-out between you and three desperados."

"It was two Manx men and an unarmed whore."

"Did you shoot the whore?"

"No, but she stretched her own neck."

The truth deflated him. "You are a year behind me, and I remain a second lieutenant invalid."

"You were with General Kearney at Bull Run!"

"I was one of half a dozen dispatch riders. Libby Bacon's father won't let me call on her. He uses the excuse that I will infect her with my ague. I know that he doesn't consider me a proper suitor."

I invited Autie to my engagement party a week before Christmas and told him a little about Victoria.

"A Colonel's daughter, and you've been crossing the Atlantic under mysterious circumstances, shooting highwaymen and getting promoted. The world is your oyster, Hud."

I handed him train tickets. "You have no excuse not to come. Wear your uniform with your gold aguilette. They'll mistake you for a French Field Marshal." I saved the best for last. "My father will invite Elizabeth Bacon to attend the party. Her father may chaperone her, but you are welcome to dance with her. I'll see to that detail."

Custer smiled genuinely, and his eyes teared, "That would be the best possible Christmas present on Earth."

"Get well. General McClellan will drive on Richmond as soon as the campaigning season begins. We can both find glory in that."

Autie nodded, "I will be there, or I will be in the grave, Hud."

. . .

The engagement party on Saturday, December 16, was subdued because of the war, the weather, and the season. My mother cared nothing for eclipsing Christmas in the name of putting on a show, but many of the people she wished to have present were with their troops, either standing picket duty to protect Washington or in the mud and snow, drilling troops. Judge Bacon and his daughter, Libby, were present, as was Autie Custer, whose uniform hung on him due to his prolonged illness. It didn't keep him from doting on Libby Bacon, and my father restrained her father at my insistence.

Victoria looked radiant, and the official date of Easter Sunday, April 20, 1862, was announced. I spoke with my mother, suggesting that organizing a date could be preempted by unpleasant news of the war. We will do what we must. Viscount Lyons agreed to give Victoria away. He sent a telegram."

"That unpleasant business with the *Trent* could bring the British into the war on the side of the Confederacy. Minister Lyons is still in the middle of the matter. Who knows when it will be resolved?"

My mother stared daggers at me for bringing up the war and politics at a festive moment.

The party included a sumptuous feast. Libby Bacon sat on one side of Autie, and I on the other. He could only take thin broth and some buttered bread. I worried that if the pattern continued, he could die of starvation. Even in his weakened state, he managed two dances with Libby: a waltz and a Virginia reel.

* * *

My brother and sister arrived on Christmas Eve, as did both grandfathers.

My brother introduced Françoise de Hauteclocque, a

short but well-proportioned lady who he said was a descendant of a patrician family. "Her father introduced the A 2-4-0 steam locomotive."

I raised my hands in mock surrender.

He explained, "It is a wheel arrangement where there are two leading wheels, four driving wheels, and no trailing wheels. It's the most modern design for passenger and freight service. We will be incorporating this design on our railroads here. They're currently only made in Belgium."

I kissed his wife's hand.

A black servant followed them, carrying brightly wrapped packages.

I introduced Robert to Victoria, and he seemed to be very taken with her. "Where did you find such an angel, Henry?"

"I could say, Scotland, but we met two Christmases ago in Port Royal, South Carolina."

"Where did you fight the duel? Surely Victoria was not witness to you taking the life of another man." Robert looked over at her.

"Aye, I was present and saw it all. Henry was fearless. He stood his ground while the other man fired, then, when his opponent turned to run in a cowardly way, he did the honorable thing and ended his flight."

Robert seemed surprised, "I didn't know that Henry shot the man in the back."

Victoria clarified, "He fired through the man's spine, and the ball emerged from his throat."

Françoise de Hauteclocque said, "I didn't know that men still behaved like men in this country. Bravo, Henry."

Robert stared at her. Robert settled his differences with people in court

"Robert would fight a duel if a man offended my honor," She pronounced.

"I know he would," I confirmed. "It's in the Hudson blood

to defend the honor of our women by taking a life here and there."

Victoria, sensing the game entirely and taking in Robert's pale behavior, said, "My Henry killed two highwaymen on the road to Wales outside Liverpool. It was in all the papers. A woman of the town aided the criminals."

Françoise said, "Last summer? That was you, Henry? I read the account while in Brugge. It was in all the papers. An American, traveling in a coach, was accosted by thieves armed with pistols. They tried to kill the driver, and the American passenger emerged holding a cavalry pistol, and a gun battle ensued. They fired and missed while he was cool and calm and shot them in the heart again and again so that you could see daylight pass through them."

I shrugged.

"It had to do with defending my honor," Victoria announced, "and protecting my virtue from the unspeakable acts they planned to commit on my person."

Victoria had been in London at the time.

Françoise put her lace-gloved hand to her mouth in horror.

"The papers spared my reputation by omitting those details and my name."

"Of course," Françoise nodded, "It is clear to me now." Turning to Robert, she said, "My husband would do no less."

Robert, who was too squeamish to clean a trout he caught, changed the subject, assuring her of his violent inclinations, and leading her into the parlor for a brandy, the servant following.

My sister, Louise, and her husband, Matthias Horn, with their boy, Charles, arrived without the theatrics that accompanied Robert's entrance. As with Robert, Matthias Horn had black servants bring presents and place them under the large Christmas tree in the parlor.

Matthias, Robert, my father, Charles, my grandfathers, Ellijah Hudson, and Leslie Forsythe gathered around the fire in the study. A butler brought crystal tumblers with two fingers of Sazerac, a rye whiskey-based cocktail, as an aperitif before we were called to dinner.

Leslie regaled them with tales of the *Seraphim* running the Union blockade. "Of course, I deeded the ship to Henry, and he stood there on the quarterdeck, running fifty thousand pounds sterling worth of opium chests into Port Royal."

Robert looked at me with his mouth open.

"He ran out that nine-inch turreted Dalghren gun, and none of the Yankees warships would take the bait."

Elijah said, "Henry, tell us about Bull Run. You were there, weren't you?"

"There's not much to say, Grandpa. I was a second lieutenant then on General McDowell's staff. I delivered dispatches regarding the movement of our army against theirs, and I'm distressed to add that we lost and retreated to defend Washington City from the Rebels."

"That's a quick promotion to captain," Elijah said, sipping his Sazerac.

"I'm a first lieutenant, with a brevet to captain. It's quick, but there was a need within my cavalry regiment for me to command a company."

"A company in the Regular Army, not the Volunteer Army," My father added. "The First United States Cavalry. He commands a company of veteran horse soldiers screening McCall's Division opposite Hampton's Legion."

Robert said, "The paper's write of Colonel Wade Hampton and his gray horse cavalry."

"The horses are not matched," I replied. "I've seen them and Colonel Hampton, who rides a tall sorrel stallion."

"You've seen him?" Robert asked.

"Yes, opposite my post at The *Kerryman* Tavern at

Mountville on the Snickersville Turnpike. We've fortified the tavern with the new three-pound ordnance rifles and C battery, 3rd US Artillery, manning their pieces."

"Regular cavalry and regular artillery," my father emphasized. Not volunteers. He lifted a rolled map from a case and spread it on a round Italian marble table. Everyone gathered around it. "You all know George McClellan." Everyone nodded.

Robert said, "He was chief engineer and vice president of the Illinois Central."

My father continued, "They call him the Young Napoleon. He commands the army now. When I met him in Washington, he did me the favor of showing me where Henry's fortification was on this map."

The map was not annotated correctly, but it would have been bad form for me to have corrected some of the details. "George said that Henry's first cavalry was the linchpin of Washington's defenses there, holding the Turpike. He quoted Thomas Babington Macaulay, who wrote *"Lays of Ancient Rome," and compared Henry to Horatius, the* Captain of the Gate. 'Then out spake brave Horatius, The Captain of the Gate: 'To every man upon this earth Death cometh soon or late. And how can man die better Than facing fearful odds, For the ashes of his fathers And the temples of his Gods.'"

I had to put a stop to all of this. "Did General McClellan actually say that?"

My father, the presiding judge of the Michigan Federal Bench, raised his right arm to the square and said, "Every word of it, and it terrified me that you would die defending a patch of bloody soil ever since."

Robert, a bright lawyer in his own right, challenged the group in his own way, "How does a lieutenant of cavalry end up on a blockade runner in South Carolina while he's defending Washington?"

My father, a solemn and serious man, said, "He was under secret orders from Secretary of the Navy Gideon Welles and President Lincoln - orders that I saw with my own eyes. I can say no more about that, but Henry did that between his service as an aide to Major General McDowell and his accepting of his cavalry command in the wilderness of Mountville, facing down Wade Hampton's entire legion, which outnumbered him fifty to one. And that little lass he is engaged to is the niece of Lieutenant Colonel Sir Iain McKay of the Coldstream Guards—the Queen's Household Guard. He was offered a lieutenancy, purchased for him, but he turned it down, didn't you, son?'

I nodded and pursed my lips. "The story sounds a lot grander than it is when you tell it."

"Applesauce!" My father exclaimed, "You do us all proud, son."

Robert gulped. My father didn't lie. My face was beet red. We were called to dinner and joined the women in our Christmas Eve festivities.

My bedroom was downstairs in the new house. Victoria slept in an upstairs bedroom, and between us, the stairs were watched by attentive servants. She was more remote to me than if she'd been on the Moon.

CHAPTER 16

Detroit Michigan
December 27, 1861

I will never forget the date. Word of the death of Prince Albert of Saxe-Coburg and Gotha on December 14 was not printed in the Michigan papers until two days after Christmas. The same day, below the fold was news that Spanish forces, acting as part of the tripartite alliance with Britain and France, landed in Veracruz, Mexico, also on December 14th.

Things predicted were becoming real, and though none of them impacted me directly, they all did indirectly. Victoria said, "The Queen has been wearing black in anticipation of his journey to meet his maker. Their marriage was sincere. She will take this badly."

According to the papers, British marines and French troupes de terre and troupes de la marine" were expected to land in Mexico within the week. I knew that their ambition went well beyond forcing a repayment of debts owed. They had their Austrian Archduke, with a distant claim to the title, waiting to be paraded as Emperor of the Second Mexican Empire. Ferdinand Maximilian Josef Maria von Habsburg-Lothringen, a weak man, would soon ascend to the throne, backed by a strong European army. Cotton would still be king, but it would be grown in Mexico.

December 27th was also the day when Victoria became ill. The symptoms presented as nausea, vomiting, abdominal pain, and dizziness without a fever. My mother called our family doctor, who came immediately and tutted over Victoria, while I waited outside her room.

When he emerged, he asked to speak with me elsewhere in the house.

My mother and I accompanied him to the study, where he shared his findings and concerns.

"I do not think it is Typhoid Fever because you have all been in the home with her, drank the same water, ate the same food, and Typhoid Fever is a *fever*. She's not hot. Her temperature is normal. Dysentery is an intestinal illness resulting in severe diarrhea. Though her abdominal cramping is severe, causing pain, her stool is normal, so it is not Dysentery. Malaria causes fevers, chills, and other debilitating symptoms that can include dizziness, but she has no fever or chills. I do not think she has Malaria. Measles and pox present with red spots on the skin, and she doesn't have those lesions. The lymph nodes under her arms are normal, not swollen, so I can rule out diseases that attack that system: there is no drainage, no swelling, and no fever, which would be present with an infection."

My mother asked, "What about female problems - the cramping?"

The doctor nodded, "I don't rule that out, and she is new to your home, so you wouldn't know if these extreme symptoms were normal." He looked at me.

"I'd say if I knew. She hasn't been sick beyond once a year and a half ago - food poisoning."

"That would involve diarrhea," The doctor opined. "And none of the rest of the household is ill. She doesn't have respiratory distress that would accompany influenza or pneumonia; again, no fever. For now, I'll call it Victoria's Complaint, and I will spend some time in the books. If she gets better quickly, then we may never know the source. I'll call tomorrow to see how she's feeling."

The next day, her condition had worsened. She drank weak tea and rested. I spent hours with her, holding her hand and reading to her until she told me that she didn't feel well enough to be read to. I had begun to annoy her, and the passages from the Bible didn't make any sense to her.

The third day, she told me, "I could be sick because I'm taking the Gypsey cure to relieve women's irregularities."

"What kind of irregularities?"

She looked aggravated, "A stoppage of nature."

"But we're not doing anything - together."

"Men are so stupid. I think I'll tell the doctor and get his opinion," she said at last. "I'll ask your mother to leave the room first. She thinks that we've been properly chaperoned since we met."

After she spoke to the doctor, he took me into the study and showed me a bottle of clear liquid, asking me to smell it.

"It smells like spearmint."

"Yes, it does, and if I were a doctor for the poor, that's what I'd think she had. Some sideshow barker sold her water and mint with epsom salts or alcohol, perhaps."

"But that's not what you think?"

"She says that she received bottles from a Gypsy who brought them from Europe. I've had other women in Detroit and Lansing who have taken similar draughts of mint-smelling cures for pregnancy."

I could feel myself blush.

"Don't be silly, you're a man and she's a woman and you're both normal, doing what nature demands of you. Society, on the other hand, presents different requirements. I researched and, based on the wisdom of wise women, secret apothecaries, and other home remedies, it often contains rue, hellbore, mistletoe, foxglove, and pennyroyal, a type of mint —Mentha pulegium. I think the pungent smell is pennyroyal, not spearmint. It doesn't grow in America. It's a European herb."

I just looked at him.

"The use of herbs like pennyroyal can be toxic, especially when taken for long periods. The dose can be cumulative and cause severe liver and kidney damage. It depends on the duration and concentration."

"She's been taking it for a long time."

"I had a similar situation with another patient here in Detroit two years ago, which prompted me to read what medical authors had written. Otto Wallach, the father of terpene chemistry, started his research in 1818, isolating and classifying terpenes from essential oils. The ingredient in Pennyroyal that gives it its flavor and scent is called Pulegone. Concentrated Pulegone causes a variety of ailments in those who ingest it. The ailments that result will cause a failed pregnancy. In this case, I have no idea what the Gypsey combined it with and no way to find out unless you can find the specific Gypsey who brewed it."

"I think she's in England."

"Would she respond to a telegram?"

"She's a Gypsey."

The doctor nodded. "If Victoria is strong enough to fight it, the symptoms will subside and she'll get well."

"And if they don't subside."

"There isn't anything that I can do except prescribe

laudanum for the pain. If the symptoms become more acute, she's in God's hands."

"NO!" I wailed. "It's all my fault."

"Listen to me," the doctor said, "It most certainly isn't your fault. And it's not hers, and I wouldn't even blame the Gypsey. Blame is easy, but it's rarely fair. Allow Victoria the dignity to fight this on her terms. She was concerned that your family would blame you, you'd blame yourself, and that you'd ride out into Confederate lines as a suicide. That is not what she wants. Victoria wants to be your wife, and at this point, best guess, it's fifty-fifty. If it goes against her, she wants you to live your life to the fullest. Go to her, hold her hand. Cuddle her if she'll let you, and tell her you love her. That's what will do her the most good. I gave her half of a teaspoon of laudanum, and she'll be sleepy, but she should be awake enough to respond."

I took advice, stayed home, fed Victoria broth, and started calling her Vica to differentiate her from the Queen of England.

"It sounds too much like Viccar, which is what we call the priests in the Church of England," she complained.

"They wear dresses too, don't they?" You can tell where this is going. I kept it light-hearted and reduced the amount of laudanum she took, and she started to improve. Her urine, which had been dark, became lighter.

I extended my furlough by a week, though I felt guilty about doing that. Then on January 1, 1862, as Victoria predicted, and as I reported, Jackson's Army of the Valley struck with the same units we'd shared with my commanders.

Even though the Federal Army had a month to prepare, Jackson's men pushed them back. The question of whether he could cross the Potomac and move on to Washington from the northwest remained in the balance as the Confederate campaign progressed, and the Federal Army responded slowly due to the cold and snow, despite having access to the battlefield by rail.

Virginia demanded that I return to the Army and my regiment, and I left on January 3rd. The doctor judged that she was out of danger.

My mother started playing games to have me recalled to a recruiting position in Michigan, but I nipped that in the bud and pulled the root.

I arrived in Washington City on Saturday, January 5th, 1862, at about noon, and went to see Redmayne, my tailor, to get fitted for warmer uniforms. I ended up ordering six. They were the standard dark-blue, single-breasted officer's frock coat; a shorter, more practical jacket; sky-blue trousers with yellow piping; and a yellow collar on the coat. I wore a dark blue kepi with crossed swords and a forage cap with a yellow band indicating that I was a cavalry officer. Redmayne had a heavy blue balaclava made with yellow piping to protect against the weather.

In the afternoon, I reported for duty at the War Department because I was unsure of the location of the First US Cavalry's bivouac. I spoke to an aide to General McClellan, who told me that the President had ordered the commanding general to form the Five Corps, but that getting it done presented a problem for the slow, organizationally bureaucratic McClellan. The organizational changes had not yet impacted the cavalry screen, and the First US Cavalry was still stationed at the Tavern.

He noted that I had returned from furlough. Because I had focused on Virginia McKay's recovery, I had not checked in with George Custer before leaving Detroit. The Army still had him listed on a medical furlough in Monroe, Michigan. I had plans to push for his transfer to the First Cavalry, but I could not do that until he recovered and returned to duty.

The news from Banks' Division was not good, and he continued to maneuver in the face of Jackson's men. Rosecrans came up from the West to oppose Jackson. None of that immediately impacted B. Company, First Cavalry Regiment.

The main bulk of my regiment was still in transit by steamship from the Pacific Coast to Panama, where they'd march overland and board a different steamship. Companies D and G were still stationed on the frontier in the New Mexico Territory. They were expected at the end of the month, whereafter Colonel Beall would retire from service on February 1st. George A. H. Blake would then assume command. Almost completely reconstituted, the regiment would be attached to the 2d Brigade, Cavalry Reserve.

Wade Hampton still demonstrated in front of the Tavern from time to time, but he had not overrun the command, to everyone's surprise, except mine. I brought two pack mules to the tavern with bottles of Pennsylvania Monongahela Rye filling the panniers of the first. The second had bottles of absinthe, Peychaud's Bitters, waxed bags of brown sugar to keep the moisture out, and twenty pounds of lemons.

Sergeant Nelson helped me offload half of the contents.

On Sunday morning, after reveille, colors, a brief address to the platoon of cavalry, the battery of 3rd artillery, and the company of infantry on loan to my garrison, we enjoyed a breakfast of Johnny cakes, bacon, and eggs.

First Sergeant Horatio Fontaine (Rash) Nelson and I reloaded two of the panniers and secured them to the pack frame.

"Are you sure that you know what you're doing, Captain?"

"No, Rash, I never know what I'm doing, but sometimes it's better to have more balls than brains."

Second Lieutenant Bryce Martin, from Autie Custer's

THE CONFEDERATE CIPHER

Class at the Academy, saluted me, "Do you have instructions for me, Captain Hudson?" It galled him that I was a class behind him and was a brevet captain, but I knew him to be a steady man.

I returned his salute. "If I'm not back by nightfall, you may report me dead and assume command."

Riding Bayard, and taking a white flag of truce in hand, I rode forward through about four inches of old snow that had frozen and unfrozen, making it crunch as I moved.

Not a hundred yards from the barricade that surrounded the tavern, I was challenged by two Confederate pickets in uniform with bayonets on their rifled muskets. "That's far enough, Captain Federal. State your business. I recognize your flag of truce."

"I'm here to parlay with Colonel Wade Hampton."

"If he doesn't want to parlay, he'll send you into imprisonment."

I nodded. They led me about fifty yards farther south to where mounted pickets were having their breakfast of bacon and biscuits.

"What did you find there Zeb?"

"A Yankee with a white flag looking to parlay with the Colonel."

A sergeant of Confederate Cavalry said, "So I see, what do you want with the Colonel?"

"Please inform Colonel Hampton that Captain Henry Hudson is here to accept the surrender of himself and his men."

"You've got a mouth on you."

Another man said, "He's that fella that sent drinks out to us."

The sergeant squinted at me, "Are you he?"

"I am."

"I will have to blindfold you."

"Can you do it while I'm mounted?"

They threw an empty flour sack over my head and led my horse even as I led the mule about a mile and a half into the Confederate headquarters. Hampton's Legion was spread around a comfortable-looking home and a barn.

"You can take off the flour sack, Captain." I recognized Hampton's voice. "How are you this Sunday morning, Henry?"

"I have been on furlough, so I missed sharing a New Year's drink with you, but I'm back."

Hampton smiled mischievously. "I heard your fiancé was ill. I hope that she is feeling better."

I had no idea how he came by the information, but I nodded. "She is much improved." I shrugged toward the pack mule. I brought this for your mess."

He unbuckled a flap and said, "Lemons. Where did you find lemons in the middle of winter?"

"I'm a part-owner of a shipping company."

"That's right—the Peninsular and Oriental Steam Navigation Company."

"It imparts some privileges. It's not cold everywhere. We have been supplying the Spanish Army, which is now landed and assembling in Mexico."

"Dismount and help me bring all this into the officer's mess."

I did, and I helped him.

He laid the ingredients on the table and asked, "Sazerac?"

"To your continued health for the new year."

I showed his steward how to rinse the glasses with the absinthe, creating a distinct aromatic layer. Then I added Peychaud's Bitters, "It is a key ingredient, known for its floral and slightly spicy notes." I tore open the waxed packet containing brown sugar. "Now, a little sugar to balance the bitterness of the bitters and add sweetness to the drink."

THE CONFEDERATE CIPHER

Turning to Colonel Hampton, I handed a bottle of Pennsylvania Monongahela Rye. "This may be more difficult to come by unless you take more territory than we are willing to cede."

He laughed and poured into the glass.

Taking my pocket knife, I cut a twist of lemon, which I squeezed slightly to release its aromatic oils, thereby contributing to the overall flavor profile.

I made one for myself and toasted him, "To happier days."

Colonel Wade Hampton, terror of the Union, said, "I can drink to that, Hud." He used my nickname. He'd been speaking with Nate Beaufort.

As many as could shared a drink.

"Would you stay for our religious service, Hud?"

"I must be getting back. My men will worry about me being hung from one of these big trees."

"Very well, you've known where my headquarters are before now. I see no need for a blindfold. Thanks for the drink and the thought that went into it from me and my command."

I mounted, tipped my kepi, and rode North, escorted by his cavalry, leading my pack mule.

He wanted me to report back on the fortifications that lay between us, manned and supported by artillery. Some of the more distant pieces had a peculiar look. I would have liked to give them a closer perusal, but since I was closely escorted, that was not possible. Could they be Quaker guns? A "Quaker gun" is a dummy piece of artillery, typically a wooden log painted or tarred to resemble a real cannon, used as a deception tactic to make an enemy believe a fortification is more substantial than it actually is. The name alludes to the Quakers' anti-war stance, as these non-lethal, harmless "guns" could not cause any harm, similar to the Quakers' refusal to use violence themselves. I studied the tactic at the Military

Academy. They were used to deceive the British during a Revolutionary War engagement at Rugeley's Mill.

We studied Carl von Clausewitz's work, *On War* (Vom Kriege), and found that deception, both then and now, has always been an essential component of war. The morale of an army, essential in winning any engagement, is essentially a function of perceptions.

When I came into sight of the *Kerryman* Tavern, I heard a bugler play, *Officer's Call*. We had visitors. My men were giving me fair warning.

There were a lot of blue uniforms just out of sight behind the tavern with horses in the trees. I figured two or three companies of cavalry, but I didn't see a guidon. The national flag hung limply from the covered porch, not our flag, which, equally limp, had been raised in the morning on a pole.

General McClellan and Brigadier General Porter walked out onto the porch, and I dismounted and handed my horse and mule to First Sergeant Nelson. I saluted, and they returned my salute.

"What were you doing?" General McClellan looked interested. General Porter looked cautious.

"I took a New Year's drink a mile down the turnpike to Wade Hampton. I've been on furlough and was not able to toast his health until now."

"His health?"

"He could have ridden down on us at any point in time and could have killed or captured this redoubt. I appreciated his courtesy. He acts like a gentleman even amid a war."

General McClellan shook his head. "What if he does attack?"

"Then I will try to kill him before he kills me, but I don't expect that today will be that day—or am I wrong, sir?"

He shook his head, "No, you're not wrong. Do you know his strength?"

"He has six hundred or more in his cavalry companies and possibly two more infantry companies acting as security very close at hand. They seem well supplied with many stacked bales of hay for his mounts. I guess that his whole force is present, twelve hundred, all well equipped, well supplied. He has our captured artillery pieces from Bull Run."

"So if asked, I can tell people you were on an intelligence mission."

"You can, General, because I was. Their defense is layered. General Beauregard, the engineer, has his 36,000 men prepared to receive us should we wish to dislodge him."

"Then I will presume, Captain Hudson, that you think it is folly to assault him frontally in our march to Richmond?"

I looked at Brigadier General Porter, who nodded and smiled.

"Yes, though it is presumptuous of me, I would not recommend that we go on the offensive through General Beauregard's prepared defenses."

"As it happens, I agree, Captain Hudson. We came, Fitz and I, to congratulate you on your prediction of General Jackson's attack on New Year's Day. I think we will stop him at Blue's Gap tomorrow or the day after. To be successful, Tom Jackson has to do more than he's done, and were it not for your information, we wouldn't have been in place, and there would be another last-ditch defense of the Capitol."

Normally, one does not gainsay the commanding general, but I pointed out. "You created defenses for Washington, sir, that are almost impregnable, Forty-eight forts and strong points, with 480 guns manned by 7,200 artillerists. I appreciate your thanks, sir, but you have secured Washington against anything Jackson's few thousand could have thrown at it.

General McClellan smiled and continued, "The nation also owes you a debt because of that, because of your work with the Navy Department, where Secretary Welles can't sing your praises high enough and your exemplary service during the Battle of Bull Run on General McDowell's staff, and what we have observed today - you riding through the Confederate lines getting the accurate lay of the land and riding back out to report. Captain Hudson, you are relieved of your service with the First United States Cavalry and are officially transferred to my staff as an aide-de-camp, possibly as my liaison to Alan Pinkerton. You know Pinkerton, don't you?"

"Yes, sir."

"Of course you do because he knows you, and as with so many others, he sings your praises."

"I know him more in his role as a railroad detective."

"Come now, don't be so modest." He says you were key in helping him break up that spy ring in Washington six or seven months ago. Those women."

"I played a small part, General."

"Taken together, you're playing a significant part, and I want you on my staff. I'll have the orders prepared, but I want you packed and at the War Department on Monday afternoon. Settle your business here at the tavern and report, Captain."

"May I bring Sergeant Nelson with me?"

Brigadier General Porter asked, "What is his full name?" He had a pad of paper and a pencil.

"First Sergeant Horatio Fontaine Nelson. We call him Rash."

"He was raised in rank for this assignment?"

"Yes, sir, he was, and he is young, but he's smart and willing, and it would help to have his wisdom at hand."

General Porter nodded.

When the commanding general stood, we all stood. We

shook hands, and he departed for Washington with his staff and bodyguard.

As I packed, I reflected on the journey that took me from home in Detroit to my early graduation from the Military Academy, and now, back to the War Department.

The War Department
Washington D.C.
Thursday, January 16, 1862

I will briefly summarize the events of the past ten days. I receive daily telegrams reporting on Victoria's health, and I'm happy to report that she is improving, is back on her feet, and is working as my mother's understudy at the house. I visited a different Corps command each day and spoke to the staff about their concerns and the various Confederate brigades they faced.

My Uncle Samuel arranged for me to live in a house built on an unpowered barge that had been moored to a dock in the Anacostia River near the Navy Yard. It wasn't a mansion, but it had been built with comfort in mind as much as any house barge can be. There was a spacious bedroom, two guest rooms on a higher level connected by an exterior stairway, a lovely kitchen with a large coal stove which heated the whole structure, and an icebox for when I could get ice. It had a comfortably furnished parlor with glazed windows that overlooked the river. The head was fully enclosed, and the river current carried away whatever you deposited. A servant's barge with two bedrooms attached by hemp ropes to brass capstans at the stern floated thirty feet downriver. There was a line that I could pull that would ring a bell on the servant's barge to alert them to a need. At the moment, with ice on the river, the servant could run to my barge on the river without getting wet. On most occasions, she would walk across a gangway to the shore, up the shoreline to my gangway, and onto my barge.

A water boat refilled the large freshwater tank on the house barge as needed. It couldn't do its duty when there was ice on the river. During the winter, servants would haul water by hand or bring it in large bottles carried by a donkey named Balaam after a Biblical character. Likewise, a collier brought coal by water when the river was free of ice. A coal shed ashore stored several tons of lump coal for times when the collier couldn't navigate the river.

I had one negro servant named Enid, who was about 30 years old and childless. She cooked dinner five days a week. I suspected that she was a runaway slave, but I never asked. She worked for my Uncle before my arrival. Because we were in Washington City and she didn't have a last name, I called her Enid Washington. She liked that. She worked for food and board for my uncle. I paid her $12 a month, which was the pay for a private soldier and more than a laborer made. The 1861 Revenue Act required that she be taxed at a flat rate of 3%. I kept everything above board.

The barge offered more privacy than the Willard Hotel, which was packed with senior officers and government officials.

A yardarm had been affixed in the middle of a sundeck that faced downriver. I hoisted a First US Cavalry guidon and a national flag to the line that descended to the deck.

A stable adjacent to the barge on land served the needs of my horses, the donkey that came with the place, and a feral black cat named Hannibal that hated everyone but was a good ratter. I heard him stalking vermin on the roof of the barge house at night.

We received word that General Thomas Jackson resigned his commission because he failed to take Hancock Town and cut the Potomac in his New Year's Raid. General McClellan

THE CONFEDERATE CIPHER

was ecstatic and bought me a steak dinner in celebration, crediting my information for his humiliation. The fact that the Confederate high command refused to accept Jackson's resignation didn't matter. The military genius, Stonewall, had been stopped.

There were two men on the staff whose surnames invited mockery, and ultimately, it got me in minor trouble. Major Johan Fahrtzinger's last name had a habitational origin, meaning it was derived from a place called Fahring in Bavaria. Fahrtzinger became *Fart-slinger* after eating three pickled eggs for breakfast, German sausage, and sauerkraut. The gas that came from the good major was eyewatering, and the discharges were regular and of a timber and volume that defy description. Major Fahrtzinger, USV (United States Volunteers), was plump, about forty years of age, with a round face and a long, waxed mustache. He had been an engineer officer in the Prussian Army; as he reminded us all in broken German, Prussia had played its role as the most powerful state within the German Confederation. His departure was said to be political, and there was no doubt that he was a gifted engineer. He arrived on the scene as the US Army was assembling a volunteer army and received his commission. He had connections, or he wouldn't have ended up on General McClellan's staff.

The Regular Army, a smaller, pre-existing force of professional soldiers, formed the core of the Union Army. The Volunteers, on the other hand, were state-raised units mobilized for the duration of the war and significantly outnumbered the Regular Army. Major Fahrtzinger never fully embraced the difference between the two.

Major Jurgen Sackreuter, USV's surname meant plunderer or pirate, and he had a large, narrow head with skin that stretched tight over his face without much flesh to soften it. *Sackrider* was somewhat the opposite of Fartslinger in that his German name was the only thing German about him. He was a coal mining engineer from Pennsylvania. He spoke with a Pittsburgh accent, also known as Pittsburghese, characterized by the use of "yinz" as a second-person plural pronoun. He, too, joined the Volunteer Army as the nation expanded its recruitment efforts. General McClellan assigned him to work on the feasibility of tunneling under rivers the army may wish to cross without alerting the Confederates as to our intentions.

Major Sackrider and I got along well, and Major Fartslinger and I didn't. Though to be fair, Fartslinger was red-faced and mad as a stump-tailed bull at fly season all the time, and it was difficult to determine who was on his bad list at any point. How could you have your dander up every day? I was glad George Custer wasn't around to prank him. Gunshots would have been exchanged.

By the end of the day on Thursday, much of the news was of our Navy's success. Secretary Welles met with the incoming Secretary of War Edwin McMasters Stanton and General McClellan. I was there as part of General McClellan's staff.

Secretary Welles stood and said, "Our sailors and Marines landed by boat from the USS *Hatteras* this morning and destroyed a Confederate battery at Cedar Keys. They also destroyed seven small vessels loaded with cotton and turpentine, which were ready to run the blockade, a railroad depot and wharf, and the telegraph office. A small detachment of 15 Confederates from the 4th Florida Infantry was taken prisoner. Four of these were released, and eleven escaped before the expedition withdrew. Cedar Keys is no longer an effective base from which the Confederacy may operate.

"Seven new armoured river gunboats have been commissioned with a new design, to be built on the Mississippi. They are of uniform design and built from the keel up in shipyards owned by James Buchanan Eads. These City-class gunboats are our first ironclad warships. The gunboats will form the core of the Union Army's Western Gunboat Flotilla. We expect them to participate in almost every significant action on the upper Mississippi and its tributaries. The first four gunboats will be built at the Carondelet Marine Ways in St Louis, and the other three at the Mound City Marine Railway and Shipyard facilities.

"In North Carolina, *USS Albatross* destroyed the British blockade-runner *York* near Bogue Inlet, where the vessel had been run aground. It has been a good day for the Navy."

I had a pleasant discussion with Secretary Welles, who was in a good mood. He asked me to come to his office the following day.

Then I walked downstairs when the meeting ended and telegraphed Victoria (at my parents' home in Detroit) that I wanted to get married immediately and wanted my father, the judge, to perform the ceremony. I didn't want to wait. There was a war, and everything around me was uncertain.

The war - the real war - had not reached me. I played parlor games at sea, at Bull Run, and at my post at the *Kerryman*. Hampton's Legion spared me because he wasn't a butcher, but the war would go on, and the Napoleonic tactics of which officers on both sides were so proud would slowly change as enough men died.

Both navies were building ironclad steam rams to operate in the littoral oceans and on the rivers. The age of sail power ended. Eventually, engineers would design steam locomotives that did not require tracks, and they would roll over horsemen with their pistols and sabers. I could see it. The face of war would never be the same.

The English and French textile industries would absorb whatever damage an absence of Southern Cotton caused.

They'd buy from India or Mexico or somewhere I hadn't heard of, and life would go on.

One potential route to Richmond might begin at Fortress Monroe on the Peninsula, with General McClellan leading the volunteer army west, flanked by the James and York Rivers, which the Union would control with steam-powered ironclad gunboats. It was a good plan, and it made strategic sense. The lines of supply and communication could be maintained along the York River. Alternatively, the James River, although less navigable, ran through Richmond itself. The Federal army would lack neither food nor ammunition. Neither would the Confederates, whose supply lines would compress as the massive Federal Force ground its way toward Richmond.

Would it be enough, given that the Confederacy claimed most of the best officers in the army and navy?

Friday came with a light snow, and I rode Glory from the barge house to the Navy Yard and from there to the War Department, stabling my horse with General McClellan's staff. Our horses received excellent care.

A telegram arrived from my father, and it was simple and to the point.

> Bvt Captain Henry Hudson (Cav), War Department, Washington, D.C., Making arrangements. STOP Mother is vexed but will attend. STOP. Will advise. Judge Charles J. Hudson

I signed out to the Navy Department, Office of Secretary Gideon Welles, and walked through the snow the few blocks' distance.

Secretary Welles invited me in, an orderly served coffee and sweet biscuits, and he came to the point. "We know something of the fate of the screw steam frigate, *USS Merrimack*. She was commissioned in 1856 and served as the flagship of the Pacific Squadron. Last year, she underwent repairs at the Norfolk Navy Yard when Virginia seceded from the Union. To prevent the ship from falling into Confederate hands, the US Navy burned her to the waterline. Unfortunately, the fire only reached the waterline, leaving the hull and machinery largely intact. The Confederacy salvaged the remains, built an iron box superstructure on the original copper-clad hull, and mounted six guns and four rifles on her." He waited for my reaction.

"So they constructed a battery ship. With sloped sides?"

"We think so. Shot will be deflected."

I recalled, "The French used their steam batteries most notably in the Battle of Kinburn in 1855, where they proved effective against Russian shore defenses. The Russian balls bounced off."

"Precisely."

"Our Army and Navy had observers in the Crimea and must have watched the British and French steam batteries in action. They carried heavy ordnance for bombardment. They could be used at very close range comparatively and were used in calm water." I reflected on my readings at the Military Academy. There was an argument at the time as to whether they should belong to the army or the navy."

Secretary Welles said, "I knew you'd be well read, Captain Hudson. The very thing is afoot today. They have renamed the *USS Merrimack* the *CSS Virginia* and intend to sink our fleet at Hampton Roads by ram and by gunfire and break the blockade. If they succeed, they will control the sea lanes opposite Fortress Monroe."

I completed his thought, "So much for our planned campaign. The Confederates know of our plans as soon as they're formulated. Washington, DC, is a nest of spies."

He nodded, "I mentioned to General McClellan that I'd like to put you on it and find out what you learn. He agreed yesterday. We may have a surprise of our own for them, but it is not complete and may not be complete until after the March deadline for the fleet to sail for Fortress Monroe with the Army aboard. The less said of that, the better."

I nodded, "I will do my best, Secretary Welles." We rose, and he shook my hand, asking me to keep him informed of what I learned.

He added, "The Pinkertons have been of little use, but General McClellan puts great store in them."

GENERAL MCCLELLAN'S leadership style emphasized meticulous organization and training, which necessitated a substantial staff to support those efforts. And it only grew larger. There were four general classes—first, the popinjays: Officers who were vain, conceited, excessively talkative, and given to pretentious displays. They were almost always US Volunteer officers who were appointed to rank in their states based on political connections. You would never see them out in bad weather or taking a risk.

Second, there were logisticians. Most of them worked long hours to organize the volunteer army and deliver the necessary equipment, provisions, and victuals to sustain their operations. The supporting naval operation, which would move 120,000 men, horses, artillery, and equipment, grew to the point that it would employ more than 100 steamships, nearly 200 schooners and other sailing vessels, and over 80 barges. All of these had to be protected from the spectre of Confederate steam rams like the *CSS Virginia*. Most of the transport ships and a significant number of the warships were propelled by the use of sail and were constructed of wood. A steam ram like the *Virginia* (former *Merrimack*) could run them down, gore them with its ram, and sink them. Their cannons may be an antecedent, but the ram could keep going so long as the boilers had coal to burn.

Third, there were the drillmasters. Most of them were graduates of the US Military Academy, and they knew how to drill because that activity comprised about half of their daily routine. For most of their careers, they drilled their men. The war offered them an opportunity to put their discipline and experience on the drill field to use, turning volunteers into soldiers. After the War with Mexico, Congress disbanded the volunteers and reduced the Regular Army to an authorized strength of 865 officers. While the main reason for the decrease in officer numbers was post-war downsizing, factors such as age, infirmity, or even personal disputes also led to resignations or departures from the service. The onset of the Southern Rebellion meant that age or infirmity were overlooked to acquire experience. Even if they might not have been physically suited to be front-line commanders, they knew how to train.

Fourth, there were specialists of all sorts like Major Jurgen Sackreuter, the tunneler; Major Johan (Fartslinger) Fahrtzinger, the engineer; balloonists; experts in making and deploying pontoon bridges; and people like myself, who could have possibly been lumped with the popinjays but had other, less conventional skills that General McClellan found valuable.

Armed with the basic information provided by Secretary Welles, I began gathering information on the *CSS Virginia*, which was nearing completion at the Gosport Navy Yard. I heard a rumor that the steel plate being manufactured for her structure was still in production at the Tredegar Iron Works in Richmond. Lieutenant Colonel Sir Iain McKay provided more specifics during my visit to the British Mission. I was invited to high tea after the Trent Affair was resolved earlier in the month, when the Federal government released the two Confederate Ambassadors, James Mason and John Slidell. Minister Lyons had been instrumental in resolving the dispute.

President Lincoln very much wanted to hold the Confederates in prison until the end of hostilities. Minister Lyons affirmed that it would mean England would come in on the side of the Confederates with their fleet and their army. Lincoln said, "One war at a time," and let them go.

Iain McKay handed me a document containing specifics on the Confederate ship, and they were impressive. It had 4-inch-thick iron plating on its deck and two layers of 2-inch iron plating, angled at 36 degrees on the casemate— the armored structure on the deck. The casemate itself was also constructed with 24 inches of oak and pine. Iron covered, the ship measured 275 feet long, 38 1/2 feet across its beam, and 27 1/2 feet deep. Outfitted with ten guns, it resembled a floating barn roof.

The two British Navy experts assisting the Confederates said that it would be ready in all respects for combat by the end of February.

CHAPTER 17

The Federal Courthouse
Washington D.C.
Saturday, February 1, 1862

The federal courthouse at Market Square was closed because there was nothing in session on the weekend, and my father pulled strings to have Victoria and me married there, with him officiating under the laws of the District of Columbia. We had the building to ourselves and four dozen guests my mother invited. The wedding feast following the ceremony would take place in the rotunda.

My father looked resplendent, my mother glowed, and George Custer, who had just returned from his medical furlough, looked like death warmed over. He must have lost thirty pounds that he could not afford to lose. Nevertheless, he was there, hair trimmed, and stood next to me as my best man.

Victoria had come to know Adeline Stone, whom I had

befriended, and Adeline was her maid of honor. Richard Bickerton Pemell Lyons, 2nd Baron Lyons, the British Ambassador to the United States, gave the bride away with Sir Iain's permission.

My mother spared no expense on the decorations, which included thousands of fresh flowers in the middle of winter, during a war. The tables, the food, and the liveried staff were offset by a sea of blue uniforms, a few Zouave officers wearing their North African-style French uniforms, and a few redcoats accompanying Sir Iain. The women used the occasion as an excuse to wear their best. The orchestra included a large string section. General McClellan gave the toast, and Secretary Gideon Wells gave a speech. President Lincoln, who sat at the table with us —my family and the British delegation —initially declined to speak, then decided to say a few words.

> "Friends, countrymen, loved ones, we gather here today not just to witness a joining, but to celebrate the enduring power of the human heart. For far too long, we have been divided by circumstance and strife. But here, in this moment, we see a new union forged, a new chapter begun.
>
> "This union, like our nation, is built on a foundation of shared purpose and mutual respect. Like a sturdy oak, it will weather the storms of life, the trials and tribulations that come to all. It is not a union of fleeting fancy but one of enduring commitment —a testament to the strength of two souls intertwined.
>
> "Let us, therefore, raise a glass to these two individuals, who have chosen to walk this path together. May their love be a beacon, guiding them through darkness and illuminating their way. May their bond be as strong as the principles upon which our nation was founded, and may their happiness be as vast as the prairie."

He knew how to give a speech without droning on. He told me that he received a letter from William H. Seward regarding a meeting with Baron Gerolt, the Prussian minister. Earlier in the week, he issued General War Order No. 1, outlining military operations for February 22, 1862, Washington's Birthday. Additionally, he was involved in discussions and correspondence regarding the ongoing conflict, particularly about General David Hunter's actions in Kansas. There were no days off for President Lincoln. His wife, Mary, was ill and could not join us.

Victoria and I danced, cut the cake, danced again, ate some dinner, and then were allowed to leave as the party progressed. A carriage took us to the house barge, which my Mother also decorated, and we spent our first night together as man and wife.

We were comfortable together. We'd been together on and off for years now, and we'd discussed starting a family. She had concerns that using the Gypsy's potion in the past might not allow for that, and I confess I shared her feelings on the matter. For the moment, we put it behind us as we shared time in our tiny floating home on the Anacostia River, encased in ice as it was. The coal stove kept the place warm, as did the quilts around us.

We didn't do much on Sunday besides sleep late, make love, eat breakfast, and then make love again. With the tempo of the war accelerating, there were no furloughs, and on Monday, I returned to the War Department. I arranged for Autie Custer to be posted with the Second US Cavalry, which served as a component of the Reserve Brigade for the Army of the Potomac. Severe weather kept them in garrison in the Capitol as a defensive force.

Autie joined us for dinner on the barge on Wednesday, and Victoria laid out a feast for him in an attempt to help him gain some weight back. He'd been promoted to First

Lieutenant, which I reminded him was also my rank. The brevet captaincy was a temporary elevation. We spoke of our Academy days, and of Libby Bacon, who occupied his mind since Victoria's and my engagement party almost continually.

"The president spoke at your wedding, Hud. That will never be my lot, even if Judge Bacon consents for Libby and me to be wed."

"It was a Saturday afternoon down the street from his house. Where else would he get a free meal and have the opportunity to politic with his army and the other people there? It was convenient and nothing more. You know my mother. She excels at organizing parties, and the president is a politician."

"So what is it like being married?"

Victoria and I answered at the same time, "Comfortable."

Custer nodded. "It's too cold to open a window, so I'll leave some cigars behind that I brought for us to smoke."

"I'll save them until you can return and we can smoke them on the deck."

Autie said, "I never thought about living on a ship this way, but I admit that it is cozy. Though living with a Scottish lass, I expect that you'll have to get accustomed to eating haggis for supper." There was a twinkle in his eye. Autie knew that I hated haggis as much as I hated grits. Victoria liked haggis, liver, and pickled anything, all of which I avoided.

I looked over at her, "How can I kiss lips that eat haggis?"

She threw a napkin at me playfully, and Autie sensed that it was time to go.

BEING MARRIED CAUSED me to take a long, hard look at myself. I wasn't pleased with what I saw. Money never mattered to me when I was growing up. There was always more, and it was practically inexhaustible. Because of family ties, I had been singled out and treated well. My arrival at West Point, while forced, introduced me to many men from the South whom I was now obliged to kill as they were obliged to kill me. My odd friendship with Colonel Wade Hampton stemmed from my friendship with Nate Beaufort. My wife was affiliated with the British faction, though I suspected it less now as she adapted to life as an Army officer.

The officers' wives organized social functions several times a week, and she was home when I returned from the War Department. She stayed busy in her role, which she slipped into with apparent ease. Life changed for all of us. Before she attended a card party with the officers' wives or donated money to the soldiers' relief, she asked for permission.

Given her independent nature, I found it odd that she suddenly became so submissive. She spoke to me of the women she met and what she learned from them. Women played a vital role in supporting their husbands' careers through social networks, maintaining appearances, and providing a sense of normalcy amidst wartime. She tried to be more like the other officers' wives, though I never demanded it of her.

Even though I was a brevet captain, a relatively humble company rank, I was part of the commanding general's staff. Abraham Lincoln spoke at my recent wedding, and it was no secret that we had influence and means. Victoria was personally close to the British Ambassador, and as a result, she was still invited to receptions among the diplomatic community. I accompanied her when I was able, attending plays, dances, and concerts. Her circle of friends included many wives of colonels and brigadiers who had been inducted into the volunteers through political friendships. Anyone who was on a first-name basis with the President became someone you would invite to your party.

Other than Autie Custer, I had nobody that I would call a friend. I knew all of General McClellan's staff, but I wasn't drawn to any of them. I didn't have the history with them that I had with Custer. My circumstances meant that there weren't many people with whom I clicked.

So I was personally isolated, even though I was constantly going here or there with Victoria. We had hired an enclosed carriage for the winter months, which came with a driver and a footman. Sometimes I invited Sergeant Horatio Fontaine Nelson to accompany us, when it wasn't uncomfortable, because of the appearance of inappropriate fraternization with non-commissioned officers. Rash Nelson was married to a tall, homely woman, a few years older than Victoria, who adopted Victoria. She was a seamstress, and Victoria arrived at their home with bolts of cloth, which they used to make their clothing.

I mentioned Special War Order No. 1, which called for a coordinated land and naval attack on Confederate forces no later than February 22; a supplemental order designated General Joe Johnston's Confederates at Manassas and Centreville as the target. They called it the *Urbana Plan*.

All this time, I watched the soldiers being trained and the equipment being staged in wharves for eventual transport to Fortress Monroe if that plan were to be carried out. President Lincoln pushed General McClellan to move against the Confederates. One of General McClellan's excuses to delay was my information on the presence of the *CSS Virginia*, which threatened the movement of our fleet.

Finally, on Saturday, March 8, the Confederates made their move against the Federal Squadron at Hampton Roads. The *CSS Virginia* rammed and sank the *USS Cumberland*, a

THE CONFEDERATE CIPHER

wooden sloop-of-war, despite the *Cumberland's* crew fighting valiantly. The *Virginia* engaged the *USS Congress*, a wooden frigate, forcing it to ground. *Virginia* bombarded the *Congress* until it caught fire and surrendered. Then the floating barn roof took the *USS Minnesota*, a steam frigate under fire. It ran aground attempting to escape.

The Confederacy had a good day, and its papers trumpeted the one-sided battle, heralding a new era of control over the oceans and navigable rivers.

The next day, the Federal warship *USS Monitor* arrived, smaller and with less gravitas than the *CSS Virginia*—a cheese box on a cracker against a barn roof. *USS Monitor* engaged the *CSS Virginia* in the first battle between armored warships. The two ships fired at each other for several hours, with neither able to inflict decisive damage due to their iron armor. The battle ended in a tactical draw, with both ships sustaining damage and eventually withdrawing. T*he Monitor's* commander, Lieutenant John Worden, was temporarily blinded when a shell from the *Virginia* exploded near the pilothouse. The *Virginia* was forced to retire due to low ammunition and the falling tide, and risked running aground.

Thus unmasked, the *CSS Virginia* was not able to prevail, giving hope to the troop and cargo transport ships loaded and prepared to sail.

Spies passed General McClellan's plan, and Johnston retreated on March 9th, establishing the Confederate Army of Northern Virginia behind the Rappahannock. Rather than pursue Johnston, McClellan marched our army out to inspect the abandoned entrenchments at Manassas. There, he discovered the Quaker guns that I have previously discussed. I had reported the possibility that some of the artillery I had seen may have been part of a deception, but the Commanding General dismissed it.

Almost immediately, McClellan adopted the alternative plan that I had previously discussed, which would have the Volunteer Army disembark in stages at Fortress Monroe and advance up the Virginia Peninsula to Richmond. Preparations had been made for that eventuality. Did spies report on those preparations? That was another question. The reliability of the people who swore allegiance to the Union was always in doubt, as loyalties were often divided. Then there were the Confederate spies and, of course, the British, who liked playing both ends against the middle.

On March 11, President Lincoln removed General McClellan as general-in-chief, leaving him in command of only the Army of the Potomac, ostensibly so that McClellan would be free to devote all his attention to the move on Richmond. President Lincoln, ever the diplomat, poured oil on the water and stroked the easily stroked, massive ego of the Young Napoleon.

At tea with Victoria and Maude McKay at the Chandler house, Maude mentioned that the *CSS Virginia* was being repaired at a dock on the Elizabeth River. She read, paraphrasing from a sheet of paper.

> "During the first day of the battle, Flag Officer Franklin Buchanan, commanding the *Virginia*, climbed out from behind the ship's armor protection and fired a carbine from the top deck at the *USS Congress*, hoping to hit her captain. Marines on the Congress returned fire accurately, and he was brought low by a sharpshooter's minie ball, which struck his thigh."

She paused, as if trying to read the script. "As of the reporting, there was no telling whether he would succumb to the wound. He was replaced in command by Roger Jones, who served as a gunnery officer on the *Merrimack* before it was transformed."

She stated that even before the engagement with the *USS Monitor*, the *CSS Virginia* had lost its ram the previous day. It broke off in the *USS Cumberland*, creating leaks in the bow structure. It received damage to its smokestack and armor plates, with two cannons disabled due to shell hits to the shutters. Numerous external fittings were destroyed, and the loss of both of its wooden twenty-two-foot cutters, which had been reduced to kindling.

To summarize, *Virginia* had a leaking bow and a severely degraded smokestack, which further reduced its already slow speed. The Union ships, though destroyed, exacted a toll. She handed me the list of damage from the first battle, compiled by British spies, and promised a list of damage resulting from the second engagement with the *USS Monitor*, whose arrival, she said, "came as a shock."

I said, "Maude, you know that I will pass this on to Secretary Welles at the Navy Department."

She smiled and nodded, patting Victoria's hand, "Aye. It's just another wedding gift, dear."

WITH THE THREAT of the *CSS Virginia* removed for the moment, I was returned to other staff duties and placed under Major Fahrtzinger, who did little.

Autie Custer came to me and expressed his dissatisfaction with the Second Cavalry. He asked me to get him assigned to General McClellan's staff.

It required a deftly worded letter and Fart-Slinger's endorsement. I brought him a jar of pickled eggs the next morning, along with the letter, and asked him for help with my arduous duties. He endorsed it and went to work on the eggs. I took the signed request to Brevet Lieutenant Colonel

Albert V. Colburn (Cavalry), who asked me, "Why are we assigning a *cavalry* first lieutenant *and* you, a captain to the engineering department, and Old Fartslinger?"

"I think that it's a *need of the Army*, Colonel. Only very junior men will agree to work in a confined office with Major Fahrtzinger."

He scrutinized me, "You commanded that outpost with the First Cavalry's under-strength company facing down Wade Hampton's entire Legion, didn't you?"

"Yes, sir."

"I guess you're no coward, both you and Custer are Academy men?"

"We graduated early, *needs of the Army*."

"I'll approve this for George Armstrong Custer, but the two of you need to be out swinging sabers as soon as we can have you replaced by junior engineers. An office is no place for a cavalryman - like me, too."

Armed with the second endorsement, orders were cut requiring First Lieutenant Custer to join the (bloated) staff. He and I would not be noticed. There were even French nobility on the staff, and the General played up to both Prince de Joinville and Comte de Paris to the exclusion of junior men.

Following General McClellan's demotion, a new War Board replaced the general in an advisory role to the President and Secretary of War. The board included Adjutant General Lorenzo Thomas, Quartermaster General Montgomery C. Meigs, and other heads of the War Department bureaus. The shift meant that Major Fahrtzinger and his small kingdom, which now included Sergeant Rash Nelson, were nearly invisible. When outsiders came in with an engineering question, they were driven away by the pervasive odor. Autie Custer and I were usually doing field work with First Sergeant Nelson when the Major was in the office.

THE CONFEDERATE CIPHER

We weren't exactly shirkers or *coffee coolers*. There was a need for officers who would aid in organizing logistics and who would deter feather merchants who might be inclined to steal army equipment. We had a close call with Lieutenant Colonel Jacob Bowman Sweitzer, who observed us performing the saber dance with a sutler-type individual who was loading instead of offloading.

He was on his knees, crying, when Colonel Sweitzer walked up and asked, "Aren't you three part of Fart Slinger's engineers?"

"We are, sir," Custer said, "But this here contractor was supposed to deliver ammunition to the army, not to *take it from the army*. We were instructing him in his responsibilities."

Colonel Sweitzer looked at me and said, "Captain, aren't you the famous duelist?"

"Captain Henry Hudson, sir."

"Yes, we could have a duel between you and this belching, shitting civilian. Sabers?"

"We could indeed, sir."

"I'm a man of peace," the thief sobbed.

The colonel looked into his wagon and found cases of whiskey. "It's almost St. Patrick's Day, isn't it, Custer?"

"Yes, Colonel Sweitzer, almost March 17th."

He spoke to the sutler, "Skedaddle and leave the wagon or I'll sanction a duel with the captain, who is a famous Confederate killer."

The colonel confiscated the alcohol, we unloaded the ammunition, and he took the wagon with his mount halter tied to the back of the wagon. None of us mentioned the ample supply of punch for toasting at General McClellan's headquarters when St. Patrick's Day rolled around.

Autie Custer had a history of problematic behavior

related to drinking, and I spirited him away from Headquarters before he was able to embarrass himself.

I plead guilty to the charge of being a featherbed soldier. I was home at night with Victoria, and we shared our experiences of the day we passed, but I knew that situation wouldn't last much longer. General McClellan slowly but surely prepared for his move to Fortress Monroe, and we would be sent in advance to prepare the way.

It's never healthy for one's career to prank one's superior officer, but Autie took particular joy in putting one over on Major Fahrtzinger. He substituted pickled duck eggs for the Major's pickled eggs with no noticeable reaction. He substituted fertile, well-developed pickled duck eggs for the unfertilized variety. The major ate them whole, swallowing the fragile bones and pinfeathers, and didn't notice, which spurred Autie to even greater heights.

Reading accounts in the papers of President Lincoln's interactions with our boss, General McClellan, inspired Autie. The President said, "The army is merely McClellan's bodyguard," as the general was doing so little. He also reportedly made a joke about constructing a two-hole outhouse for the general, saying by the time the general decided which hole to use, he would *beshit* himself.

I cautioned my friend that there were people in our midst who would share his uncautious words to his detriment if he wasn't more cautious. However, he was Autie Custer, and caution wasn't part of his vocabulary.

The day to board the transport ship arrived, and I bade farewell to Victoria and walked up the gangway to the steamship *Elm City*, which the U.S. Army Quartermaster's Department acquired to transport troops.

I didn't take either of my horses because I thought it likely that I'd be in the thick of things, examining enemy fortifications before the army moved. Scouting was what the cavalry did, and both Autie and I were in the Engineering Department for that purpose. Autie wasn't much of an artist, but I did well in my engineering coursework. I told him that his job was to shoot anyone who disturbed me while I drew the enemy's works. I had purchased three of Henry's repeating rifles for our use and three thousand .44 metallic rimfire cartridges, also designed by Benjamin Tyler Henry. The rifle held 15 rounds in its tubular magazine, plus one in the chamber for a total of 16 shots. I thought that between Autie, Sergeant Nelson, and me, we should be able to get out of any trouble that we got ourselves into. I also bought twelve-gauge short-barreled coach guns to replace our sabers.

It didn't sit well with Autie, who felt that the saber was at the very heart of a cavalryman's soul. I'd given it a lot of thought and went with the shotguns. Autie could leave his behind if he chose to. I explained to my friend that we were essentially engineers on horseback. It brought a scowl.

The McGruder Line
Aprin 1862

BRIGADIER GENERAL GEORGE STONEMAN'S men ran into flooded areas, laced with rifle pits and slapped together fortifications that the Confederates had constructed, which defied their passage on horseback. Stoneman, a cautious cavalry commander, had been Autie Custer's boss when he served with the Second US Cavalry. They were men who were stylistic opposites. We were there when he reported the fortifications along the river that General McClellan wished to cross.

Major Fahrtzinger and Major Jurgen Sackreuter were present when we heard of the obstacle.

Major General McClellan complained that the beautifully drawn Coastal Survey maps at hand were inadequate. The roads ran the wrong way. The Warwick River, which appeared to be a small blue line on paper, an insignificant creek flowing parallel to the James River, was instead a significant barrier that cut completely across his line of march. To bolster the defensive value of the river, the Confederates damned it in five places, creating lakes and training heavy artillery on the boggy intervals.

Colonel Sweitzer said, "Sackrider, you may get your big chance to dig a huge tunnel under that river."

"It's not that simple, Colonel Sweitzer."

"It never is, Sackrider."

"What type of material is under the river, and how stable is it? Tunneling through soft ground, hard rock, or fractured, clay-like, or porous areas requires different techniques. The interaction between the river and groundwater must be clearly understood. I need to understand the groundwater flow pattern, pressure, and the impact the tunnel will have on the natural water table. This is crucial for preventing water from leaking into or flooding the tunnel. Then there is the scour depth. How much erosion does the riverbed experience during floods? You need to know the maximum potential scour depth to ensure the tunnel is deep enough to remain safe and covered. That's for starters, Colonel."

"Fortunately, we have engineering cavalry scouts. Captain Hudson! It's time to earn your pay."

They had a map on the wall with a few details. "See if they can be flanked on Mulberry Island."

The situation with the Army of the Potomac remained static, but I was sent forward to sketch the enemy's works.

At first light, Autie, First Sergeant Nelson, and I rode forward on swayback mounts over swampy ground toward the overgrown Warwick River in a misty rain. We rode up

THE CONFEDERATE CIPHER

Lee's Mill Road as far as Lee's Mill, which sat on the Warwick River, and even though three men isn't much of a shooting opportunity for artillery, they shot across the river at us. I looked around and saw stakes pounded into the ground, each with a red bandana tied around it.

"We're flagged; range markers! They have the ranges down here."

We turned around and ran the horses back to a point where we couldn't see the river or the Mill. I looked at Autie and said, "I hope these brass carbine cartridges are waterproof."

"What do you have in mind, Hud?"

"We'll cut through that marsh yonder to the south and have the horses swim the river. With luck, there are no artillery markers in the slush."

Autie replied, "That's a horrible idea."

So we moved south slowly through the mud and the slew until we entered the Warwick River. Nothing moved on the other side of the river. We were comfortably around a bend where guns would have targeted us.

"I see a snake in the water," First Sergeant Nelson said.

"I'm sure there are thousands of them and that they all bite venom, Horatio," I replied, starting to get irritated at the complaints.

Having crossed the river through thick brush, we slowly made our way up through the other side. Nobody shot at us.

Sergeant Nelson held our exhausted mounts, and Autie and I shed our boots because of the thick mud. We walked barefoot, with the ooze sliding between our toes, as we stepped with sucking sounds.

"I can't believe you talked me into this, Hud. I'm a cavalryman, not an infantry engineer. I'm a commander of Mongol cavalry that charges the enemy from the front."

I whispered, "Lower your voice, and if you want, get on

the horse, charge forward. Once they shoot at you, I'll know where they are. I can mark it on a map."

He made a funny face at me, but he lowered his voice and didn't charge forward, howling and waving his saber.

The mosquitoes were thick as flakes in a snowstorm, and it was all I could do to keep from slapping them and making noise. We resisted the urge to slap, but there were places on our faces where the blood ran down like small creeks after a summer rainstorm.

Before we got too far, we heard voices and smelled bacon cooking. There was cumulative smoke mingling with the morning mist from more than one fire. They burned green wood. It gave off its own fragrance and accounted for the smoke. It made sense. The smoke would keep the skeeters at bay.

Following a game trail west through tangled willows, we hoped to catch sight of the enemy. We found one, squatting, doing his morning business with his muddy, butternut-colored trousers around his ankles. He saw us, took in our blue uniforms, and opened his mouth.

Autie told him, "The sound you make will be your last."

"I am your prisoner," he said, wiping with a fist full of broad leaves and pulling up his trousers.

We led him north through the swamp, meeting up with Sergeant Nelson on the way, and continuing for the better part of a mile before I stopped.

"Them are fancy rifles, y'all have," He commented in a whisper, referring to our Henry lever-action repeating rifles.

Sergeant Nelson said, "You load once and shoot all day." He showed him a cartridge. "The powder is inside, it's don't get wet."

I made him sit on a deadfall. "What's your name, soldier?" I asked.

Looking up at us, he appeared to be in his teens.

"Private Alexandre Dugas of the Beaver Creek Rifles."

"Is that because you're from Beaver Creek?" Custer asked.

"My people are from Tangipahoa. Not many people have heard of it, but most of the boys is from St. Helena Parish." Private Dugas said. My family owns orchards there. We sell what we grow, mainly in Baton Rouge."

"How old are you?"

"Sixteen."

Custer menaced him with his rifle, "If you want to reach seventeen, you'll tell us what we want to know."

Private Dugas gulped. "I joined up without my ma and paw sayin I could. They needed me to work the place, but all the boys were joining to protect our rats."

I asked, "What rights are those?"

He looked confused, "I ain't sure, but you Billy Yanks want to take them away and that ain't right. Not one bit."

Sergeant Nelson tried to take notes with a pencil on wet paper, but soon gave up.

"Which regiment are you with?" I asked.

"The Louisiana Tigers," Private Dugas said, sticking his chest out—"Beaver Creek Rifles are Company G under Captain James H. Wingfield."

I said, "Tigers are the Fourth Louisiana?"

"Yes, sir."

"Were you at Bull Run?"

"No, I just joined, and they marched me here with replacements."

"Who Commands the Tigers?"

"It was Colonel Barrow, but I heard that he just resigned, and Lieutenant Colonel Henry Watkins Allen took his place. Colonel Barrow thought it was unfair that his regiment was put in a swamp just because we're from Louisiana. It's said that we bayou boys like the swamp but 'taint true. Tangipahoa is not swampy ground."

"How many men are in your regiment?" Custer prodded him with his rifle barrel.

"I don't know, sir, maybe four hundred. There are only thirty-one in G Company."

"I noticed works, where do they begin and end?" I asked.

"I don't rightly know. It's about five miles, they say. The trenches start by the mill and follow the river for a fair distance, and then they end at the James River on the other side of the swamp. We, the Louisiana men, have been building works across this swamp to stop you. Most of Major General Lafayette McLaws' Division is on the high ground."

I asked, "Which units are on your left and right?"

"Company K, the Packwood guards are on our right, and Company D, the West Feliciana Rifles are on our left. The Lake Providence Cadets, from Carroll Parish, are somewhere behind us. They're C company, acting in support and reserve."

"Do you know which company of artillery covers the bridge?"

"Yes, sir, that would be the Richmond Howitzers."

"How's your food holding out?"

"It ain't ma's cooking, that's for sure. We keep a pot of stew boiling and add to it as needed. It boils the swamp water. We put what we can catch, snakes, frogs, and such, into it to make it better."

Custer asked, "Is it better with boiled frog in it?"

The private shook his head sadly.

Armed with that intelligence, we released Private Dugas and instructed him to explain his absence by telling his sergeant that he had gotten lost.

It took us most of the day to return to General McClellan's headquarters and report. I showed Colonel Sweitzer where I thought they were building redouts. "Based on what

THE CONFEDERATE CIPHER

our prisoner said, they have two Louisiana Regiments along the line, holding a five-mile stretch, and they are none too pleased to have been singled out to be in the swamp. Our prisoner didn't know much about units outside of his, but they're part of McLaw's Division.

"Can we put a brigade through the swamp?"

"To get to what? I think they're in place to link Magruder's men to the James River. They're a picket wire, not real defensive works. You'd wear out a brigade to hold a swamp and nothing more. Johnson's Divisions are on the high ground. We'd fight our way into the swamp and end up fighting uphill to get out. You'd lose half of our strength with only holding a swamp to show for it."

"What about the roads, Custer?" The colonel turned to him.

Autie gulped. "They're gumbo, Colonel. We saw some wagons toiling on our way up and back. They were up to the axles. I saw a mule go entirely out of sight in one of those chuck holes. All I could see were the tips of his ears."

The colonel looked at Custer with disbelief.

"It was a small mule, Colonel."

Colonel Sweitzer shook his head at Custer and said, "We're going to move General Erasmus Darwin Keyes' Fourth Corps forward to face Macgruder, Sumner's Second Corps will face Longstreet, and Heintzelman's Third Corps will occupy D. H. Hill and will move on Yorktown."

He wasn't asking for my opinion; he was informing me.

Autie and I conducted a raid on a redoubt dug into Mulberry Island two days later, with twenty men. We captured documents showing that the Confederates had fourteen redoubts across the Island, connecting Fort Crafford, which housed the Advance Battery, and the Warwick Line. The positions had been under McLaws' command for at least sixty days.

Colonel T. G. Hunt of the 5th Louisiana, who commanded Fort Crafford complex, had been ordered to move to Minor's farm, 12 miles from Yorktown, about a mile and a half from Fort Crafford, on April 5th to act as a flank guard to Ft Crafford and Mulberry Island.

Colonel Sweitzer said, "I think that you can take Mulberry Island off your list. Focus on the fortifications along the river and Yorktown. Major Fahrtzinger will focus on Yorktown, and Major Sackreuter will look for a place to dig a hole under the river. Assist them as necessary."

I had my orders.

General McClellan's plan called for General Heintzelman's III Corps to fix the Confederate troops in their trenches near the York River, while the IV Corps under General Keyes enveloped the Confederate right and cut off their lines of communication. Even though we brought information that Magruder held the right and Longstreet's men were entrenched behind the Warwick River in the center, McClellan and his senior staff listened to the Pinkerton assumption that the Confederates had concentrated only in the immediate vicinity of Yorktown.

I found the dysfunction disturbing.

At General McClellan's musty command tent, I waited with the rest of the staff for young Napoleon to return. When he walked in, soaked to the skin, trailed by some senior officers, he learned that a series of wires had arrived. The first and possibly the heaviest blow was that Fortress Monroe, with its 12,000 men, had been removed from his command.

"It's the staging area for the whole campaign," he shouted at us! "They can't do this!"

Colonel Sweitzer said, "It gets worse, General. McDowell's Corps, which was awaiting sailing orders at Alexandria, has been detached from our command and ordered to stand in defense of the capital."

McClellan snatched the order and read it by lantern light. "They have created a Department of the Rappahannock under McDowell and a Department of the Shenandoah under Banks, and the Army of the Potomac hasn't fired a shot besides Captain Hudson's chauvanch on Mulberry Island!"

He looked General Porter then at me, "They've cut my cullions off, Hud. That's a third of my army, gone with the snap of a telegraph key. Without those 12,000 at Fortress Monroe, I can't replace battlefield losses."

McClellan said to General Erasmus Keyes, "The plan remains the same. You shall push your Fourth Corps forward to the Warwick to face Macgruder and pin him in place." To the grizzled old Sumner, he said, "Your Second Corps will push Old Pete Longstreet back, which will allow General Heintzelman's Third Corps to pivot on D. H. Hill, and you can take Yorktown. He put his hand on Heintzelman's shoulder and squeezed gently with fondness. It will all come down to you, Samuel. They can't hold the line without Yorktown, even if they do presently occupy the high ground. Bull Sumner will have your back."

AUTIE and I shared a tent with a floor made out of doors and wood we took from rebel homes. It wasn't bad, considering life in a tent, and we were out of the mud. We ate at a makeshift officer's mess that offered the same basic food as that available to the rest of the army: Hardtack, a hard, dry biscuit made of flour, water, and salt; Salt pork or salt beef; Flour or Cornmeal for making soft bread or biscuits; Coffee: Often distributed green, requiring that we roast and grind it; Sugar and molasses: for sweetening. Salt, rice, beans, dried peas, and sometimes dried fruit or desiccated vegetables. A good cook could make it palatable—the senior officers' mess poached the best cooks who did a good job for them, leaving us with the worst of the lot.

Major Fahrtzinger sent First Sergeant Nelson on a mission to survey sutlers for jars of pickled eggs and saurkraut. When he came back empty-handed, the major threw a tantrum, and the surgeon gave him laudanum to calm his Teutonic nerves.

I telegrammed Victoria asking her to find a source of pickled eggs or to have Enid pickle some, jar them, and crate them for shipment. Ten days later, a supply wagon brought a crate containing twelve one-gallon jars filled with pickled eggs, and the fart slinger was back in business.

In the meantime, Autie, Rash, and I captured two more prisoners and interrogated them. The first came to us wounded after a small squadron of Confederate Cavalry jumped us with sabers and pistols. We fought them off with our Henry rifles, killing two and wounding the third. The wounded man was hit in the gut. He said that his name was George Kirby, a corporal with Company F, Third Virginia Cavalry, under Captain Telemachus Taylor. Taylor commanded their patrol across the river when he met us. The dying Corporal Kirby was chagrined that a company was set to flight by three Yankees, better rifles notwithstanding. I agreed to write a letter to his family in New Kent on his behalf if he told us about his command. He agreed. They had been screening for Longstreet's Division, which had about two thousand men on the line. The Virginians had been riding back and forth to convince the timid McClellan that they had greater numbers. He laughed and spat up blood at the deception. "We'll whoop you Yanks! You'll see." He died, and I sent the letter as promised.

The next prisoner was a spy that we found skulking

THE CONFEDERATE CIPHER

behind Heintzelman's Corps, wearing civilian clothes. Sergeant Nelson searched him while Autie and I covered him with our rifles. He discovered three blank pages in the man's haversack.

"See, I ain't no spy, you don't have nothing. I'm on my way home."

I lit a match and waved it under the paper, finding writing.

Autie asked me, "Can I shoot him?"

I said, "Yes." And he shot the spy in the heart with his pistol."

The spy looked surprised as he died.

I took the pages back to camp, heated them over a coal oil lamp, and transcribed them. They were written in code. Decryption was straightforward, involving shifting letters using the same key that John Summerhaze taught me. I didn't disclose to anyone that I had the key, but I could read what the spy wrote —essentially an accurate account of the Federal artillery attached to the Second and Third Corps.

General McClellan sent the Pinkertons forward to count Confederate soldiers. They returned with inflated numbers that couldn't possibly be accurate. Alan Pinkerton was in camp and visited our mess. I invited him into Autie's and my tent and poured him a generous drink of good Scotch. "I'm sorry it's in a tin cup, but we are on campaign, Alan."

"I thank ye, Henry."

"What news do you have for General McClellan?"

"It's not good. We may be facing two hundred thousand Confederates in Joe Johnston's command."

As he laid out his methodology, I deduced his mistakes. Pinkerton assumed every Confederate regiment was at full strength. Based on what we heard, they were significantly under strength. His agents took the Confederate bait and counted the same units multiple times as they moved through an area, leading to inflated figures. If a thousand men were seen at one location and then moved to another, Pinkerton's agents would report having seen two or even three thousand men."

"So you say we may be facing two hundred thousand Confederates? Double our number? How can that be?"

"Honestly, Hud, he likes the number." Pinkerton looked down into his cup and took a sip.

"You are pleasing him by pandering to his concerns?"

"The count is the count."

"Why are you here in my tent, Alan?"

"I don't know, Henry. Sometimes the war and these people are too much, and you are an easy fellow to speak with. You listen well and you don't judge."

That tells you how much Alan Pinkerton misjudged me. "To speak fairly, I expect that we outnumber General Johnston and are better supplied, even though his back is to Richmond. I go forward to examine their works every day at different points, have taken prisoners, and have a general sense of our enemy. They are potent fighters and have the advantage of the defender, but if you push, they will fall back if they don't have a decisive advantage."

"What do you say to General McClellan?" Pinkerton asked.

"I forward my drawings, observations, and interrogation reports through Major Fahrtzinger."

General McClellan changed his plan and decided to lay siege to Yorktown. I toured our fifteen ten-gun batteries of thirteen-inch siege mortars, which were being installed within two miles of the town. They would throw 400 tons of shells into the city per day and would be ready to begin by the first of May.

CHAPTER 18

On the Warwick River,
York County, Virginia
Sunday, April 13, 1862

*G*eneral McClellan received increasingly strident messages from President Lincoln to attack the Confederate force opposing them. The president had intelligence that contradicted what Pinkerton's spies had been presenting. He called me to the building, which he used as his headquarters.

"You have taken prisoners and have interrogated them, Lieutenant Hudson?"

"Yes, sir."

"And does their information conflict with the information that I am receiving through my intelligence department?"

"My information provides a very incomplete picture of the main Confederate force. I was ordered to focus on

Mulberry Island in the hope of finding a way to flank them. Louisiana Regiments are drawn up along a line of redoubts, which in themselves are weak, but their purpose is to connect with a battery on the James and to provide a picket wire that will alert the main forces if it is broken."

"And Mulberry Island is a swamp."

"Yes, sir."

"In three days, I am sending General Keyes' Corps forward at the dam. I'm told you have been there."

"Yes, sir, to the mill and to the dam the Confederates constructed to flood the river near the mill several times."

"Very well, take Lieutenant Custer, First Sergeant Nelson, and four of Berdan's sharpshooters forward in the morning and attempt to seize a prisoner in the area of the dam so that we may interrogate him before General Keyes' assault."

The general motioned to an adjutant to write orders detaching some of Berdan's men.

Once I had the orders in hand, I saluted, left, and Autie Custer, who had been waiting for me outside, asked what the general wanted. I told him, and he whistled.

"They've been more alert lately, Hud. They know we're snatching their pickets."

"They've also had more pickets on our side of the river lately, and it may be that we can grab one of them skulking and bring him back. We'll have the sharpshooters to give us more punch if we meet another cavalry patrol. We were lucky that the last one ran."

"After we emptied our magazines into them."

We were empty and down to our pistols. If they had turned, they would have had us all. The repeating Henry rifles had been worth their weight in gold.

It rained all night, and we left before the Sun rose to reach the dam by sunrise. The rain abated somewhat to a drizzle, decreasing the mosquito scourge, but even so, we were soaked through by the time we traversed Lee's Mill Road and turned north to follow the river from a distance.

The four picked men of the 1st Sharpshooter's Regiment, Berdan's Sharpshooters, all rode well and sat on their horses with their rifles across their laps. We poached them from General Heintzleman's III Corps, where they fell under Brigadier General Fitz John Porter's First Division, Dan Butterfield's Third Brigade.

The sharpshooters, led by a sergeant named Hay, arrived in the evening before we departed, wearing their famous green uniforms. The distinctive dark green color was intended to reduce visibility; their uniforms featured non-reflective, hard black rubber buttons rather than shiny brass ones. They also wore green wool forage caps and trousers.

They weren't happy to learn that we would ride down Lee's Mill Road. They preferred to walk. I explained that, since we were departing from the Warwick Courthouse, it made sense to get at least halfway to the Mill on horseback because nobody would see us through the rain squalls. If we obtained the desired prisoner, it would make sense to spirit them away on horseback in the event we were pursued.

All four picked men carried personal weapons rather than the Army's Model 1855 Springfield Rifle Musket. They said that they anticipated the issue of the new Sharps breech-loading rifle, noted for its accuracy, speed, and ability to load from a prone position.

After we presented our passes and moved through the forward works, First Sergeant Nelson rode ahead, cutting for enemy cavalry sign as he rode. The rain meant there were no tracks. I don't know what good finding tracks would have been. Keyes' cavalry reserve patrolled the area. We ran into Companies F and H of the 6th New York Cavalry in the area before. Their shod horses left the same tracks that the Third Virginia Confederate Cavalry and Mathews Light Dragoons did. It seemed like an ego problem. Nelson worked hard to be the old seasoned professional in a sea of newly arrived young men.

We dismounted, and I ordered Sergeant Nelson to remain behind with the horses and one sharpshooter while the rest of us stalked toward the Warwick River, maybe a hundred yards in front of us. There was more abundant growth of taller trees adjacent to the river.

My first inkling of a problem came when our horses began whinnying behind us. The sharpshooters were on it. Horses called from the direction of the river, and we dropped. Cavalry moved through the heavy brush in front of us, and we saw blue uniforms. Sgt. Hay shrugged at me, and I mouthed, "Sixth New York." We marveled that they didn't explore the presence of other horses on the Union side of the river. They may not have wanted to provoke a confrontation.

Ten minutes after they moved on, we walked to the Warwick River, where the rain kept visibility low. The sharpshooters moved like ghosts. Autie and I wore dark blue officers' uniform patrol jackets with light blue trousers trimmed with broad yellow stripes. Our uniforms were adorned with polished brass buttons, gold braid, and furnishings, and the wisdom of green uniforms became evident.

Sergeant Hay motioned us to get down, and he walked silently forward with another sharpshooter covering his back. I heard men talking. "I caught two catfish here on the Sabbath." Our side of the river had less overhanging brush and would be easier to fish from. Then silence. I saw Sergeant Hay prodding two gray-clad, shoeless infantrymen in my direction.

Suddenly, I heard the rattle of musketry from across the river and felt a sharp, burning pain across my chest. I backed up into the brush, and Autie said, "They got you, Hud, you're bleeding."

THE CONFEDERATE CIPHER

I looked down, and the front of my patrol jacket from under my breast down was covered in bright red blood. I felt rubber knees and suddenly nauseous and threw up in front of me, bending over and holding onto the trunk of a tree for support.

Sergeant Hay and the prisoners came up next to me. "Let me see, Captain."

I opened my jacket, and he looked at a broad red gash along my ribs that continued to my back. "It looks like a ball fired from some distance hit your ribs at an angle, and it rode your body around. I've seen these before. If the bleeding worsens, you'll bleed to death. If it doesn't worsen, you should visit the surgeon and have him clean and dress the wound."

Sergeant Hay had an arid but sharp wit.

When we arrived at the horses, we bound the prisoner's hands and lashed them to the saddles. Two of them took First Sergeant Nelson's mount, and he rode behind Autie.

At the dressing station in the rear, the surgeon pulled a round bullet from my back with forceps and showed it to me. "Pistol ball, Captain, looks like a thirty-six. I'm going to use iodine on the wound, stitch it, and then apply a bandage. The stitching didn't hurt nearly as much as the iodine did. He had me lie down and gave me a fortifying drink of brandy.

Autie Custer showed up later and brought me two slices of soft, fresh bread with salt beef, which we called salt horse, stuffed between them. I ate it and chased it with mild beer, which was less likely to cause illness than water in camp.

Colonel Schweitzer was pleased, and so was everyone else. He said, "I was told that a Confederate ball found you, but you'd live." He felt it was a fair trade for two prisoners the Pinkertons could interrogate.

I told Autie later, "Somehow it's less fair of a trade if you're the one who's shot."

Custer nodded.

I said, "I'm going to our tent to lie down."

> Headquarters, Army of the Potomac,
> Camp Winfield Scott,
> in the vicinity of Yorktown, Virginia.
> Tuesday, April 15, 1862

On April 15, 1862, I received orders routed through my commanding officer, who, in this case, was Major General George McClellan, commanding the Army of the Potomac. Major General McClellan endorsed the orders and forwarded them to Colonel Jacob Sweitzer, who likewise endorsed them and brought them to me.

The orders detached me from General McClellan's staff. They ordered me to report to Edwin M. Stanton, the Secretary of War, signed by Major General Edward D. Townsend, Adjutant General.

They came with a sealed envelope. I broke the seal, withdrew the paper, and read.

> (Bvt) Capt. Henry Laughton Hudson (Cav.) US Army
> HDQRS, Army of the Potomac,
> Eng. Fld., Div.,
> Camp Winfield Scott, York Cnty, Virginia
>
> Sir,
>
> You are to travel to the War Department for reassignment to the Navy Department pursuant to a finding by the Secretary of War that the needs of the Navy warrant this action.
>
> You are authorized a one-week furlough beginning on the date of your arrival in Washington, D.C., following your reporting.

> I have the honor to be,
> Very Respectfully
> Your Obt. Servant
> (signed) R.F. Cross
> Major & Adjut.

General Keyes probed the Confederate defenses at Dam No. 1 near Lee's Mill, but did not breach the Confederate defenses.

General McClellan ordered them back and opted to continue the siege rather than an immediate assault on the Confederate works.

Two weeks later, on May 3, on the night before General McClellan's planned bombardment, Confederate forces evacuated their positions at Yorktown, moving toward Williamsburg. The next morning, the Federal army occupied the Confederate fortifications and captured the defensive artillery intact. The Confederates retreated with their field artillery intact.

I didn't know any of that happened at the time. I was with Victoria on the *Seraphim*, bound for London, England, in the master's cabin. With the stitches along my ribs removed, I enjoyed her ministrations as she delicately applied a salve to the healing gunshot wound.

"It missed the watch my grandfather gave me when I left home for the Military Academy in 1958. I had it in my breast pocket under my uniform blouse."

Victoria looked up at me, "Was that lucky? It could have been deflected and shot your nose off." She touched my nose gently.

I nodded. "You never know, do you?"

The Series will continue with ***Hudson's Scouts***

EPILOGUE

George A. Custer was promoted to (bvt) Captain on June 5, 1862, while serving as a temporary aide-de-camp to Major General George B. McClellan. He was demoted to First Lieutenant on July 17, 1862, when McClellan was removed from command (the first time).

George B. McClellan led the Army of the Potomac down the James Peninsula, southeast of the Confederate capital at Richmond, Virginia. During this campaign, he exhibited the timidity and sluggishness that later doomed his military career.

Queen Alexandrina Victoria was the daughter of Prince Edward, Duke of Kent and Strathearn, and Princess Victoria of Saxe-Coburg-Saalfeld. She inherited the throne at the age of 18 after her father's three elder brothers died without leaving any surviving legitimate issue. She married her first cousin, Prince Albert of Saxe-Coburg and Gotha, in 1840. Their nine children married into royal and noble families across the continent, earning Victoria the sobriquet "Grandmother of Europe." After Albert's untimely death in 1861,

Victoria plunged into deep mourning and avoided public appearances for years.

ACKNOWLEDGMENTS

Some years ago, when I first became interested in the British Secret Service's involvement in the War Between the States/War of Northern Aggression and began researching it as a historical project, I found that reliable information on the topic was hard to come by.

Several pointers led me to the Henry E. Huntington Library in San Marino, California. It is one of the world's great independent research libraries, with some 12 million items spanning the 11th to the 21st centuries.

Every year, researchers from over 30 countries make more than 20,000 visits to the Library's reading rooms, and thousands of remote researchers use the Library's virtual services and digital collections. Some 75 Library staff members play a critical role in cultivating and expanding access to the collections, creating new opportunities for discovery and engagement, and ensuring that collections are preserved for the future.

Becoming a documented *reader* with physical access to their collections was not an easy task. At the time, I was employed as a Supervising District Attorney Investigator at the Orange County, California, District Attorney's Office, Bureau of Investigation, Organized Crime/Grand Jury Unit. I was also serving as an officer in the United States Naval Reserve with a Top Secret SCI clearance with a special background investigation and polygraph.

Graduate degrees from the Naval Postgraduate School and the California State University systems were likewise insufficient. They wanted to see a PhD and, preferably, a postdoctoral studies endorsement from a major university.

Because my portfolio wasn't good enough to get me through the door. It took intervention from the US Intelligence Community, cosigned by both of California's US Senators, to finally gain grudging acceptance, but it was worth the effort. I greatly acknowledge the assistance of the Henry Huntington Library in providing research reference materials that were used as a portion of the factual basis that underscores both this and future volumes of the *Duelist Series*.

Doing research at the Huntington Library remains a fond and moving experience.

In addition to the dedication page, there are friends and colleagues from Great Britain's domestic (M. I. 5) and foreign (M. I. 6) Services, the Special Air Service, and Royal Marines 62 Commando, with whom I've rubbed shoulders over the years, who formed the curiosity base that led to the research in the first place. The British Official Secrets Act constrains me from offering named praise, but you know who you are.

Unfortunately, many of my old friends have passed, so to my friends beneath the sand - thank you.

Thank you to my dear friend, the late John Derva, Oslo, Norway, who died in December 2025 before this book could be published. John was an intelligence officer of great renown and a cherished brother from another mother. My deepest condolences to his wife and daughter. I spoke with John about this book series, and his encouragement helped to make it real.

Thank you to another dear friend, the late Colonel M. Cordell Hart, US Army/Central Intelligence Agency, and Southern gentleman, with whom I traveled in China and Asia, worked with at the Interpol General Secretariat (Lyon, France), and elsewhere. His friendship, brotherhood, and wisdom shared over many years can't be overemphasized. He is interred at Arlington National Cemetery among our honored dead. *sic transit gloria mundi!*

When I first tried my hand at writing some fifteen years past, I reached out to my friend and colleague, the late Detective Lieutenant Jack (Wo Fat) Willoughby, New Orleans Police Department, who was struggling to write some true crime novels. Jack generously introduced me to a real author who took a wicked red pen to what I had written and chopped my work into bloody sushi. It made me better. Knowing Jack (former Army/National Security Agency) also made me better. I'll see you on the other side, where it's always double drill and no canteen.

—Larry B. Lambert, Blue Ridge, Arizona

ABOUT THE AUTHOR

Larry B. Lambert spent much of his adult life in government service. He has had the opportunity to travel and operate in places and situations that are denied to many people.

ALSO BY LARRY B. LAMBERT

Non-Fiction

The Orange County Bankruptcy: An Investigative Summary

Fiction - Based on a True Story

White Powder: A Novel of the CIA and the Secret War in Laos

Exiles from Eden

Fiction - Cartel Wars

Bloody Mexico

The Old Whore

Science Fiction

Red Mist (with Jules Smith)

Loki's Fire (with Jules Smith)

Broken Toys

Historical Fiction

The Confederate Cipher (book 1)

Hudson's Scouts (book 2)

The Crow Creek Expedition (book 3)

Short Story Collection

Virtual Mirage

The Shorts

Conduct Unbecoming

Editorial Credit

Hunting in the Shadows (by Michael Watson)

Made in the USA
Coppell, TX
21 January 2026

68865252R00203